Social Studies and the Press

Keeping the Beast at Bay?

a volume in
International Social Studies Forum: The Series

Series Editors:
Richard Diem, *University of Texas at San Antonio*
Jeff Passe, *University of North Carolina*

International Social Studies Forum: The Series

Richard Diem and Jeffe Passe, Series Editors

Social Justice in These Times (2004)
edited by James O'Donnell, Marc Pruyn, and Rudolfo Chávez Chávez

Social Studies and the Press

Keeping the Beast at Bay?

Edited by

Margaret Smith Crocco
Teachers College, Columbia University

INFORMATION AGE
PUBLISHING

Greenwich, Connecticut • www.infoagepub.com

Library of Congress Cataloging-in-Publication Data

Social studies and the press : keeping the beast at bay? / edited by
Margaret Smith Crocco.
    p. cm. -- (International social studies forum, the series)
  Includes bibliographical references.
  ISBN 1-59311-336-6 (pbk.) -- ISBN 1-59311-337-4 (hardcover)
  1. Social sciences--Study and teaching. 2. Journalism. I. Crocco,
Margaret. II. Series.
  H62.S7247175 2005
  302.23--dc22
                        2005013017

Printed in the United States of America

CONTENTS

ACKNOWLEDGMENTS

I would like to thank Stephen J. Thornton for providing the title for this book and Gene I. Maeroff for helping shepherd this project through its infancy.

PART I

GETTING TO KNOW YOU

CHAPTER 1

BEAUTY OR BEAST?

Margaret Smith Crocco

INTRODUCTION

Virtually all my life, I have had a love affair with the *New York Times*. My affection for this country's newspaper of record was bolstered each time I wrote a letter to the editor and saw it published. Far more regularly, the paper expanded my knowledge about a myriad of topics—from news of the region, country, and world, to science, cooking, and pop culture. Every Sunday, I pored over its many sections. Besides the "Week in Review" and "Book Review," my favorites include the "Sunday Style" section with its wonderfully sociological wedding announcements. (I must admit that my taste in these matters puzzles and amuses family and friends.)

For only a fifth of that life, I have been a social studies professor at Teachers College, Columbia University. That role catapulted me into a new relationship with the paper when I became the subject of an article in the "Metro" section. As a result of this experience, my ardor cooled a bit. As any veteran of dealing with the press will tell you, the neophyte can get bloodied pretty quickly, even when the journalistic encounter seems to have taken place on the friendliest of terms.

This book chronicles the longstanding and mutual attraction social studies and the press have felt for each other for almost 100 years. Its

Social Studies and the Press: Keeping the Beast at Bay?, 3–14
Copyright © 2005 by Information Age Publishing
All rights of reproduction in any form reserved.

chapters provide instructive insights into how mainstream journalism has viewed a unique educational field—one whose founding mandate was to provide citizenship education in a democracy. Likewise, a number of authors return the favor by sharing teaching strategies designed to help bolster critical media literacy in schools.

Several chapters reflect the degree to which social studies finds itself embattled these days: on the right, from pundits seeing its professors as symptomatic of the "tenured radicals" lurking throughout academe; and on the left, from the "turf battles" promoted by historians who consider social studies an example of the decline in rigor within American schooling over the last century.

Despite this tumultuous state of affairs, the book is not animated by defensiveness but by high regard for the importance of the press in a democracy and the critical need for vigilance on the part of American citizens in the face of consolidation within the industry. Likewise, the book pays homage—of a sort—to the pervasive influence played by the media in shaping the lives and attitudes of today's youth.

One of the main goals of this book is to encourage constructive engagement by social studies educators with the press. As this book reminds us again and again, the field has been the subject of intense media scrutiny since it was introduced as a formal school subject early in the twentieth century. Some members of the social studies community have welcomed, indeed encouraged, this attention; others have found it thrust upon them. One of the messages here is that if the field is to do a better job in protecting its public image from detractors and maintaining its importance in the face of encroachments related to the literacy emphasis of the No Child Left Behind Act of 2001, then it needs to pay attention to the lessons imparted in these chapters.

As Carlos Cortes argues in Chapter 3, the information media serve as social studies' main competitor these days. One reason for the degree of attention the press has accorded social studies since its inception has been due to the field's intimate relationship with the core values of American society, especially nationalism and patriotism. As most readers surely know, much of the attention the press showers on social studies concerns what American students know, or more accurately do not know, about this nation's history.

Taken as a whole, this book strongly suggests the importance of raising the visibility of critical media literacy within the social studies. Ignoring this subject, as Carlos Cortes and Michael and Ilene Berson make clear, puts today's students at risk of lacking a form of literacy arguably more important to their futures than the current preoccupation with reading primary sources and other historical documents.

MY STORY

As everyone knows, Andy Warhol once quipped that Americans share a desire for "fifteen minutes of fame." Let me share my moment in the bright lights of the media here. Such fame as this may deliver will be in keeping with the ironic spirit of Warhol's comment but more importantly will help explain how this book came about.

Between 1996 and 2001 in my role as professor of social studies and education at Teachers College, I investigated the changing landscape of high schools in New York City and the effects of the "small school movement" on social studies. Since the early 90s, the city had been engaged in launching small schools intended to stem the high dropout rates associated with large, impersonal high schools. These schools were hiring our students and giving them responsibility for creating curriculum in what was called "humanities," an amalgam of history and English. In an effort to keep class size and school costs down, and to encourage teachers to get to know their students better by spending more time with them, the curriculum found in these schools was interdisciplinary. Math and science were also combined into one offering, with a single teacher responsible for both, as was the case with humanities.

I wanted to learn more about the new environments in which so many of our graduates were finding jobs. So, with financial support from a dean's grant, I assembled a team and began research on how these small schools were handling a traditional school subject, social studies. We sent out surveys, analyzed publications, pursued fieldwork, reviewed reports of supervisors of our student teachers, and interviewed administrators, teachers, and New York City Board of Education representatives. We published our findings in the *Journal of Curriculum and Supervision* (Crocco & Thornton, 2002) in an article called "Social Studies in the New York City (NYC) Public Schools: A Descriptive Study."

In the article, we applauded the gains made in reducing the dropout rate due to the caring environment created by teachers in these high schools. However, we also raised a few concerns about the interdisciplinary approach which had substituted humanities for social studies. Although we found that the curriculum was by no means uniform across the many new schools we studied, we did find a disturbing trend in some of them. If a humanities teacher had received his or her teacher preparation in English, then the humanities curriculum, not surprisingly, tilted toward English. Moreover, we found that in some schools only history, and not civics and economics, was being taught. Even where students received 4 years of history instruction, large topics such as the Civil War were not part of the curriculum. As a result of our findings, we questioned whether the subject of social studies was getting short shrift in the new small high schools.

At Teachers College, our public relations director thought our scholarly article might be of interest to a broader audience than readers of the *Journal of Curriculum and Supervision*, and decided to send a copy to the *New York Times*. Several days later, one of its reporters, Anemona Hartocollis, called me for an interview. We spoke for about an hour but her spin on our article soon became clear. What was of real interest to her was the fact that our study added grist to the mill of criticism swirling around small schools at that time.

In the hurly-burly world of NYC educational politics, small schools were under siege, with critics calling them too expensive and bureaucrats insisting they follow requirements related to curriculum and assessment enforced in the traditional high schools. One of the signature features of the small schools, graduation-by-portfolio, had provoked the wrath of education officials who wanted all students in New York State to take Regents exams.

At the end of our 60-minute conversation, even so naïve a media neophyte as I knew what was coming. Hartocollis summed up our conversation by commenting that our study suggested that restructured schools were doing a poor job. Despite my assertions that such a global conclusion was not supported by the study and that the study's aim had been to discover what appropriate teacher education in social studies for small schools would look like, my protests were of no avail.

Two days later, the headline in the paper read: "Study Faults Small Schools on Social Studies" (Hartocollis, 2002). The opening line intoned: "A study by two Columbia University professors has found that many of New York City's small high schools teach a diluted version of social studies that does not adequately prepare students for citizenship's demands." After four paragraphs of describing our study, which was reduced to its critique of the problems related to the humanities curriculum, the reporter introduced the opposing viewpoint, represented by Avram Barlowe, chair of the social studies department at Urban Academy, one of the best new small schools in the city. Naturally, Barlowe hotly disputed the allegations in our study, interpreting its findings as an attack on his already embattled school.

Subsequent events raised the stakes significantly. Other small schools banded with Urban Academy to declare a moratorium on accepting student teachers from the program in social studies at Teachers College. I received calls from jazz critic and educational gadfly, Nat Hentoff, who was eager to talk about the state of civics in the city's schools. Diane Ravitch called to commiserate with me about my treatment by the media and to share the irony she found in having two Teachers College professors engaged in a critique of what many would call "progressive education." Colleagues at Teachers College questioned my judgment in having spoken with the reporter in the first place, especially my assumption that 25 pages of nuanced scholarly writing could be productively captured through the sound bites of the modern media. The president of Teachers College took calls questioning why its professors were seemingly speaking out against small schools, especially at a time when they appeared to be losing the war against the Regents tests. In short, we had a lot of explaining to do around Teachers College—to our graduates who taught in these schools, our students, other professors, and the college's administrators.

AN UNRECIPROCATED RELATIONSHIP

This extremely brief and admittedly modest experience in the media limelight left me bruised yet intensely curious about the ways in which social studies, a school subject steeped in this nation's history and core values, had fared in the media over the last century. This interest was also fed by the concert of right-wing voices criticizing social studies at that time.

For example, one month later the *Weekly Standard*, a journal with a conservative bent, ran an article titled "Anti-Social Studies" (Hymowitz, 2002). The tagline for that article read, "So many ideas for improving the curriculum—all of them bad." What intrigued me in the escalating rhetorical wars over the next year was the degree to which such attacks on social studies had a history. A quick search on Lexis-Nexis suggested that controversy about social studies is just about as old as the field itself. During the 1940s and 1950s, *New York Times* journalist, Ben Fine, took an ongoing interest in social studies curriculum and instruction in New York City and national schools. In 1955, the *Times* ran an editorial with Fine's byline, titled "Teaching of Social Studies in High Schools is Found Inadequate to Today's Needs" (Fine, 1955, p. E9).

Around the same time, Columbia historian Allan Nevins explicitly blamed social studies for having eaten into the study of history in the nation's schools. In 1977, the American Historical Association and the Organization of American Historians, along with the National Council for the Social Studies (NCSS), prepared a joint position statement titled "History in American Schools: A Call for Renewed Emphasis." However, this document was never officially adopted, undoubtedly due to resistance within NCSS. In the early 1990s, Princeton historian Sean Wilentz (1997) once again scapegoated social studies as the cause for students' lack of understanding of the nation's history in an editorial featured in the *New York Times*.

Much to my surprise, I found a deep and wide popular literature about social studies within the mainstream media. My research indicated that battles between history and social studies, American children's alleged ignorance of American history, and the textbooks wars in Texas and California had all drawn considerable media attention.

Given this pattern, I expected to find some degree of commentary or investigation of the media's treatment of social studies by its scholars, but found myself stymied as the search went on. To the best of my knowledge, no one had investigated the relationship between social studies and the press. Of course, social studies scholars often write about controversial issues, and in recent years a few have addressed the importance of media literacy in the social studies curriculum. Perhaps this silence meant there was nothing of interest to say, but I doubted that conclusion. Given the long history of commentary by journalists about social studies, surely its scholars could provide a critique and not just defensive reaction to the analysis of their field offered by the press.

At one level, it is hardly surprising that social studies has long been controversial—even within educational circles. Its mission of creating better citizens for this democracy launched an educational enterprise that has regularly served as a lightning rod for public discourse about the means and ends of citizenship, democracy, and schooling. In recent years, debates over multicultural education, global education, and patriotism in the wake of 9/11 have all pitched social studies squarely into the heated battles of the "culture wars." But again, this is not new news: During its infancy in the 1930s, social studies professors' calls for the field to serve as an engine of social reconstruction precipitated accusations that they were promoting Communism. It seems quite natural that the media have been interested in social studies. And it seems quite appropriate, therefore, that the field return the favor.

CONSTRUCTIVE ENGAGEMENT

As a first step in opening up a new chapter in social studies' relationship with the press, I enlisted the help of Gene Maeroff, former education editor of the *New York Times* and now affiliated with the Hechinger Institute on Education and the Media at Teachers College, Columbia University. Together, we prepared a proposal for an "Invited Presidential Symposium" at the 2003 meeting of the American Educational Research Association (AERA) in Chicago, Illinois. On this panel, which drew over 200 people, a number of prominent social studies professors offered their views on the subject of social studies and the press from a variety of vantage points. James A. Banks considered multicultural education; Merry Merryfield, global education; Carole Hahn, civic education; Michael Berson, 9/11 and young children; and Stephen J. Thornton, social studies and urban schools. I served as moderator of the panel and Gene Maeroff offered a journalist's reactions to the five presentations.

Several of the original participants in this symposium have expanded their AERA presentations for this book: Merry Merryfield, Michael Berson, and Gene Maeroff. In this chapter I have retold the story which Steve Thornton presented at AERA. Interestingly, Carole Hahn felt she did not have enough material to comprise a full chapter for this book. Her story of the International Education Association's Civic Education Study, nevertheless, reveals something about what the press finds worthy of reporting.

When Hahn and her research team called a press conference to announce the positive results of the U.S. study of civic education, which found U.S. students doing the best in civic education of all nations surveyed, the press gave this news little attention. Good news, as Hahn discovered, does not travel very far.

In the AERA symposium, James A. Banks discussed the many forms of alternative media which exist in this country and cautioned the audience not to consider the press monolithically. This is an important, but easily overlooked, consideration when we talk about the media. The two chapters in this book written by professional journalists focus their attention on the print media, where it is far more likely that subjects get serious attention than generally is the case on television or radio.

Although not all the AERA presentations eventually became chapters for this book, Gene Maeroff's commentary on the symposium is included here. Maeroff offers his perspective on the presentations as a veteran education writer whose reactions and insights extend well beyond the boundaries of the original event.

The AERA symposium took place on April 21, 2003. National events over that winter and spring had rapidly unfolded toward an invasion of Iraq. Disturbing articles ran in the mainstream press and education-related news outlets about the challenges, even the dangers, confronting social studies teachers in discussing the war in their classrooms. Sadly, but perhaps unsurprisingly many individuals defined *patriotism* and *dissent* in ways rather less than nuanced and frighteningly out of sync with historic traditions of civil liberties in this country.

As these events unfolded, journalism itself was experiencing a wave of introspection. In 2003, Columbia University's new president, Lee Bollinger, announced that acclaimed writer Nicholas Lemann would take over as dean of the School of Journalism after a protracted search due to concerns over the mission of the school. The son of a newspaperman, Bollinger called for rethinking how journalists get trained for their work, citing the need for better preparation about world and national affairs.

Over the last decade, a number of books have addressed concerns with the state of journalism, for example, James Fallows' (1997) *Breaking the News: How the Media Undermine American Democracy*; Herbert Gans' *Democracy and the News* (2004); Michael Schudson's (1995) *The Power of News*, and Susan D. Moeller's (1999) *Compassion Fatigue: How the Media Sell Disease, Famine, War, and Death*.

In the last several years, the trickle has become a torrent of writing on the media and democracy, including such prominent works as Robert W. McChesney's (2004) *The Problem of the Media: U.S. Communication Politics in the Twentieth Century*. Some of the debate became quite partisan as journalists argued that the press leaned left (e.g., Bernard Goldberg's, 2002, *Bias: A CBS Insider Exposes How the Media Distort the News*) or that it leaned right (e.g., Eric Alterman's, 2003, *What Liberal Media? The Truth about Bias and the News*). Bill Moyers (2004a, 2004b) jumped into the fray, with well-publicized speeches about the status of independent journalism in the current climate of extreme partisanship. The editors of the *New York Times* on May 26, 2004, in an unprecedented move, "published a mea culpa for the paper's one-sided reporting on weapons of mass destruction and the Iraq war" (Schell, 2004).

Of course, little of this publication frenzy about the media has pertained directly to education. This lack of attention makes Maeroff's and Colvin's chapters in this book even more important. In his groundbreaking work (1998), *Imaging Education: The Media and Schools in America*, Maeroff provides a rare examination of the relationship between schooling and media at a time when national interest in education was on the upswing.

In 2000, education found itself at the top of politicians' and citizens' list of concerns. Maeroff's book attempted to explain the role of the press in shaping support for public education. Despite this laudable intention, social studies did not appear in the index to this volume. The 15 contributors to the book had other educational concerns—standardized test results, school desegregation, and college selection, among them.

Interest in education as a topic for the public spotlight has waned since that time. Given media consolidation it should not come as a surprise that many areas within education get scant coverage. For example, a study done by the Hechinger Institute indicates that a majority of newspapers do not assign anyone to cover prekindergarten issues, somewhat surprising given the emerging importance of this field (Colvin, 2004).

In addition, schools and colleges of education find themselves on the defensive. With the re-election of George Bush in 2004, the prospects for bringing high-stakes testing into secondary schools and offering alternative paths to teaching certification have gained steam. In light of these challenges, all educators and teacher educators—whatever their field—

need to understand better how the media operates and how the media can be used to support, rather than defame, public education. Just as Berliner, Bell, and Biddle (1996) exposed in their book, *The Manufactured Crisis*, political forces are at work which have taken aim at public education and its defenders. Teachers and teacher educators must be strategic in offering alternative perspectives to those who would categorically condemn public education.

PREVIEWING THE BOOK

Social Studies and the Press is organized into five parts. Part One, "Getting to Know You," contains three chapters. Besides this one, the other two include a chapter by journalist Maeroff and another by historian Cortes, author of *The Children are Watching: How the Media Teach about Diversity* (2000). Social studies educators need to understand what messages their students take from the media or risk finding their own lessons about these topics ineffectual at best and irrelevant at worst.

Part Two of the book contains four chapters providing a set of historical perspectives on the relationship between social studies and the press. Ron Evans (2004) and Linda Symcox (2002) draw on their books chronicling aspects of the culture wars. Tedd Levy, past president of the National Council for the Social Studies (NCSS), offers an insider's view of the relationships between NCSS leaders and members and the press over the last 20 years. Richard Paxton, a former journalist, examines the ways in which historical knowledge and the teaching of history have been depicted by the media. Paxton demonstrates just how easy it is to get the story wrong when it comes to education.

In Part Three, Mark Sass and James McGrath Morris tell tales of media scrutiny which, although highly personal, could happen to any social studies teacher. The other three authors in this section are education professors, Merry Merryfield, David Sadker, and Catherine Cornbleth recounting their own Andy Warhol experiences. Merryfield and Sadker have long been associated with two fields—global education and gender—at the heart of public controversies over the last 20 years. Cornbleth's chapter describes another central battleground of the culture wars—multiculturalism. Here she describes her experiences in writing *The Great Speckled Bird: Multicultural Politics and Education Policymaking* (Cornbleth & Waugh, 1995).

Part Four provides a set of three practice-oriented chapters which provide stimulating examples of how educators might think, teach, and respond to topics related to social studies and the media. Veteran social studies authors, Doug Selwyn and Alan Singer along with Singer's former student Michael Pezone provide two chapters with rich descriptions of practices which will stimulate readers' thinking about how to do critical media literacy in today's classrooms. Michael and Ilene Berson contribute a chapter that focuses readers' attention on the depiction of trauma and violence in the media and the often unacknowledged threat such coverage poses to children. Constructively, they also suggest measures teachers and parents can take to mitigate the adverse effects of saturation by such stories in homes today.

Two chapters comprise Part Five on the "New Media and Citizenship Education." Howard Budin reflects on the democratic potential of self-publishing on the Web in light of new theorizing about citizenship education. Judith Cramer investigates several examples of "blogging" and skillfully mines their implications for the future of journalism, politics, and citizenship education.

The book concludes with three chapters—one by a past president of NCSS, Rick Theisen; one by former *Los Angeles Times* education writer Richard Lee Colvin, now director of the Hechinger Institute; and one by E. Wayne Ross, former editor of *Theory and Research in Social Education*, the scholarly journal of the College and University Faculty Assembly of NCSS. Theisen's chapter offers concrete ideas for dealing with the media. His chapter draws on his experiences as spokesman for NCSS at an American Enterprise Institute forum in Washington, DC, titled "Social Studies and the Battle for America's Soul." Other participants in this forum were Senator Lamar Alexander, Dr. James Leming, Dr. Lucien Ellington, and former Secretary of Education William Bennett (*The Social Studies Professional*, 2003). The event was precipitated by the Thomas B. Fordham Foundation's publication of its screed, *Where Did We Go Wrong?* (Leming Ellington, & Porter-Magee, 2003).

Colvin's chapter is an insightful and self-critical recapitulation of journalistic failures in reporting successfully on the history wars of the 1990s. Colvin's findings speak directly to the challenges facing all educators in getting their messages and stories out to the journalists who deal with the tyranny of deadlines in writing complicated stories about education.

E. Wayne Ross's chapter offers a sobering assessment and a picture of possibilities for engagement with the press by a seasoned academic adventurer in the world of journalism. Perhaps no other social studies scholar has so consistently served as a public intellectual for social studies than Ross. Here he offers a number of examples of his highly proactive relationship with the press over the last 10 years—as letter writer, editorial writer, and source about all things educational for numerous journalists. For scholars interested in making their voices heard on a larger stage, there could be no better model.

It is my hope that this book will stimulate thinking about the ways in which social studies can engage more effectively with the media. By that I mean several things. First, social studies scholars need to teach about and sometimes against the media. Second, social studies educators need to learn more about the media and understand its impact on our students. Finally, social studies scholars need to embrace the political and policy-oriented aspects of their work and seek out the press. If we do not define ourselves, we will be defined by others—historians, right-wing pundits, or individuals with a vested interest in bringing down public education.

Of course, I recognize that social studies is not the same as public education, but its work for citizenship education does inhabit a critical space in our educational universe. In the public arena today, clearly the media help shape future citizens' core understandings of what it means to be an American. Since civic as well as cultural values lie at the heart of so much public debate (Frank, 2004), one thing is clear: Social studies educators must do a better job in insuring that the many little publics comprising this nation recognize full well the contribution citizenship education makes to this nation's civic vitality.

REFERENCES

Alterman, E. (2003). *What liberal media? The truth about bias and the news.* New York: Basic Books.

American Historical Association, Organization of American Historians, National Council for the Social Studies. (1977). *History in American schools: A call for renewed emphasis.* Unpublished manuscript. New York: NCSS Archives, Special Collections, Milbank Library, Teachers College, Columbia University.

Berliner, D., Bell, J., & Biddle, B. J. (1996). *The manufactured crisis.* New York: Perseus.

Colvin, R. L. (2004, December 10). *Survey reveals lack of coverage on pre-K issues by nation's media.* Retrieved December 21, 2004, from www.tc.columbia.edu

Cornbleth, C., & Waugh, D. (1995). *The great speckled bird: Multicultural politics and education policy making.* Mahwah, NJ: Erlbaum.

Cortes, C. (2000). *The children are watching: How the media teach about diversity.* New York: Teachers College Press.

Crocco, M. S., & Thornton, S. J. (2002). Social studies in the New York City public schools: A descriptive study. *Journal of Curriculum and Supervision, 17*(3), 206-231.

Evans, R. (2004). *The social studies wars: What should we teach the children?* New York: Teachers College Press.

Fallows, J. (1996). *Breaking the news: How the media undermine American democracy.* New York: Vintage.

Fine, B. (1955, January 2). Teaching of social studies in high schools is found inadequate to today's needs. *New York Times,* p. E9.

Frank, T. (2004). *What's the matter with Kansas?* New York: Henry Holt.

Gans, H. (2004). *Democracy and the news.* New York: Oxford.

Goldberg, B. (2002). *Bias: A CBS insider exposes how the media distort the news.* Washington, DC: Regnery.

Hartocollis, A. (2002, April 10). Study faults small school. *New York Times,* p. B7.

Hymowitz, K. (2002, May 6). Anti-social studies. *The Weekly Standard,* pp. 27-29.

Leming, J., Ellington, L., & Porter-Magee, K. (2003). *Where did social studies go wrong?* Retrieved December 21, 2004, from http://www.edexcellence.net/institute/publication/publication.cfm?id=317

Maeroff, G. (Ed.). (1998). *Imaging education: The media and schools in America.* New York: Teachers College Press.

McChesney, R. W. (2004). *The problem of the media: US communication politics in the 21st century.* New York: Monthly Review Press.

Moeller, S. D. (1999). *Compassion fatigue: How the media sell disease, famine, war and death.* New York: Routledge.

Moyers, B. (2004a, May 19). *An eye on power.* Speech given at Newspaper Guild/Communication Workers dinner. Retrieved December 21, 2004, from www.tompaine.com

Moyers, B. (2004b, September 11). *Journalism under fire.* Speech given at Society of Professional Journalists conference. Retrieved December 21, 2004, from www.tompaine.com

Schell, O. (2004, July 19). *Why the media failed us in Iraq.* Retrieved October 15, 2004, from http://hnn.us/articles/printfriendly/6209.html

Schudson, M. (1995). *The power of the news.* Cambridge, MA: Harvard University Press.

Symcox, L. (2002). *Whose history? The struggle for national standards in American classrooms.* New York: Teachers College Press.

Theisen Presents NCSS Position at Forum: AEI's Social Studies and the Battle for America's Soul. (2003, November/December). *The Social Studies Professional,* 178.

Wilentz, S. (1997, April 20). The past is not a "process." *New York Times,* Sec. 4, p. 15.

CHAPTER 2

SPREADING THE NEWS ABOUT SOCIAL STUDIES

Gene I. Maeroff

Just how well do the media mediate? After all, film, television, and espe-cially newspapers and magazines play a crucial role in connecting the public with social studies, as Margaret Smith Crocco (2003) notes in writ-ing of the "mediating influence of the press in translating our research into digestible form for the public." Not only research but the content and teaching of social studies, as well, are within the purview of the mediating influence of the media.

One might suppose that the public could get along without the media performing this function. There are other ways to learn about social stud-ies. Lay people, after all, could subscribe to research journals. They could obtain and review curricula and lesson plans from schools, districts, and states. They could go into classrooms and observe social studies teachers. We know, however, that such behavior is totally impractical. Chances are that even the most diligent parents of students do none of this.

And why should they? Whether it is news about business, sports, or government, people turn to the media. Members of the general public did not visit Iraq to gauge the progress of the invasion. They did not fol-low presidential candidates in person across America to hear what they were saying. Few even attend all of their favorite team's games, home and

Social Studies and the Press: Keeping the Beast at Bay?, 15–23

away. They depend on reports by the media. Given this mediating role, I offer five propositions as a framework for considering matters involving social studies and the media:

- Much of what the media define as news revolves around tension and/or conflict. This makes a story more interesting and compelling.
- There are huge differences between print and broadcast outlets. In general, these differences lead to more thorough, more accurate coverage of news in the print media.
- Social studies as social studies does not appeal to the media, even to education reporters. But social studies can engage journalists when they see a newsworthy angle.
- Everything I have noted until this point applies equally to news about social studies research, content, and teaching.
- Finally, by and large, few journalists set out to botch the facts or to make mistakes. Like good researchers, most want to exercise care and objectivity.

News spreads fast these days, making Americans "a nation of collective witnesses," as Michael Berson (2003) puts it. The dissemination of news relied on the spoken word before the invention of moveable type in the fifteenth century, an innovation that made mass circulation newspapers possible. Newspapers essentially enjoyed a monopoly on the spread of news for several centuries. The advent of radio in the 1920s changed all that. Then, after television appeared in 1939 at the World's Fair in New York, it was just a matter of another decade or so before Americans were collective witnesses to Edward R. Murrow, Uncle Miltie, and Howdy Doody, whose shows they could discuss the next morning.

It grew clear in late November of 1963 that the new public square in which Americans figuratively gathered comprised the tens of millions of places around their television sets. First, they learned on a preholiday Friday afternoon that their president had been shot and shortly thereafter they found out that John F. Kennedy was dead. They were collective witnesses to ensuing events as they unfolded, including, almost unbelievably, the on camera assassination of the assassin. Television screens glowed through one of the nation's saddest weekends and into the next week. How can anyone forget the funeral and its regalia? This was social studies in live time.

Finally, as one takes note of the rapid spread of news to Berson's nation of collective witnesses, the arrival of the Internet represents just one more way of speeding the process. Press the button on the monitor; fire up the computer. News flows into one's home or work place with the immediacy of a ringing telephone. Newspapers? Television? Who needs them? Now, the public gets the latest news instantly and surfs the Web for embellishments.

One may lose sight, however, of the fact that someone somewhere has to gather that news and put it onto the air waves, into printed pages—and even online. With all of the rapid dissemination, journalists themselves still play a mediating role. But the implications are enormous for them when the public can get the news so fast and from so many competing sources. And in mentioning the Web, I must point out that despite its many attributes the Internet represents the triumph of the trivial, the inconsequential, and the incorrect over the forces of the fair and the accurate. Anything can get online. There is no vetting, no peer review. This is not the *Encyclopedia Britannica* or even the *World Book*. And given that a whole generation of Internet-bred Americans is coming of age not knowing better, the consequences for social studies are indeed frightening.

Returning to the work of journalists, they can no longer settle just for relating the facts of what happened and leave it at that. They must dance to a 24/7 news rhythm. Everything becomes a "second-day story" and they have to probe for angles to advance their coverage. Journalists must find ways to relate the story with information and insights that go beyond what the audience has already witnessed. This can mean straining to find something new, possibly rushing into print or onto the air before the story is really ready—or fully accurate.

Berson speaks of the dichotomy between patriotism and tolerance, and the idea of balancing these two concepts in the classroom. America's actions in Iraq illustrate the challenge. The best media outlets try to reconcile this dichotomy, much as good social studies teachers attempt to do. Some news outlets are more successful than others at attaining balance without tottering to one side or the other.

The challenge manifested itself early in the invasion, when the swift march of American troops across Iraq evoked shameless jingoism in some sectors of the media. Fox News Channel was emblematic in this regard, a role it continued to maintain in the patriotic stances of such personalities as Sean Hannity and Bill O'Reilly throughout the occupation. The inimitable Michael Moore eventually provided a counterbalance that was no less one-sided.

Even books, a medium once considered the sanctuary of more reasoned, more careful analysis, have taken on the coloration of out-and-out partisanship. The publishing lists leading up to the 2004 election illustrated this trend. Consider some of the titles:

How to Talk to a Liberal (If You Must): The World According to Ann Coulter
Cruel and Unusual: Bush/Cheney's New World Order
Rogue State: America at War with the World
Hoax: Why Americans Are Suckered by White House Lies
Can America Survive? The Rage of the Left, the Truth, and What to Do About It
Worse Than Watergate: The Secret Presidency of George W. Bush.

How are social studies professionals who wish to keep patriotism and tolerance in check to deal with such extremes? Where is the demarcation between objectivity and subjectivity? Social studies itself, whether in the hands of teacher or researcher, often sinks into this mushy ground. Facts and interpretation are not the simple matters that social studies practitioners of yore pretended them to be. When is a classroom lesson or a research article akin to documentary journalism? When is it a polemic? When is it propaganda? When is it a screed?

I considered these questions anew recently during a field visit to a second grade classroom, where I watched children learn to read from a nonfiction book about the environment. Given their age, one could expect little sophistication in the content. But the one-sidedness made me wonder who allows such books into schools. Pollution of streams, the air, and food filled the pages. There were no explanations. The pupils would have no idea that any protections exist for the environment, or that production and employment are legitimate pursuits that may sometimes take note of environmental concerns.

Issues of balance cut across social studies—well beyond the pages of a second grade reader—and one may also examine balance through the lens of the larger media. Consider Hannity, O'Reilly, and Moore, whom I have just mentioned. One may dismiss them as entertainers whose pronouncements have scant connection to the *real* news and, therefore, little to do with social studies. This response, however, ignores the fact that such commentators exert enormous influence in an era when much of what passes for news wears the garb of entertainment. Even comedians, after all, have become news commentators. Consider Bill Maher or Dennis Miller, for example. Uncle Walter left the business just in time.

The same problem exists in film. When Arnold Schwarzenegger and other cartoon-like figures roar across the screen it is clear even to the most thick-headed cinema-goer that this is fiction. Yet, let an Oliver Stone deal with the assassination of John F. Kennedy in a film and a debate erupts over verisimilitude. What are we talking about here? Filmmaker Stone trades in historical fiction—that's right, fiction. This brand of fiction flows from the mind of the auteur, no less than it does when such novelists as Gore Vidal write of Abraham Lincoln or E.L. Doctorow of Emma Goldman. Such work is not a documentary and no one should regard it as such. Yet, as social studies teachers know, young people have increasing difficulty sorting out fact from fiction and this is more the fault of Americans willfully allowing themselves to be uninformed and misinformed than it is the fault of the news and entertainment media.

Talk radio with its all-opinions-are equal mentality exacerbates the problem. The fact is that all opinions are not equal and some derive from pure ignorance and unadulterated enmity. A decade ago, when talk radio was a less pervasive blight on the media landscape, a study revealed that talk radio listeners thought they knew more about the issues than other people, when they actually knew less (Simurda, 2004). Chances are that the situation has not improved.

What are people who are serious about social studies to make of such matters? How does one teach social studies to students for whom politicians and news have become fodder for humor? How does one conduct social studies research when the line between entertainment and news grows indistinguishable?

As a corollary, Merry Merryfield's (2003) observations prod me to emphasize that social studies professionals must assiduously differentiate in their teaching and their research between news and opinion. When a Phyllis Schlafly, whom Merryfield mentions, or a Rush Limbaugh comments on global education or any other social studies topic, their pronouncements are akin to the editorials in a newspaper. They have points of view through which they filter their comments. This is quite different from the impartiality that journalists supposedly strive to convey in news coverage.

Opinion and hard news are not the same even if some Americans no longer recognize the difference. It is one thing, for instance, to describe global education as simply one of the approaches used by professors and teachers and quite another matter to deride global education as a vehicle by which pointy-headed, fuzzy-thinking social studies professionals try to undermine America and its singular vision.

Disagreements over social studies that find their way into the media, of course, are not limited to descriptions and interpretations of global education. Such disputes could very well encompass portrayals in social studies textbooks and classrooms of early European explorers of North America, slave-holding founding fathers, pioneers who seized Indian lands, and turn-of-the-century robber barons. "There is no such thing as impartial history," says historian Howard Zinn, whose own version may be as suspect as anyone else's (Holden, 2004).

The latest frontal attack on traditional notions of journalism comes from bloggers who have discovered a lifeline on the Internet. Their output exacerbates tensions between hard news and opinion. How much credence should social studies professionals give to the blogs that so many of their students read? How should a social studies teacher react to students who draw their current events reports from blogs? Officials running the Democratic and Republican national conventions were shoved into this debate when they had to decide who would receive press credentials, forcing them to consider whether bloggers are journalists and whether blogs are a form of journalism.

Such issues illustrate the potential for division in social studies. And controversy and conflict, lest one forget, are what make news. So, then, what happens when social studies scholars disseminate results of their research through the mass media, as Stephen Thornton and Margaret Crocco (Thornton, 2003) tried to do? Suffice to say that the results may not resemble what occurs when one publishes the same findings in a scholarly journal.

Crocco discovered after a one-hour telephone interview with a reporter that the reporter tried to sum up what she had said, boiling down her words to what the journalist considered the gist. Space limitations mean that only a fraction of a research report or an interview on research findings will be used. A typical story in a daily newspaper runs no more than 500 to 600 words. That is less than a page and a half in a book. The usual television story consumes less than 90 seconds. Read a passage aloud and see how little you have covered after a minute and a half. Thus, researchers cannot approach journalists as if they are dealing with a refereed journal. The media sum up topics; they seek to keep reportage brief. Limits of space and time dictate that function follows form. Still, a researcher has a reasonable right to expect fairness and accuracy of the news media.

A problem, though, is that complexity does not lend itself to short explanations and sound bites, as John Kerry so rudely learned in his labored explanations of policy. Researchers in dealing with journalists should perhaps keep in mind the abstracts that they write as introductions to scholarly articles. Such an abstract might provide a good deal of what a journalist really wants. The challenge facing researchers who follow this admonition is to be both pithy and precise simultaneously, without sacrificing accuracy at the altar of brevity. Of course, a researcher is always free to let the words on the pages of a journal speak for themselves without further comment. He or she should understand, though, that this leaves the interpretation to the journalist or whoever the journalist may contact.

Journalists get fed up with members of the public who tell them, "You're interested in only the bad news." Yet, while journalists may not like hearing this complaint, there is some truth to it. News by its very definition is aberration; it is man bites dog, not dog bites man. There will be no article in tomorrow morning's newspaper about the hundreds upon hundreds of airline flights that safely reached their destinations today.

The story, if there is one, will be about the plane that did not make it or almost did not make it. Ho-hum events are not newsy.

Journalists do not altogether ignore so-called good news, but they prefer to find an angle that makes a story worthy of their attention. So, the good news nature of a study by the International Association for the Evaluation of Educational Achievement (IEA) may put off journalists, as Carol Hahn (2003) said she discovered. Hahn's experience in trying to publicize the results of an IEA study may be instructive to other social studies researchers in at least two ways.

First, while every detail of the study was not revealed the first time around, there was, in fact, an announcement of the main findings several weeks before she sought the attention of journalists. Other findings had been withheld for the later announcement that Hahn says was largely ignored. News outlets generally refuse to pay attention to information they regard as stale, having been previously revealed on their own pages or, worse yet, by a competitor.

News is supposed to be new; that is where it gets its name. Such leading news organizations as the *New York Times*, for instance, may refuse to print a story that has run elsewhere. And a newspaper that *does* print a story that appeared elsewhere may do so without giving credit to the publication that carried the story first. Anyone doing research in the social studies should try to avoid serving up morsels to the press that journalists will regard as reheated.

Another lesson from Hahn's experience: Secretary of Education Rod Paige spoke to the same group at the same meeting, earlier in the day. He discussed No Child Left Behind (NCLB), a fairly fresh subject of great interest to the press at the time. The facts about the implementation of NCLB were still unfolding across the country and education writers welcomed Paige's input. The information about IEA had the misfortune of trying to gain a toehold on a day in a place where other news overshadowed it. Timing plays a major role in determining what is news, just as location does in deciding which real estate claims the highest price. Researchers who wish to see their findings covered ought to hope, among other matters, that it is a weak news day.

Scholarly journals operate on a more leisurely publication schedule than the daily news media, putting submissions through months of peer review and sometimes even taking years beyond publication dates to run reviews of books. Those who inhabit the academic world, like waltzers in fin-de-siecle Vienna, are accustomed to a slower, more leisurely rhythm. Journalists, on the other hand, chronicle ephemeral events. Sometimes history and current events merge, but it is the current aspect, not the history, which piques the interest of journalists—a ship from the Civil War just discovered at ocean's bottom, access for the first time to Russian archives that provide new insights into Stalin's behavior, DNA testing of an ancient lock of hair.

James Banks (2003) offers a critique that comes at the issues from an entirely different perspective, leading us to consider other questions regarding the media. He wonders, for example, about the ownership of the mainstream media and the influence on what gets covered and how it is covered. This is an appropriate topic of inquiry as many Americans may not appreciate the extent to which conglomerates have taken over the media in the United States.

- Huge corporations—Disney, Viacom, and General Electric—own the three major television networks. Quite a shift from the old days when ABC, CBS, and NBC were essentially self-contained media companies. Fox, the newest network on the block, is a tentacle in Rupert Murdoch's globe-spanning media octopus.
- Most major cable channels, which ostensibly seem independent of the networks, are actually owned in part or fully by the same companies that own the networks or by such other giant corporations as Time Warner.
- Just a few companies now account for most of the country's 1,600 daily newspapers, having gobbled up the lion's share of ownership in less than three decades. Gannett alone owns more than 100 dailies.
- Closer to home for those in education, four publishers now control most of the textbook market.

Somewhat related to Banks' critique, though he does not speak to it specifically, is the alarming overlap of news and entertainment, especially on television, as I have already mentioned. I suspect that many viewers, especially younger ones, have little interest in news that is not suffused in amusement. In elementary and secondary school classrooms, social studies teachers struggle to engage children who prefer to be entertained. Professors who are preparing social studies teachers to work in the schools must rev up the learning curve for young adults who not many years earlier were those children who cared little about the past. Add reality shows to the mix and you have the latest version of the old relevancy debate that erupted in education during the ferment of the 1960s.

And so it is that Americans gravitate to media outlets that package the news in forms that they find most palatable. The multitude of media possibilities seems to offer a limitless source of news and views, packaged in countless forms. Yet, how valuable is this cornucopia if people cannot evaluate the veracity of what they read, hear, and see? Furthermore, how valuable is diversity of choice if people opt for only those outlets that reinforce their prior dispositions? Such conditions make social studies more important than ever. The subject, as taught in schools and colleges, must arm students at all levels with the ability to act as informed consumers of the media. Social studies professionals must give students the facts and background to know when the media tries to dupe them—or when teachers or researchers try to dupe them.

REFERENCES

Banks, J. (2003, April). Multicultural education and the press. In M. S. Crocco (Chair), *Social studies and the press: Keeping the beast at bay?* Symposium conducted at the annual meeting of the American Educational Research Association, Chicago, Illinois.

Berson, M. J. (2003, April). The social studies and 9/11. In M. S. Crocco (Chair), *Social studies and the press: Keeping the beast at bay?* Symposium conducted at the annual meeting of the American Educational Research Association, Chicago, Illinois.

Crocco, M. S. (2003, April). Introductory remarks. In M. S. Crocco (Chair), *Social studies and the press: Keeping the beast at bay?* Symposium conducted at the annual meeting of the American Educational Research Association, Chicago, Illinois.

Hahn, C. (2003, April). Civic education and the press. In M. S. Crocco (Chair), *Social studies and the press: Keeping the beast at bay?* Symposium conducted at the annual meeting of the American Educational Research Association, Chicago, Illinois.

Holden, S. (2004, July 23). Activist with a topsy-turvey view of the world. *New York Times*, p. E19.

Merryfield, M. (2003, April). Global education and the press. In M. S. Crocco (Chair), *Social studies and the press: Keeping the beast at bay?* Symposium conducted at the annual meeting of the American Educational Research Association, Chicago, Illinois.

Simurda, S. (2004, Summer). Editorial pages—A future in doubt. *The Masthead: National Conference of Editorial Writers*, p. 13.

Thornton, S. K. (2003, April). Social studies in the urban context. In M. S. Crocco (Chair), *Social studies and the press: Keeping the beast at bay?* Symposium conducted at the annual meeting of the American Educational Research Association, Chicago, Illinois.

CHAPTER 3

THE "INFORMATION" MEDIA

Social Studies' Main Competitor

Carlos E. Cortés

I did not put quotation marks around "information" in order to be postmodernist cute. It is just my way of indicating that those media do far more than simply supply information.

Of course, they inform. However, recent surveys suggest that consumers tend to choose those information media—newspapers, magazines, Internet sites, talk radio shows, television news programs, cable news channels, and documentary films—that exhibit, reinforce, even promote their personal beliefs. In other words, *consumers* seek *confirmation* as well as—or instead of—*information*. For example, a summer, 2004, Annenberg National Election Survey found that only 12 of 5,501 respondents had *both* listened to Rush Limbaugh's radio talk show *and* seen Michael Moore's film, *Fahrenheit 9/11* (Rosenberg, 2004).

As I discuss in my book, *The Children Are Watching: How the Media Teach about Diversity* (2000), the media go well beyond presenting (selected) information. In a pedagogical sense, they operate in at least four other major ways.

They organize ideas. They disseminate values. They create and reinforce expectations. And they model behavior.

Social Studies and the Press: Keeping the Beast at Bay?, 25–35

In such ways, whether intentionally or incidentally, the information media teach. Reverse the equation. As research has clearly demonstrated, people learn from the media. Not only from news, documentaries, and other supposedly nonfiction sources but also—albeit often subconsciously—from reality TV, docudramas, and other hybrid forms sometimes referred to as *infotainment*. According to the Pew Research Center for the People and the Press, 21% of Americans ages 18-29 use such shows as "Saturday Night Live" and Comedy Central's "The Daily Show" as primary sources for political news, while only 23% regularly read a daily newspaper (Altaras, 2004).

But while the information media teach, what do media consumers actually learn from them? It is vital to distinguish between media teaching (intentional or incidental) and media-derived learning (conscious or subconscious). Yet many observers and analysts tend to conflate these two processes.

Consider the parallel between schools and information media. School educators cannot assess student learning merely by analyzing textbooks and lectures. Examinations clearly demonstrate the inevitable teaching-learning gap in school education.

Likewise, we can *analyze* (and disagree about) the content, nature, and intentionality of media teaching and on that basis can *hypothesize* potential consumer learning. However, we cannot be certain what consumers are learning without assessing their reception or observing behavior that appears to demonstrate that media impact. That is why conflicting *theses* are a staple of media studies. For example, there is major disagreement over the impact of repeated media coverage of global suffering (like poverty, disease, starvation, and civil strife). Does it increase viewer caring or does it anesthetize viewers, sometimes referred to as the *compassion fatigue thesis*?

Regardless of your position on that question, this example illustrates the fact that, as informal teachers, the information media do engage topics or exemplify concerns of social studies educators (National Council for the Social Studies, 2002). These include knowledge and interpretations of history, geography, government, economics, and other dimensions of the world, including ideas about civic behavior, societal values, conflict resolution, diversity, intergroup relations, global awareness, the environment, and the analytical use of evidence.

There is only one way to avoid social studies teaching by the information media and only one way to immunize yourself from media-based social studies learning—by totally avoiding those media, all of them, including newspapers, magazines, radio, television, documentary motion pictures, and, of course, the new cyberspace media (Berson & Berson, 2003). In short, when it comes to the social studies, the information mass media are a formidable competitor to school educators. Let us briefly look at those five information media teaching functions as they relate to the social studies.

PROVIDE INFORMATION

Obviously the media present information. Sometimes accurate, sometimes inaccurate. Sometimes with complexity, sometimes simplistically. Sometimes nuanced, often stereotypical. Sometimes with words alone, sometimes enhanced or sensationalized by visuals (Graber, 1990). Sometimes delivered as news, other times packaged as entertainment. Sometimes embedded in a clarifying context, other times abbreviated, fragmented, and chaotic, often as a stream of televised factoids, Internet news briefs, newspaper capsules, and radio sound bites——the media equivalent of fast food.

Take local TV news. Driven by ratings competition and their perceptions that viewers want the sensational more than the substantive, they generally operate according to the widespread *if-it-bleeds-it-leads* ideology. Some pundits have referred to local news as a series of crime stories followed by sports and the weather forecast.

How accurate are these stories? Who knows? But so what? The main teaching-learning issue is frequency, not accuracy.

Let us assume that each individual story is factually accurate. Even so, the very crime-oriented selection of much local TV news, especially if it recurs night after night, can still create a distorted community portrait. The relentless, repetitive, and skewed local news emphasis on crime and violence can create an atmosphere of community distrust, even fear. In fact, research has demonstrated that heavy TV watchers tend to overestimate the threat of violence in their own lives, what George Gerbner has labeled the "mean world syndrome" (Gerbner, Gross, Morgan, & Signorielli, 1986).

Then add another social studies teaching dimension. When local TV news focuses on crime, it is often about the violent acts of *others*, meaning those of racial and ethnic backgrounds different from the viewer and with whom the viewer may have limited personal contact. This nightly bombardment of image-heightened stories about others as criminals can contribute to intergroup stereotyping, social polarization, and a fear of venturing into areas of those who are "different" (Romer, Jamieson, & Aday, 2003).

But does that really happen? Take a viewing experience I once had with an episode of the long-running daytime television game show "The $25,000 Pyramid." Competition involves two-person teams of total strangers. A series of words appears on the screen in front of one player, who then gives clues to guide the partner into correctly identifying the maximum number of words. Victory goes to the team that gets the most correct answers within the time limit.

As I watched one morning, the word gangs popped onto one cluer's screen. Without hesitation she shouted, "They have lots of these in East L.A." (a heavily Mexican American section of Los Angeles). Responding immediately, her partner answered, "Gangs." Under competitive pressure, two strangers found instant cognitive communion via their mutual knowledge of a Latino community as being synonymous with gangs. Simultaneously they transmitted that stereotype to a national TV audience.

Unfortunately East Los Angeles does have gangs. But it also has families, schools, businesses, churches, and socially contributing organizations. Yet gangs, not such far more prevalent aspects of East Los Angeles life, had instantaneously linked these two total strangers by punching their comparable mental *default functions*. Why?

Sure it is *possible* that *both* of these strangers had independently conducted research into the East Los Angeles community and concluded that gangs were the most important element. Possible, but unlikely. Moreover, as strangers, neither would have *known* the other was also an East Los Angeles expert.

So where did they get their coinciding *default knowledge*. Where else? From the information media. The deleterious bombardment of gang-featuring local television and newspaper crime reports (a message reiterated by movies and fictional TV) has created an informal social studies curriculum featuring gangs as *the* quintessential popular vision of urban Latino communities, such as East Los Angeles.

Once again, the issue is frequency, not accuracy (Gilens, 1996). The facts presented in every news story can be 100% accurate. Each story can be organized clearly and contextualized fairly. However, the canted selection of stories about a specific group (racial, ethnic, religious, gender, you name it)—which stories are included or excluded—can reinforce or even create viewer knowledge, as demonstrated by "The $25,000 Pyramid."

ORGANIZE IDEAS

But media go well beyond deluging viewers with (selected) information and images. Through the ways that they *frame* information, both local and national information media also organize ideas (Goffman, 1974). By influencing reader, viewer, and listener cognitive structures, the information media *transform* as well as *inform*.

These media idea organizers range from newspaper columnists, Internet bloggers, television commentators, and radio talk show hosts, who spin the news and try to define the issues, to headline writers and magazine cover designers, who create and dramatize news frames. And, of course, there are those behind-the-scenes operatives on such channels as CNN and Fox News Network who cram every inch of the TV screen with unrelated, noncontextualized news bites and headlines. These informational appetizers and fast food framings organize information by simplifying multifaceted events and predigesting complex issues for viewers— part of what has been termed *the CNN effect* or the *Foxification* of the news.

Next time you listen to a TV newscast, notice how many times and in what words announcers tantalize viewers about an upcoming story before actually presenting it. By the time viewers finally receive the story, the multiple teasers have instructed and conditioned them as to *how* they should think *about* the story that is finally being presented.

The information media, particularly television, often proclaim that they provide a window on the world (or sometimes, more passively, that they merely *reflect* the world). Really? As I have sometimes challenged TV newspeople on panels and in my media workshops, if those two glass metaphors are true, why not just roll the camera over to the studio window, shoot 30 minutes of raw footage, and then show it on the nightly news? That would be a much truer window on the world ... but nobody would watch.

TV newsmakers carefully organize their content (they call it selecting, editing, and framing) in order to hang onto audiences, keep them from switching channels, and encourage them to return rather than choose their competitors. Sometimes they even explicitly organize and frame stories to provide lessons about U.S. society or the world, traditionally a social studies function (Carragee & Roefs, 2004).

In his longtime nightly newscast, CBS anchorman Walter Cronkite used to end each evening's program by assuring viewers, "That's the way it is," a classic window formulation. Need I comment that those carefully-selected, painstakingly-edited 30 minutes provided far less than the entire world's *it*.

Likewise, for the print media. The week after the May, 1992, court acquittal of the four Los Angeles policemen accused of beating African American motorist Rodney King, the May 11 *U.S. News and World Report* organized the resulting Los Angeles riots with the following cover headlines: "Race and Rage: Black vs. White: The New Fears, Cops in the Crossfire." The event was framed as Black versus White despite hours of television showing riots that involved not only Blacks and Whites, but also Asian Americans and Latinos. Maybe America's first major televised *multiracial, multiethnic* riot.

Yet *U.S. News and World Report* synthesized it for readers (or casual cover glancers) as a Black-White thing. No wonder journalism is sometimes called *the first draft of history*. However, the following week, the May 18 *Newsweek* provided a *second draft* by multiculturally *reorganizing* the event with a new social studies framework, its front cover proclaiming, "Beyond Black and White." What a difference a week makes!

When news broadcasts and newspaper stories repeatedly adopt the same narrative structures while reporting on a subject, they help to shape reader and viewer mental and attitudinal frameworks for organizing future information and ideas about those topics (Hartmann & Husband, 1972; Hawkins & Pingree, 1981). For example, in a study of the comparative treatment of Blacks and Whites by Chicago local television news, communications scholar Robert Entman (1990) concluded that:

> In the stories analyzed, crime reporting made blacks look particularly threatening, while coverage of politics exaggerated the degree to which black politicians (as compared to white ones) practice special interest politics. These images would feed the first two components of modern racism, anti-black affect and resistance to blacks' political demands. On the other hand, the positive dimension of the news, the presence of black anchors and other authority figures, may simultaneously engender an impression that racial discrimination is no longer a problem. (p. 342)

The media, then, go well beyond spreading information (and misinformation). Using such devices as framing, they also influence the organizational schematas of viewers, readers, and listeners.

DISSEMINATE VALUES

The information media transmit and promote values. This occurs although many, maybe most, information media makers do not consider themselves to be values disseminators.

Quite the contrary, I have served on panels with information media executives and newspeople who vehemently deny that they are involved in *values education*. Or, for that matter, that they even deal with values. That is why it is so welcome when an opinionated pundit, such as CNN's Lou Dobbs, clearly lays out his values position as he does through the title of his ongoing series, "Exporting America", in which he criticizes U.S. businesses for off-shoring jobs.

Ironically, one of the hottest current media-discussed topics is the issue of media values bias—generally via accusations of *other* media makers as having biases, that is. Yet that very debate is influenced by what has been called the "hostile media effect": the tendency to evaluate mass media treatment of selected topics as being contrary to—often expressed as biased against—one's own beliefs (Gunther & Schmitt, 2004). Both Rush Limbaugh and Michael Moore have accused CNN of media bias ... but in nearly opposite directions! Comparably, Tony Blair railed against the British Broadcasting Corporation (BBC) for being antiwar, while polls of British viewers revealed that they considered it prowar (Fraser, 2004).

Sometimes media values messages are delivered in the form of a purportedly neutral question. For example, at the top of its front cover, the April 6, 1992, *Newsweek* posed the question, "Who Speaks for Blacks?" A question, yes, but one replete with (possibly unintentional) values messages. That readers ought to assume—or at least consider—that there *ought* to be one person (or a selected few) designated to speak for Blacks. (Should it be Jesse Jackson or Clarence Thomas?) That the absence of *a single* Black spokesperson (or at least a small number) might suggest African American community divisiveness or organizational incompetence— cannot 35 million Blacks get their act together and speak with one voice?

My personal test for determining values bias in the information media is what I call the *substitution game*, in this case the substitution of White for Black. Try to imagine a national magazine cover asking, "Who Speaks for Whites?" When I have suggested this at media workshops, the inevitable response is painful laughter. Why? Because they could not possibly imagine that any headline writer would even *consider* such a headline.

Or take newspaper headlines that organize ideas about divisive Latino political behavior with terms like *Brown vs. Brown*, when the story itself concerns Latino politicians who are running for the same elected office. I thought that was the nature of democracy. And when was the last time you saw a headline calling attention to *the straight agenda*?

Black-on-Black violence (or crime) has become a staple for both the print and electronic media. The values message: they even do it to each other. Playing the substitution game, for a number of years I offered a prize if any of my students could find a headline proclaiming White-on-White violence. No success. Plenty of headlines about White *interethnic violence*, but never framed racially as White-on-White.

In fall, 2003, one of my students uncovered such an article in the December 22, 1996, *Milwaukee Journal Sentinel*, with a headline, "Radio program aims to turn tables on media" and a subhead, "Show gives account of 'white-on-white' crime for its mostly black listeners." It was the story of radio station WNOV reporter Teju Ologboni. Cohost of the "Word Warriors" program, he turned the Black-on-Black media values tradition on its head with an ongoing segment, "The White-on-White Crime Report," about crime within the White community.

CREATE AND REINFORCE EXPECTATIONS

The media create and reinforce expectations. As film critic Michael Medved (1992) argued in his book, *Hollywood v. America: Popular Culture and the War on Traditional Values*, "If nothing else, repeated exposure to media images serves to alter our perceptions of the society in which we live and to gradually shape what we accept—and expect—from our fellow citizens" (p. xxiii). This applies directly to social studies concerns.

In some respects, the war in Iraq became a litmus test for media expectation-setting, culminating in two April, 2004, controversies: the Internet release and ensuing widespread media dissemination of Pentagon photographs of flag-covered coffins of U.S. armed services personnel in Iraq; and Ted Koppel's April 30 "Nightline" reading of the names of American service people who had died in Iraq, accompanied by their photos.

This is not the place to play armchair psychoanalyst. What were the real motives of Tucson author Russ Kick (who requested the photographs, acquired them under the Freedom of Information Act, and put images of the flag-covered coffins on his Memory Hole Web site)? Or the real motives of media makers at newspapers and magazines who chose (or chose not) to publish the photos? Or the real motives of the "Nightline" team in presenting the names and photos of the dead service people? Or the real motives of the Sinclair Broadcasting Group, which refused to air that "Nightline" segment on its seven ABC stations?

Nor is this the place to try to wade through the extensive media debate about whether or not such actions were respectful or appropriate. Rather it is to call attention to the fact that myriad responses—by both opponents and supporters of the war, as well as by those with more nuanced beliefs—coincided in their recognition that these two media events had the potential to influence viewer and reader expectations. Those with various positions on the war concurred that those two media events *could* feed into and hypertrophy expectations that Iraq *might* become—or was becoming—another Vietnam.

Why was there such concern about those images? Certainly not because of beliefs that they might contribute to the careful analysis of the following question: did evidence about the war in Iraq tend to support or reject a conclusion that this war was becoming a Vietnam-like phenomenon? Rather, concern resulted from the fear (by some) and hope (by others) that these emotion-packed photos of flag-covered coffins and dead service people (along with Koppel's reading of their names) might foster such a media-exacerbated expectation.

Spurred by the heated media-driven debate about these two media events, April, 2004, may have marked the moment when the *another Vietnam* idea was transformed from an (often unvoiced) subtext into a widespread expectation-setting media frame. For example, the April 18, 2004, *Newsweek* posed those possible expectations with a cover announcing: "Crisis in Iraq: The Vietnam Factor. How This War Compares—and How It Doesn't."

MODEL BEHAVIOR

Finally, media model forms of civic behavior. Is not such behavior modeling one of the goals of participatory citizenship education and efforts to integrate democratic practices into the classroom?

I am not claiming rampant consumer copycatting of either media behavior or behavior dramatized in the media. Nor am I implying that people—particularly young people—will inevitably mimic what they see, hear, and read in the information media. However, media-disseminated actions *can* influence behavioral norms through role-modeling.

Take the flood of television and radio talk shows that focus on public issues. These interchanges, sometimes shouting matches or insult contests, often resemble verbal mudwrestling more than thoughtful discussion. Such talk shows may provide information (often inaccurate) and interesting, even novel, insights, interpretations and framings.

Yet, with participants vying to top each other in name-calling and coarseness of invective, as well as flexing their interruptus muscles as they try to shout each other down, what do they role model for viewers and listeners about how to conduct civic discourse? Certainly not careful evidence-based argumentation combined with interpersonal civility. In fact, in July, 2004, Comedy Central launched a parody of talk shows called "Crossballs."

Add to this sports coverage, an increasingly popular element of the information media. (According to ESPN, it attracts 94 million viewers each week.) Many young people now suffer from what has been termed "Slight Trigger Disease," the tendency to do physical battle over minor bumps or perceived wrong looks. According to James Kauffman and Harold Burbach (1997), they may be doing what they see adults do, often transmitted to them through the media:

> They see popular sports figures who seem to be always on edge, talking trash, scowling at close calls, and flashing intimidating looks at their opponents ... politicians reflexively demeaning each other...television talk show hosts encouraging guests to abuse each other verbally, often over trivial issues. (p. 322)

Will this become the media-driven social studies role model for public civic life? And what does this mean for the future of civil discourse in our society?

MEDIA AS SOCIAL STUDIES CHALLENGE

The information media, in short, have created a sweeping and pervasive social studies curriculum, albeit neither monolithic nor always intended. Yet media teaching relentlessness need not result in school educator powerlessness. However, it does create an unavoidable challenge.

Let us reframe this discussion one more way. Suppose that every school and school district in the United States eliminated social studies from its curriculum. Would that mean the end of social studies education?

Hardly. It would only mean that, by default, with schools no longer conscious participants, the information media would assume an even greater role in social studies education. Information (and misinformation) about history, government, economics, and geography would still be provided, organized, and framed—by the media. Sometimes-competing values about the environment and conflict resolution would still be disseminated—by the media. Expectations about diversity and the globe would still be created and reinforced—by the media. Public behavior, civic participation, and interpersonal relations would still be modeled—by the media.

Yet the information media are not merely social studies educators. They can also serve as a rich social studies curricular resource. By drawing upon the media and encouraging students to examine it analytically, teachers can help students develop a better understanding of the media's complex role in public knowledge construction and help them become better prepared to grapple with its omnipresent social studies teaching. These are among the critical goals of the media literacy movement.

School educators—especially social studies educators—have two options. They can ignore the media and thereby squander a rich opportunity to help develop student analytical thinking, particularly about the media. Or they can actively and consciously develop social studies critical thinking skills by thoroughly incorporating media analysis into the curriculum. In fulfilling their commitment to helping prepare students for a future of thoughtful leadership, social studies professionals need to accept this challenge and grasp this opportunity.

REFERENCES

Altaras, S. (2004, August 15). Ignorance isn't funny. *Seattle Times*, p. D4.

Berson, I., & Berson, M. (2003). Digital literacy for effective citizenship. *Social Education, 67*(3), 164-167.

Beyond Black and White. (1992, May 18). *Newsweek*.

Carragee, K. M., & Roefs, W. (2004). The neglect of power in recent framing research. *Journal of Communication, 54*(2), 214-233.

Cortés, C. (2000). *The children are watching: How the media teach about diversity*. New York: Teachers College Press.

Entman, R. M. (1990). Modern racism and the images of Blacks in local television news. *Critical Studies in Mass Communication, 7*, 332-345.

Fraser, N. (2004, May). To BBC or not to BBC: Independent journalism suffers an identity crisis. *Harper's Magazine, 308*(1848), 55-64.

Gerbner, G., Gross, L., Morgan, M., & Signorielli, N. (1986). Living with television: The dynamics of the cultivation process. In J. Bryant & D. Zillman (Eds.), *Perspectives on media effects* (pp. 17-40). Hillsdale, NJ: Erlbaum.

Gilens, M. (1996). Race and poverty in America: Public misperceptions and the American news media. *The Public Opinion Quarterly, 60*(4), 515-541.

Goffman, E. (1974). *Frame analysis: An essay on the organization of experience*. New York: Harper & Row.

Graber, D. A. (1990). Seeing is remembering: How visuals contribute to learning from television news. *Journal of Communication, 40*(3), 134-155.

Gunther, A. C., & Schmitt, K. (2004). Mapping boundaries of the hostile media effect. *Journal of Communication, 54*(1), 55-70.

Hartmann, P., & Husband, C. (1972). The mass media and racial conflict. In D. McQuail (Ed.), *Sociology of mass communications* (pp. 435-455). Baltimore: Penguin.

Kauffman, J. M., & Burbach, H. J. (1997). On creating a climate of classroom civility. *Phi Delta Kappan, 79*(4), 320-325.

Hawkins, R., & Pingree, S. (1981). Using television to construct social reality. *Journal of Broadcasting, 25*, 347-364.

Medved, M. (1992). *Hollywood v. America: Popular culture and the war on traditional values*. New York: HarperPerennial.

National Council for the Social Studies. (2002). *National Council for the Social Studies curriculum guidelines*. Washington, DC: Author.

Race and rage: Black vs. White: The new fears, cops in the crossfire. (1992, May 11). *U.S. News and World Report*.

Romer, D., Jamieson, K. H., & Aday, S. (2003). Television news and the cultivation of fear of crime. *Journal of Communication, 53*(1), 88-104.

Rosenberg, S. (2004, August 8). Unconventional coverage. *Seattle Times*, p. A27.

PART II

HISTORICAL PERSPECTIVES

CHAPTER 4

A FICKLE LOVER

Experiences with the
Media in Historical Context

Ronald Evans

The media is a capitalist enterprise, a business. Like most businesses, media, generally speaking, must turn a profit. To survive and prosper in the media world means to attract readers, listeners, and viewers. The impact of capital on media is the starting point for understanding the sometimes tortured, always difficult relationship between social studies and the media. Capital owns, operates, and shapes the media landscape in the United States. A capitalist ideological perspective "rather consistently predominates" (Parenti, 1986, p. 27). As A. J. Liebling once said, freedom of the press belongs to the man who owns one. Increasingly, the media is owned, operated and controlled by a few large conglomerates. Despite the journalist's code of ethics aimed at serving the public by reporting truth, the first obligation of the media is to make money, and to serve at the pleasure of corporate interests. This fact has serious consequences for citizens and society. As Robert McChesney writes, "corporate domination of media is a key factor in helping to explain the woeful state of our democracy" (McChesney, 2004, p. 7).

Social Studies and the Press: Keeping the Beast at Bay?, 39–54
Copyright © 2005 by Information Age Publishing

From a larger perspective, in the capitalist economy the media is one of the institutions that helps maintain the hegemony of the corporate class and the capitalist system. In recent decades, business as a system, as a way of thinking and a way of organizing property, capital and labor, has become ever more influential. A business mentality permeates the airwaves, the newsprint, and the rhetoric and management of schooling.

The structure of business, and of the media, is top down and hierarchical. Ownership exerts a level of control and interference in the media that academics would find extremely uncomfortable. The working media are beholden to media owners and corporate advertisers (Parenti, 1986, p. 19). Owners exercise control through their power to hire and fire, promote and demote, and by regularly intervening into the news production process with verbal and written directives.

Like many other cultural institutions such as corporations, schools, and universities, the media is controlled by interlocking (and interchanging) directorates. Boards of directors, school boards, and university boards of trustees are composed largely of prominent business, industrial, and civic leaders. The cultural system and institutions are not independent of the business system. Not only do schools, the media, and other cultural institutions borrow business management techniques for running their operations efficiently, the management of cultural institutions like schools is strongly influenced by interlocking directors from the business world. The media is ultimately controlled by boards of directors from the moneyed class, "linked with powerful business organization, not with public interest groups; with management, not with labor; with well established think tanks and charities, not their grassroots counterparts" (Parenti, 1986, p. 29). Thus, media is part of the establishment, with natural sympathies with business interests.

Moreover, the media is manipulated at least to some extent by foundations and foundation funded scholars and researchers. Foundations have long held prominent positions influencing education policy. Recent work in curriculum history illustrates the influence of conservative foundations on the undergraduate college curriculum since the 1950s (Selden, 2004). In social studies, the influence of foundations also has a long history. In recent years, conservative foundations bent on influencing policy and reshaping the social studies curriculum, replacing a broad approach to social studies with a more narrowly defined focus on history, geography and civics aimed at conservative goals have had increased influence. The Bradley Foundation, the Heritage Foundation, the American Enterprise Institute, Hudson Institute, Olin Foundation, Manhattan Institute, Hoover Institution, and the Fordham Foundation have funded attacks on social studies and supported endowed positions for scholars supportive of their views (Berliner & Biddle, 1995, pp. 132-139; Berliner & Biddle,

1998; Evans, 2004; Stiehl, 1997). Frequently, sponsorship of sources is concealed or left unmentioned in news reports (Paletz & Entman, 1981; Selden, 2004). These foundations and allied scholars and projects have had a profound influence on the recent policy direction of schooling, as well as on recent trends in social studies as illustrated in *The Social Studies Wars*, my recent work on the history of the field (Evans, 2004).

Who controls the news? In the day-to-day working lives of reporters, autonomy is conditional. Editors control assignments and are sometimes influenced directly by meddling owners (à la George Steinbrenner in baseball). For example, one former reporter told me that editors frequently lunch with the owner, and that there is *a ton* of ownership interference in some cases. He told the story of working for the *Vancouver Sun* under a morally conservative editor that refused to give much coverage to the city's serious drug addiction problems, and allowed no mention at all of the legalization alternative. A change of editors, to a libertarian, brought a change in policy, extensive coverage of the city's drug and drug related problems, and extended treatment of the legalization alternative (Beers, 2004). Newspapers, the media, are hierarchical creatures. Their reporting and depiction of the world reflect that fact.

Does ruling class propaganda translate into indoctrination of the public? Are we manipulated by the news? Yes, sometimes inadvertently, sometimes more explicitly. The media defines and frames issues, determining what questions, issues, and problems get the most airtime. Indeed, two prominent media scholars have offered a penetrating analysis of the mainstream media by developing a "propaganda model" to help explain media control and influence (Herman & Chomsky, 1988). Moreover, the issue-attention cycle is not a transparent phenomenon driven by issues and public interest alone. It is filtered through the lens of a media saturated by its capitalist roots. The media is "oligopolistic, standardized, and most accessible to capital" (Parenti, 1986, p. 30). This tends to lead to the homogenization of what is reported. Media sources commonly rely on a few main wire services (AP, UPI, Reuters) and reports from the leading newspapers such as the *New York Times* and *Los Angeles Times*. Media coverage appears to be influenced by, and may be characterized by, the following:

- A focus on sensationalism, on the dramatic, on news that sells, and that attracts the reader's attention. "If it bleeds, it leads," has become, "If it bares, it leads." (Willinsky, 2004). The scramble for ratings and rankings and market share (equaling money) frequently dictate coverage.
- Bad news tends to dominate, especially so it seems in coverage of schooling, with the seemingly perpetual series of crises (the literacy

crisis, the crisis in the teaching of history, etc.). Coverage is not usually supportive or positive (Kaplan, 1992; Raywid, 1984). One
study, based on an analysis of network news coverage, found four
negative stories about schooling for every positive one (Robinson,
1984). The press *delights* in stories about the failures of schooling,
but "shies away" from coverage of its successes (Berliner & Biddle,
1995, p. 171).

- The framing of news stories by using "emphasis, nuance, innuendo
  and peripheral embellishments, communicators can create a
  desired impression without resorting to advocacy" or straying too
  far from the appearance of objectivity (Parenti, 1986, p. 220).
  Framing often leads to unequal space and positioning, and treatment of topics that, while covering both sides, may omit other
  alternative perspectives.

- Image dominates as the media construct images that stand in place
  of evidence or reality, and are frequently counterfactual. The image
  that American schools are failing is a good example (Berliner &
  Biddle, 1995; Vinson & Ross, 2003).

- Media serves up a grand spectacle to consumers, providing entertainment to the masses (a new opiate) and giving power over to an
  elite. The media spectacle is dominated by "media logics": leads,
  hooks, angles are used to determine newsworthiness; a focus on
  symbols and symbolic language predominates and frames coverage
  of schooling; policymakers focus on symbolic action (Smith, 2004,
  pp. 125-127).

- Feeding frenzies frequently dominate media coverage. "A feeding
  frenzy is defined as the press coverage attending any political event
  or circumstance where a critical mass of journalists leap to cover the
  same embarrassing or scandalous subject and pursue it intensely,
  often excessively, and sometimes uncontrollably" (Sabato, 1991, p.
  6). Social studies has suffered through its share of feeding frenzies,
  as we shall see.

- Though the media cover and are influenced by a plurality of interests, some voices get more airtime and coverage than others. On
  many topics, official and government sources dominate. The same
  group of spin doctors often dominate press reports, quotes and
  tokes (statistics) (Willinsky, 2004). The press "tends to go along will-
  ingly with officialdom's view of things" (Parenti, 1986, p. 19). This
  seems especially true in education, where administrators and policymakers tend to receive most coverage.

- Government secrecy impedes collection of evidence and harms
  freedom of inquiry and democracy. Increasing levels of government

secrecy are abetted by media giants consolidating ownership (Moyers, 2004).

- Bias and omission are common in media reports, most commonly through the characteristics described above, but also explicitly in cases where ownership has an ax to grind (i.e. conservative media such as the *Washington Times* or the *Weekly Standard*).

- Key stories are frequently underreported. A consortium of media critics has published an annual list of the most under-reported stories (Phillips & Project Censored, 2004). An array of media critics has developed a growing literature analyzing and critiquing media control and influence (Herman & Chomsky, 1988; McChesney, 2004; Parenti, 1986).

- Power relations shape the media, what gets reported, and which voices are heard. Power and knowledge interpenetrate, producing knowledge industries shaped by power relations, reflecting the power and hegemony of established elites (Foucault, 1980). Framing, omission, and the consequences of the above nexus of traits result in inadequate journalism and mean that the media provide inadequate coverage on many key social issues.

One prominent media scholar, Robert McChesney, has recently written that it is "difficult to imagine much headway being made on the crucial social issues facing our nation given how poorly they are covered by the current U. S. media system." McChesney suggests that media policy debates are shaped by a "corporate insider hegemony" and marked by "lack of public participation" (2004, p. 7). In his view, media politics are shaped by eight common myths:

- the media do not matter much, reflecting reality rather than shaping it
- the corporate, commercial media system is a natural outgrowth of democracy
- debates over media policy have accurately reflected public opinion (the media policy arena is a corrupt process, a private playground serving an elite)
- commercial media provide the highest quality journalism. (n.b.: The journalist's professional code is deeply flawed.)
- the media have a left-wing bias
- commercial media seek profits and give people what they want
- no alternative to the status quo will improve matters. The choice is between corporate control or government control. (A mix is possi-

ble by forming a large, nonprofit, noncommercial media sector) (McChesney, 2004, pp. 7-11).

Edward S. Herman and Noam Chomsky, in *Manufacturing Consent*, make several similar points, though in even stronger language, in their analyses of media politics employing a "propaganda model." In their opening paragraph they write:

> The mass media serve as a system for communicating messages and symbols to the general populace. It is their function to amuse, entertain, and inform, and to inculcate individuals with the values, beliefs, and codes of behavior that will integrate them into the institutional structures of the larger society. In a world of concentrated wealth and major conflicts of class interest, to fulfill this role requires systematic propaganda. (1988, p. 1)

Their analysis focuses on the inequality of wealth and power and the ways in which it influences "mass-media interests and choices." It creates a process by which "money and power are able to filter out the news fit to print, marginalize dissent, and allow the government and dominant private interests to get their messages across to the public" (p. 2). They describe five layers of filters which fall under the following headings:

1.   the size, concentrated ownership, owner wealth, and profit orientation of the dominant mass-media firms;
2.   advertising as the primary income source of the mass media;
3.   the reliance of the media on information provided by government, business, and *experts* funded and approved by these primary sources and agents of power;
4.   "flak" as a means of disciplining the media; and
5.   "anticommunism" as a national religion and control mechanism (Herman & Chomsky, 1988, p. 2).

These filters act as a sieve, removing much of the raw material and leaving "only the cleansed residue fit to print," fixing the parameters and assumptions of discourse and making alternative choices nearly unimaginable. The filters "narrow the range" of news, sharply define which stories can become 'big' news, and create a distinct disadvantage for dissidents and for weak or unorganized individuals or groups (p. 31). In conclusion, they write, their "propaganda approach ... suggests a systematic and highly political dichotomization in news coverage based on serviceability to important domestic power interests" (p. 35).

SOCIAL STUDIES MEDIA STORMS

How has corporate domination of media influenced social studies? In the following portion of this essay I will describe several key episodes from the social studies past in which the media played a key or decisive role. Though some of the key episodes are covered in greater depth by other authors (Symcox, 2002; Zimmerman, 2002), selected episodes from my own recent work, *The Social Studies Wars* (Evans, 2004), summarized here, will help us revisit several of the most important conflagrations of the twentieth century.

In the 1930s and early 1940s a media storm of controversy and criticism centered on social reconstructionism as embodied in the Rugg social studies program of textbooks and materials. Critics viewed the Rugg materials as "against private enterprise," as a "subtle, sugar-coated effort to convert youth to Communism," as part of a "reconstructed" educational system teaching that "our economic and political institutions are decadent" (Forbes, 1939; Myers, 1940, p. 18). Later critics accused the books and others of being "un-American" (*New York Times*, February 22, 1941, p. 1). In defense of social studies and the Rugg materials the Academic Freedom Committee of the National Council for the Social Studies issued a strong statement and a packet of materials. Rugg and his colleagues at Columbia University organized a defense Committee, and Rugg engaged his critics directly, often in person (Winters, 1968). The episode left an impression that social studies was some sort of radical plot and led to the demise of the Rugg social studies program in schools. The media, and in particular the Hearst press, played a key role in creating and sustaining the controversy.

Another important controversy occurred in the 1940s and centered on charges from a respected, Pulitzer Prize winning historian, Allan Nevins, which were published by the *New York Times*. Nevins argued that U.S. history was no longer sufficiently taught in the nations schools (Nevins, 1942). Nevins' article was followed by a *New York Times* survey, and later a *New York Times* test to determine the extent of the problems (Fine, 1942, 1943). Once again, the bogey was social studies. Hugh Russell Fraser, who joined what came to be referred to as the *New York Times* crusade against social studies, blamed "extremists from NCSS and its twin brother, Teachers College," for the decline in the teaching of history. Social studies educators including Edgar B. Wesley, Wilbur Murra, and Edgar B. Hunt responded vigorously and provided evidence that U.S. history was a "universal requirement" in the nation's schools (Hunt, 1942; Wesley, 1944). The net result of the stalemate was that social studies was once again portrayed as faddish, and that attempts at innovation by *educationists* led to a dilution of the study of political history and of American heroes. In the case of this particular incident, the *New York Times* crusade against social studies was something of a plot developed by the newspaper's owner, as well as Allan Nevins, and reporter Benjamin Fine (Sunday Editor, 1942).

During the 1950s, attacks on social studies became a central part of attacks on progressive education. Mainstream critics charged in a deluge of books, articles, and media stories that social studies was antiintellectual, and red-baiting critics called it a form of propaganda for communism or socialism. Arthur Bestor, one of the most respected critics, called social studies an antiintellectual "social stew" (Bestor, 1953). After suffering defeats, and with many progressive educators at or near retirement, the response from social studies was rather anemic. The net result was the decline of progressive experimentation with curricular fusion and birth of a social studies movement centered on study in the academic disciplines. By this time the pattern of boom and bust, or innovation and reaction, had become a familiar cycle. And, once again, the nation's media played a key role giving extensive coverage to the charges from critics of education.

In the aftermath of another period of innovation, the era of the new social studies in the 1960s and early 1970s, there were, again, a number of attacks. These included academic freedom cases involving teachers Keith Sterzing and Frances Ahern in which teaching innovations were literally put on trial (Ahern, 1969; Sterzing, 1968). Book and textbook controversies occurred in Kanawaha County, West Virginia, and in the state of Georgia, the latter involving the Fenton textbook series. The most famous controversy of the period centered on *MACOS*, a project of the new social studies era described by U. S. Congressman John B. Conlan as a "dangerous assault on cherished values and attitudes" because of its "approving" depiction of euthanasia, wife swapping, cannibalism, and infanticide (Conlan, 1975). In defense of social studies, the National Council for the Social Studies (NCSS) issued statements on academic freedom, and organized the NCSS Legal Defense Fund. Shortly thereafter, the Wingspread Conference focused on understanding and overcoming the controversy (Wingspread, 1975). The incident contributed to the impression that social studies was influenced by radicals with an un-American bent, and it combined with the failure of the new and newer social studies to leave the field seemingly directionless.

Into the void stepped the revival of history in the 1980s. Diane Ravitch made the field a scapegoat for the "decline and fall of history teaching," portraying it as a vacuous form of "tot sociology" (Kirkendall, 1975; Ravitch, 1985). Critics charged that social studies was poorly defined and directed by the whims of educational fashion. The movement gathered steam with formation of the Bradley Commission and garnered substantial funding from the conservative Bradley Foundation (Bradley Commission, 1988; Stehle, 1997). The response among social studies educators was to create a new consensus definition and to support the standards movement, offering social studies as an umbrella for the teaching of history and the social sciences. The net result was an increase in course taking in history and the social sciences, notably in world history and geography, and a decline in elective social studies offerings. The episode also contributed to the further denigration of social studies as the directionless and poorly defined concoction of educationists. In each of these episodes, the media played a key role, not as a neutral bystander or *objective* reporter, but as publisher of what had become the conventional critiques of social studies.

A number of conclusions might be drawn from these episodes. First, criticisms often stick, despite defense and counter arguments. Over the years, criticisms of social studies have taken their toll on the vitality and public impression of the field. The media have framed these controversies in such a way as to give voice to the concerns of critics, while relegating the alternative voices of social studies professionals to letters on the Op Ed pages of newspapers. While it has not silenced the voices of social studies professionals, neither has it given them the placement or space devoted to critics. Second, the sum total of the criticisms over the years may have left the general impression that social studies is an unsound educational idea, developed by second-rate scholars in schools of education. Third, in each episode, it seems, politicians and policy advisors tend to embrace the traditional academic disciplines in battles over social studies. Alternatives may continue to face rough sledding. Fourth, the response of social studies educators to criticism has varied from vigorous in the 1930s and 1940s, to anemic in more recent periods. This suggests that social studies educators should consider developing a stronger response to critics including: a war chest for mounting a defense; clarification of alternative theoretical traditions in social studies with development of practices and materials in support of each; development of a new consensus with a stronger focus on the social issues at the heart of a purist, Deweyan approach to social studies; support for experimentation including unified field approaches to social studies; and, a more saavy procedure for dealing with the media and the criticisms to which it often gives time and space.

MY OWN NAÏVE EXPERIENCES WITH THE MEDIA

On a more personal note, as I write this essay, and as I reflect on the social studies past, I am coming to see my own growing number of media contacts through a different, more critical lens. My story could aptly be encapsulated by a title like, *From Naïve to Jaded*. My experiences with the media have included a number of contacts. Two of them were searing experiences. The first such incident occurred while I was a classroom social studies teacher in Portland, Oregon, and ended up becoming the spokesperson, as union representative, for a teacher rebellion against an autocratic principal who happened to be African American. The incident included, most notably, an interview by *The Oregonian* in which I was one of two teachers who were quoted in the story. My involvement resulted in threatening phone calls; racial overtones; a conversation with the super-intendent of schools ("I know, but I have to support him"); and an even-tual transfer to another school.

The second searing incident occurred while teaching at San Diego State University when I spoke out via a letter to the editor and a printed flyer in support of an English teacher who had been censured. It led to testimony at a local school board hearing, threatening phone calls, and police involvement to curb one harassing caller.

My other media contacts as a professor have been less troublesome and more rewarding, though with sometimes frustrating results as well. I have received a number of calls from reporters over the years and have made several radio appearances (PBS). These contacts include a few phone interviews in which reporters sought my expertise on social studies topics: an AP reporter on school treatment of the Clinton impeachment; an *Education Week* reporter on the social studies wars; a *Los Angeles Times* editorial writer on the conflicts between history and social studies; a Delaware reporter investigating social studies in schools; a writer for *NEA Today* writing a brief article on my recent book, *The Social Studies Wars* (Evans, 2004). In most of these more recent contacts I felt that I was treated fairly, and that my ideas were heard and understood. In one case, the resulting editorial left me feeling that the writer was simply looking for an idea or two to include, that she already had a mindset on the history/social studies wars, and that she really did not comprehend the alternative perspective embodied in much of what I told her. Once again, disappointing and frus-trating results.

If anything, my experiences, taken in context of the experiences of social studies leaders and episodes from the past, and in light of some of the realities of the media of which I am becoming more aware, have led me to be more cautious and careful in my statements to reporters. I am painfully aware that social studies is news only when the media thinks it is news, and that we must create or respond to media contacts very care-fully, fully cognizant of the context in which the media operates. Finally, I have learned that the press is a fickle lover. While media attention is exciting, it can bite back with a vengeance. I am learning to curb my excitement.

DISCUSSION

Social studies is highly political, shot through with ideological assumptions. Debate over what goes on in schools often serves as a screen on which competing visions and their accompanying anxieties are projected. Social studies is, in my opinion, the one area of school curricula that has suffered the most from media controversy. Feeding frenzies seem to occur with regularity as social studies ideas or projects come to light, which are seen as exceeding the public's "zone of toleration" (Evans, 2004). These episodes, unfortunately, serve to place boundaries and limitations around the field, defining the limits of what is permissible and what is taboo. Moreover, they have contributed to a public image that is largely negative.

Media storms and the critique of social studies by critics can be answered by facts, as in the Nevins episode and in the more recent "manufactured crisis" (Berliner & Biddle, 1995). We must respond to criticism in the interest of improving the field, improving what goes on in classrooms, and wresting some degree of power from the brokers of capital.

Though cases of direct media manipulation may seem rare or farfetched, the Rugg and Nevins episodes reveal that in the past, specific persons orchestrated or manipulated the media to serve their own vision or interests. In the Rugg case, the Hearst press, to a lesser extent the *New York Times*, and a small coterie of committed conservative critics orchestrated the textbook crisis. In the Nevins' case, Nevins and his associates had the ear of the owner of the *New York Times*. Needless to say, the ego involvement of both educators and critics is inherent in each of these episodes.

In the social studies past, anticommunism and red-baiting critics have played a strong role in at least two of the key episodes discussed above. "Anti-communism has long been an unremitting media theme, an ideological bias that pervades both the news and entertainment sectors" (Herman & Chomsky, 1988; Parenti, 1986, p. 113). Given the prominence of this theme, and the bias it reveals, it is little wonder that the media has displayed a crisis orientation in its coverage of education and social studies.

It seems, also, that reporters and the media tend to rely on academics with high prestige such as historians at elite private universities and on highly visible and vocal critics. Though the internet and other technological developments may be changing this, it has long been common for the media to rely on a few favorites for commentary. In the recent history of social studies, this seems especially true. Diane Ravitch, Chester Finn, and other well-heeled critics of similar persuasion have had a disproportionate share of the national media attention devoted to social studies, and have cast it in a negative light to further their own vision and agenda. On the local scene, it seems that the media may sometimes be easily manipulated by local cranks and small groups of visible and dedicated individuals. Comedian Woody Allen once joked, "Half of success in life is just showing up." Conservative critics have been heard partly because they show up at school board meetings. They are frequently a visible, vocal, and persistent presence.

Finally, it seems that media coverage of social studies and education has been shaped in part by attitudes toward educationists as second-rate scholars, or worse, as quacks. Media coverage during the 1950s seemed to accept this theme as a basic assumption, reflecting several antieducationist books of the era. In the more recent period, schools on the whole are seen as failing, and social studies, when given attention, is an educational backwater failing more than other areas. In sum, social studies and education have a public relations problem of longstanding.

WHAT CAN WE LEARN?

The first and foremost lesson for social studies educators is that most of us are dirt ignorant about the media and media relations. The media, with a few exceptions, is driven by capital and money. Over the history of social studies, we have had a tendency to be naïve. Key episodes from the past illustrate again and again our naiveté and ignorance in dealing with the media. We need to educate ourselves by studying the media. Perhaps media studies should be a requirement for a graduate degree in education, if not for high school graduation.

As a conclusion to this essay I would like to offer a few thoughts on improving the relationship between social studies and the media:

- Be wary. Experience suggests strongly that the media is not always supportive of social studies or education, and is frequently critical.
- Know who you are dealing with. Reporters work in a context shaped by capital. This is true with only a few exceptions (alternative magazines such as *Mother Jones*, *The Nation*, etc.). The work of reporters is influenced by editors and owners. Know the orientation and politics of the publication or outlet you are communicating with.
- Cultivate positive relations with key journalists, at the local, state, and national level, as the opportunity arises. Beers suggests that relationships with reporters can be nurtured (Beers, 2004), not by bombarding your contacts with press releases, but by the occasional communication on topics and developments of mutual interest.

- Keep your ego in check. While media attention can be sweet, and it can give us a sense that someone is paying attention to our work, it can also explode.

- Feeding frenzies will occur again, and again, and again. A wise organization (i.e., NCSS) might be prepared with press releases that can be modified to fit the occasion, or might even consider hiring a public relations consultant.

- Schools and the media are institutions of conformity in which a smooth and comfortable domination seems a natural state of affairs. Keep in mind the context. Capitalist hegemony is a creation that can lead to a *one-dimensional* system which can repulse alternative views. "Democratic unfreedom" sometimes squeezes out unpopular opinions and stories (Marcuse, 1964). We must work hard to prize alternative voices and perspectives in the classroom and in our contacts with the media. This means giving increased attention to alternative sources of news in the social studies classroom. Journalism, the media, and education are significantly interrelated in the information arena and deeply linked in the struggle for a more democratic and open society. Our relationship with the media must be understood in the context of our collaborative struggle to "redress our grievances, retake our politics, and reclaim our commitment to equality and justice" (Moyers, 2004).

- Social studies professionals might wield greater influence by forming alliances with like-minded, larger, and more powerful groups such as the NEA and other progressive organizations that are supportive of a broadly progressive vision. We have a responsibility to make our voices heard on issues confronting the field (Maeroff, 1998).

- We must learn to play the public relations game, and play it well. We face a crisis in civic understanding, a crisis in issue awareness, a crisis in critical thought, a crisis in developing in citizens the synthesis of knowledge and the commitment needed for civic participation. One thing social studies professionals could do that might make a difference would be to create a media watch committee or a consortium of those committed to advancing a progressive vision of social studies and society.

Finally, to have greater influence on the policymakers who frame and re-frame the curriculum, social studies would be well served by getting its house in order. This will require greater clarity about the possible definitions or alternative curricular approaches that may count as strong social studies. Our field is rife with confusion, mindlessness, and competing curricular ideologies. Critics frequently charge that social studies is poorly defined. Developing five to seven clearly framed alternative paths for defining social studies may be a reasonable option that could help social studies professionals clarify what they are about, assist the field in creating a more positive relationship with the media, and help to cultivate a stronger continuing presence in the social studies wars.

REFERENCES

Ahern, F. (1969). Ahern Case: Correspondence, briefs, letters, confidential legal documents, folders 1-3, box 3, series 4D, Executive Reference Files, NCSS Archive, Milbank Memorial Library, Teachers College, Columbia University.

Beers, D. (2004, April). *The media and educational policy and research.* Symposium at the annual meeting of the American Educational Research Association, San Diego, California.

Berliner, D. C., & Biddle, B. J. (1995). *The manufactured crisis: Myth, fraud, and the attack on America's public schools.* Reading, MA: Addison-Wesley.

Berliner, D. C., & Biddle, B. J. (1998). The lamentable alliance between the media and school critics. In G. I. Maeroff (Ed.), *Imaging education: The media and schools in America.* New York: Teachers College Press.

Bestor, A. (1953). *Educational wastelands: The retreat from learning in our public schools.* Urbana: University of Illinois Press.

Bradley Commission. (1988). *Building a history curriculum: Guidelines for teaching history in schools.* Washington, DC: Educational Excellence Network.

Conlan, J. B. (1975, October). MACOS: The push for a uniform national curriculum. *Social Education, 39,* 388-392.

Evans, R. (2004). *The social studies wars: What should we teach the children?* New York: Teachers College Press.

Fine, B. (1942, June 21). U.S. history study is not required in 82% of colleges. *New York Times,* pp. 1, 36.

Fine, B. (1943, April 4). Ignorance of U.S. history shown by college freshmen. *New York Times,* pp. 1, 32-33.

Forbes, B. C. (1939, August 15). Trecherous teachings. *Forbes,* p. 8.

Foucault, M. (1980). *Power/knowledge: Selected interviews and other writings, 1972-1977.* New York: Pantheon.

Herman, E. S., & Chomsky, N. (1988). *Manufacturing consent: The political economy of the mass media.* New York: Pantheon.

Hunt, E. M. (1942, October 25). History charges called untrue. *New York Times,* p. 6D.

Kaplan, G. R. (1992). *Images of education: The mass media's version of America's schools.* Washington, DC: National School Public Relations Association and the Institute for Educational Leadership.

Kirkendall, R. S. (1975). The status of history in schools. *Journal of American History, 62,* 557-570.

Marcuse, H. J. (1964). *One-dimensional man: Studies in the ideology of advanced industrial society.* Boston: Beacon Press.

Maeroff, G. I. (1998). Conclusion: Toward greater responsibility by all. In G. I. Maeroff (Ed.), *Imaging education: The media and schools in America.* New York: Teachers College Press.

McChesney, R. W. (2004). *The problem of the media: U. S. communication politics in the 21st century.* New York: Monthly Review Press.

Moyers, B. (2004). Address to newspaper guild/communications workers of America. Retrieved May 19, 2004, from http://www.TomPaine.Com.

Myers, A. F. (1940). The attack of the Rugg books. *Frontiers of Democracy, 7,* 17-21.

Nevins, A. (1942, May 3). American history for Americans. *New York Times Magazine,* pp. 6, 28.

Paletz, D. L., & Entman, R. M. (1981). *Media, power, politics.* New York: Free Press.

Parenti, M. (1986). *Inventing reality: The politics of the mass media.* New York: St. Martin's Press.

Phillips, P., & Project Censored. (2004). *Censored 2005: The top 25 censored stories.* New York: Seven Stories.

Ravitch, D. (1985, November 17). Decline and fall of history teaching. *New York Times Magazine,* pp. 50-53, 101, 117.

Raywid, M. A. (1984). Education and the media or why they keep raining on your parade. *Contemporary Education, 55*(4), 206-211.

Robinson, M. J. (1984). How the networks cover education: Schools are not the media's pet. *American Education, 8*(1), 18-21.

Sabato, L. J. (1991). *Feeding frenzy: How attack journalism has transformed American politics.* New York: Free Press.

Selden, S. (2004, April). *Fifty years of sponsored neo-conservative challenges to the undergraduate course of study*: Linking *capital, culture, and the undergraduate curriculum.* Paper presented at the annual meeting of the American Educational Research Association, San Diego, California.

Smith, M. L. (2004). *Political spectacle and the fate of American schools.* New York: RoutledgeFalmer.

Stehle, V. (1997, June 30). Righting philanthropy. *The Nation,* pp. 15-20.

Sterzing, K. (1968). Sterzing Case: Correspondence and Clippings, Confidential Legal Documents, folders 2-4, box 44, series 4D, Executive Reference Files, NCSS Archive, Milbank Memorial Library, Teachers College, Columbia University.

Sunday Editor. (1942). Sunday Editor (*New York Times*) to Allan Nevins, February 7, 1942, "1941-1942" folder, 1942 Correspondence, box 54, Allan Nevins Papers, Columbia University Archives, Butler Library, Columbia University.

Symcox, L. (2002). *Whose history? The struggle for national standards in American classrooms.* New York: Teachers College.

Vinson, K., & Ross, E. W. (2003). *Image and education.* New York: Peter Lang.

Willinsky, J. (2004, April). *The media and educational policy and research.* Symposium at the annual meeting of the American Educational Research Association, San Diego, California.

Wesley, E. B. (1944). *American history in schools and colleges.* New York: Macmillan.

Wingspread. (1975). Wingspread Conference folder, Box 2, Accession # 850625, NCSS Archive, Milbank Memorial Library, Teachers College, Columbia University.

Winters, E. F. (1968). *Harold Rugg and education for social reconstructionism.* Unpublished doctoral dissertation, University of Wisconsin, Madison.

Zimmerman, J. (2002). *Whose America? Culture wars in the public schools.* Cambridge, MA: Harvard University Press.

CHAPTER 5

HEADLINES AND FURROWED BROWS

NCSS Engagement with Social Studies Critics and the Press

Tedd Levy

When an opinion has taken root amongst a democratic people, and established itself in the minds of the bulk of the community, it afterwards subsists by itself and is maintained without effort, because no one attacks it. Those who at first rejected it as false, ultimately receive it as the general impression; and those who still dispute it in their hearts, conceal their dissent; they are careful not to engage in a dangerous and useless conflict.

—Alexis de Tocqueville, *Democracy in America*

For more than 80 years, the National Council for the Social Studies (NCSS) has represented educators who trace their roots to a 1916 report on, *The Social Studies in Secondary Education.* The field was essentially born with this report although numerous questions remained over a curricular scope and sequence, the significance of individual disciplines, the nature and quality of teacher preparation, and other issues that have continued to be sources of controversy and media attention (Hertzberg, 1981).

Social Studies and the Press: Keeping the Beast at Bay?, 55–66
Copyright © 2005 by Information Age Publishing
All rights of reproduction in any form reserved.

In an attempt to resolve these early issues, a group from Columbia University called a meeting in Atlantic City in 1921 to launch the National Council for the Social Studies and selected Edgar Dawson its first secretary. Although the organization remained small and dependent on support from the National Education Association and especially the American Historical Association (AHA), by the mid-1930s it began to play a more independent role and in 1935 held its first annual meeting. This was followed in 1937 with its own journal called *Social Education* with Professor Erling Hunt of Teachers College, Columbia serving as editor, and in 1940 Wilbur Murra was appointed its first full-time executive secretary (Davis, 1996).

From then until now, the issues present at the founding of NCSS remain points of contention. From then until now, the criticisms have remained remarkably consistent, and continue to be expressed with intensity and conviction. And from then until now, with rare exception, the proponents of social studies have been defensive or ineffective in communicating a clear vision of their purposes or practices.

The observations in this chapter highlight a few key events and are based on a review of selected publications, discussions with former NCSS presidents, and my experiences as a teacher and longtime member of NCSS, including several years on the board of directors and as president. Several important topics related to NCSS, the press and social studies are discussed elsewhere in this publication.

CRITICS ON THE OFFENSIVE

With general enthusiasm in the 1920s and public despair in the 1930s, little national media attention was given to social studies until just before World War II when critics raised questions about the content in social studies textbooks. Severe and repeated criticism of social studies and NCSS began in the early 1940s with articles published by *The New York Times*. The charges regularly concluded that students were ignorant of U.S. History and the culprit was social studies.

This period also marked the beginning of a running battle over the content being taught in social studies classes. It became part of a larger effort to replace what critics saw as integrated social studies with its focus on issues with a discipline-oriented and nationalist view of history and government.

Led by executive secretary Wilbur Murra and *Social Education* editor Erling Hunt, the youthful and feisty NCSS offered energetic responses but many unsubstantiated attacks reverberated throughout the land and the critics had an impact on the public consciousness far beyond the cries of foul by NCSS and its supporters.

With the ending of World War II and the early stages of the Cold War and an emerging civil rights movement, social studies teachers faced flare-ups of complaints involving subversive textbooks, teacher loyalty, and pressures to teach about the evils of communism or the benefits of the free enterprise system.

Other critics directed their attention toward instructional materials and urged more content in U.S. history about women, people of color and the contributions of all socioeconomic classes (Evans, 2004).

NEW SOCIAL STUDIES

Prompted by the shock waves from the launch of Sputnik by the Soviet Union on October 4, 1957, federal officials turned to the schools to promote mathematics and science, subjects thought to be essential in the Cold War race in space. In one of its most significant educational actions, Congress passed the National Defense Education Act of 1958 which placed the federal government in the position of actively supporting efforts to improve education in the sciences, mathematics and languages.

This also seemed to acknowledge the criticism prevalent during the 1950s that the schools were a wasteland as Arthur Bestor, the chief antagonist proclaimed. He further thought the term "social studies" should be abolished and a separate history teachers' association formed. For its part during this period, NCSS responded by preparing yearbooks and other publications for its members that provided a greater focus on individual disciplines and academic scholarship.

At about the same time, Jerome Bruner wrote a profound little book called *The Process of Education* in which he argued that disciplines have distinctive structures, that learning can be done by inquiry, and that any subject can be effectively taught in some honest form to any child at any level.

With support from the National Science Foundation, university researchers began examining traditional subjects and preparing new curriculum materials in mathematics and science. However, social studies was not receiving federal assistance or attention until Charles Keller, director of the John Hay Fellows Program, sparked interest by calling for a revolution in social studies.

Many social studies projects based on Bruner's theories and with federal funding emerged—Harvard Public Issues; the Amherst College history units; Carnegie-Mellon history; Purdue University's economics program; the High School Geography Project; the Anthropology Curriculum Study Project; Sociological Resources for the Secondary School, and even an organization of project directors, the Social Science Education Consortium. And, in an April 1965 article in *Social Education*, Edwin Fenton and John M. Good identified the major characteristics of the projects and named them the "new social studies" (Fenton & Good, 1965).

These were enthusiastic times and social studies educators, often through their participation in NCSS, were exploring a more focused discipline based education. These invigorating new developments would come to an abrupt end with conservative attacks and resulting controversy over *Man: A Course of Study.*

MACOS, as it was called, was a popular elementary level anthropology curriculum which encouraged students to compare the values, tools, languages, and social organizations of different cultures. Some aspects of the program caused concern, including a segment that taught about Netsilik Indians in the Arctic and their practices of infanticide and mercy killing. Complaints soon reached Congressman John Conlin (R-AZ) who attacked the program in the U.S. House of Representatives. Eventually Conlin convinced Congress in 1975 to end funding for *MACOS*.

Brian Larkin, NCSS executive director at the time, responded to the criticism in a statement in *Social Education*. It did not make it to any newspaper or magazine. As would occur many times, NCSS was unable to gain access to the press that carried the attack and was left to using its own publications to convey information to its members, but not the public.

NCSS past president, James Shaver, himself a major contributor to the new social studies with work on the Harvard Public Issues program and on the follow-up Utah Analysis of Public Issues Program, says today that in the 1960s and 1970s critics of social studies were writing popular books and getting attention in the press. "If there was any similar effort or public exposure by NCSS, it escaped my attention. And I've not noticed any change since. That is, social studies is rarely a news topic and NCSS is never mentioned as an educational participant or a news source" (J. Shaver, personal communication, July 1, 2004).

In any event, the Conlin attack on *MACOS* essentially ended further efforts in the new social studies.

ESTABLISHING THE RIGHT STANDARDS

The New York Times returned in the 1980s to publishing articles remarkably reminiscent of the 1940s claiming, once again, that history was in trouble and the culprit was social studies. A small band of prolific critics—Diane Ravitch, Chester Finn, Lynne Cheney, and William Bennett—all alumni of the Reagan presidency, reintroduced the aged argument that "social studies was causing ignorance of history."

With access to foundation money, close ties to federal officials and easy access to the national media, the little group launched or promoted several influential efforts to reshape American education, including the introduction of specific standards for what students should know and be able to do in history and other disciplines.

Perhaps the most influential critical attack in recent years was published as a page one opinion piece in the *Wall Street Journal*.

"Imagine a version of American history in which George Washington makes only a fleeting appearance and is never described as our first President," the piece began. "Or in which the foundlings of the Sierra Club and the National Organization for Women are considered noteworthy events, but the first gathering of the U.S. congress is not" (Cheney, 1994, p. 1).

With these attention grabbing words, Lynne V. Cheney, who funded the development of national standards while head of the National Endowment for the Humanities, condemned the standards for highlighting minor, "politically correct" figures and focusing on the negative aspects of U.S. history. If the standards are adopted, Cheney warned, "much that is significant in our past will begin to disappear from our schools."

Her comments unleashed an avalanche of criticism in news columns and op-ed pieces repeating her charges. Quick to pile on were many conservative syndicated columnists, American Federation of Teachers (AFT) president Al Shanker, and the howl was amplified by radio talk show host Rush Limbaugh.

Noting that Cheney used examples from the sample teaching activities but not the standards themselves, the *New York Times* concluded in an editorial that "reading the standards and support material is exhilarating. Students will rejoice in learning from them, teachers will cherish using them" (Nash, Crabtree & Dunn, 1997, p. 196).

An op-ed writer at the *Chicago Tribune* concluded that Cheney "is using the standards as an excuse to initiate a discussion that has nothing to do with education and everything to do with politics" (Nash, Crabtree & Dunn, 1997, pp. 196-197).

"In early weeks of the controversy," project director Gary Nash later wrote, "many op-ed writers and talk-show hosts threw grenades at the standards without reading them, but metropolitan editorial boards and journalists did their homework. These editorials and news reports highlighted misrepresentations of the guidelines and acknowledged the merits that reviewers found in the books" (Nash, Crabtree & Dunn, 1997, p. 194-197).

However, as it did after the 1943 *New York Times* history test and with the 1975 *MACOS* controversy, the U.S. Congress moved quickly to show support for American history and values. In a resolution proposed by Senator Slade Gorton (R-WA) and later modified and approved 99 to 1, they denounced the standards for failing to respect the contributions of Western civilization.

JUST OFF THE PRESS

During this period when national standards were being prepared for individual subjects, but not social studies, it became evident to NCSS that steps had to be taken if social studies was to remain a viable part of the school curriculum. With some $25,000 of its own funds, compared to the millions available for the federally funded standards projects, NCSS established a task force to prepare social studies standards.

Upon completing this project, and wishing to provide its account to the public, NCSS leadership arranged for a press conference, an event rarely initiated in the normal routine of its operation. Former President Robert Stahl recalls the time when NCSS was ready to launch its social studies curriculum standards:

> NCSS sent out over 50 letters to news organizations, including major newspapers, wire services, TV networks, and local contacts whom members of NCSS knew in the Washington, DC area to attend the session at the National Press Club in downtown DC. We did all that was customarily done and I heard that some of the press folks were called the week before as a reminder of the session.
>
> I flew in from Phoenix, as NCSS President, and [Executive Director] Martharose Laffey was there. We brought about 100 copies of the Executive Summary and about the same number of the full published standards. All was ready. We had our little speeches prepared. Finally at about 5 minutes after the session was to begin, two people from the same press agency showed up and said they had about four stories to do, and had about a half hour to spend. These were the only two who showed up.
>
> One said she would try to get something in *Education Week* on the releasing of the NCSS standards, and that she would just get the information for her short article from the NCSS Press Release and the *Executive Summary*. We invited the two to meet with us later that day if they had more questions or needed more information, but got no takers. Martharose and I stayed the full hour and a half, and left deeply disappointed. I received no inquiries from the press after this session, and to the best of my knowledge, Executive Director Laffey also received none.
>
> In hindsight, I believe NCSS did a commendable job in doing what was needed to put on a high-quality press conference. It was not a failure on our

part that only two individuals came or that the NCSS curriculum *standards* did not get broader coverage after this event. The negative press and controversy over the national History Standards and the growing anticipation of the National Geographic Society-sponsored Geography Standards were grabbing the attention of the press at the time. R. Stahl (personal communication, June 28, 2004).

ACCESS BY A FEW

In a study of 37 articles from 10 newspapers that reported on the Cheney essay condemning U.S. history standards, it was concluded that the controversy was promoted by a small number of people and groups. (Avery & Johnson, 1999, p. 224).

The study found that of 174 citations regarding the controversy, only 5 were from classroom teachers. The voices of those who were responsible for teaching history were largely absent. Instead, university professors, particularly those who teach history, received attention. And, it almost goes without saying, that no students were interviewed.

The authors of the study conclude that U.S. history in the schools plays a pivotal role in shaping the national identity and is likely to remain controversial. But they were struck that the press reported the conservative voice without its liberal counterpart, and the voices of university academicians without those of classroom teachers (Avery & Johnson, 1999, pp. 220-224).

Their nonstartling but important conclusion is that "those with greater access to the media have a better chance to shape the course of public debate, and ultimately, to determine educational policy" (Avery & Johnson, 1999, p. 224).

ATTENTION TO A FEW

A search of online archives for recent years of the widely read and influential *Education Week* provides clear evidence of a subject under attack. Not including short announcements of grants or awards, the titles of articles about social studies tell the story:

"Cheney Strives to Keep Putting Her Stamp on History," 6/16/04

"Book Accuses Social Studies Group of Ignoring Racism," 12/3/03

"Arts, Foreign Languages [Social Studies] Getting Edged Out," 11/5/03

"'Contrarians' Launch Salvo at Social Studies Traditions," 9/3/03

"History Invading Social Studies Turf in Schools," 1/22/03

"Educators Split Over What to Teach Come Sept. 11," 9/4/02

"US History Again Stumps Senior Class," 5/15/02

"Concentration on Reading, Math Troubles Social Studies Educators," 2/20/02

"Attacks Alter Instructional Landscape," 9/26/01

In recent years, *Education Week* has reported in a paragraph or two the election of new NCSS officers and occasionally on the annual meeting if there was some controversy. There have been no articles about any aspect of the organization or the educational views of any of its leaders.

Who are the individuals whose comments do make the pages of this publication? Obviously, whoever is Secretary of Education receives considerable coverage. From 2000 through July 2004, then Secretary of Education Rod Paige was referred to 580 times. No one else comes close, but other frequently noted personalities provide an interesting list of who gets press attention and who is driving the education discussion in this country. See Table 5.1.

During this same period, no president or other individual in a leadership position at NCSS was mentioned more than a few times. NCSS, itself, was referred to a mere 39 times.

Other less political, less conservative, and lower profile educators provide an interesting contrast shown in Table 5.2.

One can conclude that either *Education Week* over-reports information from the personalities or pronouncements of the politically conservative critics, or that these critics are saying and doing much more than others.

Table 5.1. Conservative Critics Number of References	
Person	*2000-2004 (through July)*
Chester Finn	174
William Bennett	133
Lamar Alexander	129
Sandra Feldman	84
Diane Ravitch	75
Lynne Cheney	62
E.D. Hirsch	57

Table 5.2. Academic and Other Observers Number of References	
Person	*2000-2004 (through July)*
Alfie Kohn	34
Ted Sanders	33
Larry Cuban	30
David Tyack	7
David Berliner	4
Ted Sizer	2

On the other hand, no individual rises to the status of an authoritative voice for social studies or NCSS.

In fact, many professional organizations are themselves too weak or meek or scrambling to protect and promote their own fields of endeavor. They are simply not in the same league with critics who are well-financed, clearly focused, politically connected and media savvy in pursuing their agenda of altering the cultural landscape and removing social studies from the curriculum.

It should also be noted that NCSS leadership comes from teaching ranks with background in local or state educational organizations or from professorial ranks in education departments with professional or academic experiences. Critics come from foundations or so-called think tanks, federal government, and occasionally more prestigious universities. In addition, they often have close ties and considerable support from the corporate world where there are additional critics of education in general and social studies in particular. They know little or nothing about NCSS because it has not risen high enough to be on their radar screen.

A number of characteristics emerge when the press reports on NCSS and social studies (as well as public education in general). Most notable, of course, is that there is little coverage until it is provoked by an individual or organization seeking to use the press to advance its agenda. Only a few papers have education reporters and fewer still run regular columns on educational issues.

Some other observations that readers might look for when reading their favorite daily include:

- *Battles and Bottom Lines*. Education news is commonly reported using military or corporate metaphors, generally a battle between two opposing groups. This framing of the story, plus a number of code words ("educationist" for professor of education, etc.) and stereotypes distorts reality and understanding.

- *Roundup the Usual Suspects*. Articles are often a roundup of unsubstantiated opinions from reliably available critics based at colleges/universities, government agencies, or cause-driven think tanks. It is easier to use snappy comments from educational celebrities than to delve into often abstract and complex issues or gather information on the experiences of teachers, students or parents

- *Beware all generalizations*. Reliance on national spokespersons causes articles that report generalizations that do not apply to all situations, or school systems, or communities. Reporters often fail to distinguish between levels in school systems, miss the fact that time and resources restrict what is taught, rarely note student characteristics or concerns, and fail to give sufficient attention to the realities of teaching.

*   *An (un)informed source reports.* Anecdotes are presented as facts. Politically motivated studies are given as much credence as academic research. Reporters are susceptible to the attention-getting gimmick, for example, tests that are designed to highlight how much students do not know.
*   *Those who do not know history, report it again as news.* Reporters do not know, or use, educational history (or history, in general) to help give readers a perspective or context for understanding events.
*   Reporters and newspapers have an important role in educating the public.

A MEEK MEGAPHONE

Social studies educators and NCSS suffer from the contradiction of preaching participation in community affairs but are professionally timid in promoting their own profession. Relations with the press, other media and the general public have not been high priorities nor do they seem to be now.

In the 1970s NCSS developed a "Tool Kit" to improve communication with the public and strengthen local social studies councils. In 1974, *Social Education* editor Dan Roselle wrote a pamphlet, "What Parents Should Know about Social Studies." Little further effort has been directed toward parents or the larger community.

Since the 1980s, many federal initiatives have promoted what conservative advocates call *traditional* history or geography while discrediting, reducing or eliminating social studies from the curriculum. At the elementary school level social studies has largely been replaced by reading programs.

NCSS past president, Donald Bragaw, believes that "NCSS has never had good or bad relations with the press because it never considered public relations to be a significant role for it, despite attempts by several Presidents and Boards to both prioritize and foster that role" (D. Bragaw, personal communication, June 29, 2004)

"Education is a "dull" topic for most people," Bragaw asserts, "but Social Studies professionals should be in the forefront of commenting on the issues of the day, taking controversial stands, etc., and putting a public face on social studies" (D. Bragaw, personal communication, June 29, 2004).

NCSS—A STORY WITHOUT A LEAD

Critics of social studies have powerful allies in the government, corporate, foundation, and the media world. NCSS lacks these alliances and has questionable support from professional organizations and the national teachers associations.

To remain viable, genteel professional organizations need, more than ever, to get their message to the public, energize their members and influence policy makers. If the social studies profession, under the NCSS leadership, does not clarify and convey the value of its content and methodology, it is likely to follow rhetoric and penmanship to the curricular graveyard.

This means that NCSS cannot avoid significant issues by not including them in their publications. It cannot hide from critical educational issues but must risk an opinion and take a stand. It means that it has to recognize and reward its press friends. It means that it has to change its mindset from reaction to action.

"Dependence on 'position papers' became the PR device," Bragaw recalls of times past. "Only the organization never promoted or hyped any of them in the public press arena to my knowledge. I have never seen the headline: 'Social Studies Organization Takes a Stand on ...'" (D. Bragaw, personal communication, June 29, 2004).

The public has little conception of social studies, past president James Shaver writes. It is not a question of "whether the public or policy makers understand and support NCSS, but whether they are even aware of the organization. The same can be said about the awareness of many social studies teachers" (J. Shaver, personal communication, June 29, 2004).

By 2004, NCSS was working with several organizations in a Campaign for the Civic Mission of Schools. Part of that effort was to work with national media to increase understanding and support of public education for democracy. Further, the staff and leadership realized that what had been done in the past was insufficient. There is a staff member responsible for press relations but the culture of the organization remains timid. The president at that time, Jesus Garcia, proposed a program to highlight positive aspects of social studies. The organization had identified members who could respond to press inquiries. Attention was given to the press and public relations at leadership institutes and annual meetings but all agreed that much more needed to be done. However, that concern without much action has been expressed frequently through the years.

Given the organization's notoriously deliberative nature and the enormity of the task, one wonders if they are able to act quickly and effectively enough to make difference or, if after all these years, the critics will not only have their say, but have their way.

REFERENCES

Avery, P. G., & Johnson, T. (1999). How newspapers framed the U.S. history standards debate. *Social Education*, 4, 220-224.

Cheney, L. V. (1994, October 20). Hijacking America's history. *Wall Street Journal*, p.1.

Davis, O. L., Jr., (Ed.) (1996). *NCSS in Retrospect*. Washington, DC: National Council for the Social Studies.

De Tocqueville, A. (1971). *Democracy in America*. New York: Washington Square Press.

Evans, R. W. (2004). *Social studies wars: What should we teach the children?* New York: Teachers College Press.

Fenton, E., & Good, J. M. (1965). Project social studies. *Social Education*, 3, 206-208.

Hertzberg, H. W. (1981). *Social studies Reform, 1880-1890*. Boulder, CO: Social Science Education Consortium.

Nash, G. B., Crabtree, C. & Dunn, R.E. (1997). *History on trial: Culture wars and the teaching of the past*. New York: Alfred A. Knopf.

CHAPTER 6

DISPATCHES FROM THE CULTURE WARS, 1994-2004

Linda Symcox

It has been 10 years now since Lynne Cheney launched a new campaign in the culture wars. She wrote an opinion piece in the *Wall Street Journal* (Cheney, 1994) attacking the soon-to-be-published *National Standards for History* (University of California at Los Angeles, 1994), and sparking an 18-month debate over the teaching of history.[1] Her argument carried enormous force because it was couched in traditional patriotic terms. She accused the *Standards*, and by implication the view of history they expressed, of denigrating America's cultural and political achievements. In so doing she trivialized and oversimplified the task of teaching history and critical thinking skills to K-12 students. Through a clever tactic of counting how many times various historical figures were mentioned (or not mentioned) in the *Standards*, she was able to mischaracterize the *Standards* as a laundry list of America's failures and shortcomings. According to Cheney, the *Standards* valorized America's downtrodden, made rogues of traditional heroes, and retold America's story primarily as one of white male greed, racism, misogyny, and economic opportunism. America's history, she claimed, seemed so "grim and gloomy" in the newly-written guidelines that they ought to be dumped. Ingeniously she made her argument by citing omissions in the *Standards*, rather than by citing the dozens of standards that were devoted to the uniqueness and goodness of the American democratic experiment. She kept her message short and simple for maximum effect.

If Cheney's immediate goal was to discredit the *Standards,* and by implication to cast doubt on the government agencies that had paid for their development (the National Endowment for the Humanities, NEH, and the U. S. Department of Education), she was extremely successful. The *Standards* were trashed and the NEH lost much of its funding over the next few years. However, if her larger goal was to help her husband Dick Cheney's presidential ambitions by serving as a culture warrior for the right, it took time for success to materialize. Bob Dole, not Cheney, won the Republican nomination in 1996, and Cheney went off to run Halliburton until he was nominated for vice-president in 2000 (Jacoby, 2004). But whatever her ambitions at the time, I doubt that she could have imagined the profound and long-term cultural impact her accusations would make. Her single article ignited a firestorm which would be enthusiastically fueled by the print and television media, and legitimized by politicians in Congress who needed an ax to grind (Nash & Ross, 1997; Symcox, 2002). In fact, the U.S. Senate voted to condemn the *Standards* by a vote of 99-1, a bigger majority than voted for the Gulf of Tonkin Resolution of 1964 (Symcox, 2002).

In a sense, however, none of this was particularly new: Cheney had simply triggered another clash in a conflict that had been repeating itself for most of the past century. This was not the first time that an innovative approach to teaching history and the social studies would come under attack, nor would it be the last. In 1943 Harold Rugg, one of the founding fathers of the social studies movement and the social reconstructionist movement, found himself in the crossfire during an earlier episode in the culture wars.

Twenty years earlier Rugg had developed a unique textbook series, designed to help students examine what he considered to be the fundamental challenges faced by contemporary American society. By 1939 Rugg's *Man and His Changing Society* had sold over 1 million copies (Kliebard, 1986, p. 175). Each volume in the series dealt with a different social issue, and many of his ideas were very radical for the time, foreshadowing the social historians and critical pedagogists of the late twentieth century. For example, in Rugg's discussion of immigrants, he expanded the definition to include the story of involuntary immigrants who were brought to America as slaves. During the Depression he wrote other textbooks challenging unbridled capitalism and recommending regulation as a cure for the current economic malaise. Rugg's textbooks found a sympathetic audience during the Depression era of the 1930s. Literally millions of American school children grew up reading them. However, by 1939, with the external threat of war looming, criticism of American society could not be tolerated. Instead, a groundswell of patriotism, expressed in opinion pages across the country, criticized and condemned Rugg's textbooks. In 1940, Rugg's textbooks, after nearly 20 years of success, were suddenly attacked as unpatriotic and taken off the market by his publisher. They were accused of debunking the nation's heroes, finding fault with the Constitution, condemning the American system of private ownership and capitalism, and undermining traditional morality—the same accusations that Cheney would later level at the *Standards* (Armstrong, 1940; Symcox, 2002).

Fast-forward 30 years, and the social studies curriculum was again in the headlines. The same cycle was about to repeat itself. This time the curriculum under attack was part of a massive reform effort funded by the federal government to revitalize public education in the wake of Sputnik. Harvard psychologist Jerome Bruner left his lab to lead this K-12 reform effort during the mid-1960s, and by 1969 he had won two national awards for his innovative sixth grade social studies program, *Man: A Course of Study (MACOS)*. The program was based on the emerging discipline of anthropology, and by using an inquiry approach it gave sixth graders the task of probing basic human commonalities across cultures. However, in spite of his success within the educational establishment, Bruner soon found himself in a firestorm of public controversy (Dow, 1991, p. 135). The program's anthropological subject matter, such as the harsh realities of the Eskimo life revealed in graphic documentary films, proved unacceptable to conservative parents and politicians, both for its graphic detail and for its implied cultural relativism.

By 1975, with the newly formed Moral Majority flexing its political muscles, conservative parents in several states campaigned effectively against this federally-funded course by writing harsh opinion pieces in local newspapers. In mid-1975 the *MACOS* controversy reached Congress, when Representative Conlan of Arizona argued that the *MACOS* program was an affront to traditional American values. He opposed *MACOS* because he believed that the program encouraged children to doubt the existing social order and that it made them susceptible to foreign values and beliefs. Within a short period *MACOS* disappeared from the curriculum and Bruner was back at Harvard devoting himself to more scholarly pursuits (Dow, 1991; Symcox, 2002, pp. 19-24).

What is interesting here is that in each of these cases—Rugg, Bruner, and the History Standards—the attacks came from the political right, not the left. And during each of these clashes the media seemed largely to have accepted and propagated the conservatives' critique. In fact, I believe that if one were to conduct a content analysis of how the press has reported issues in the social studies at least since the 1940s, one would find that the overwhelming weight of criticism has come from the right. Certainly during the *Standards* controversy and many of the textbook controversies of the 1990s, criticism of the way we teach history rarely, if ever, came from the left, even though the history curriculum in the nation's schools tends to be traditional in tone and content. Ever since the resurgent political right launched a new phase in the culture wars during the late 1970s and early 1980s, the left has been on the defensive and has responded only spasmodically, belatedly, and ineffectually to the attacks from the right. The left has failed to develop a counter argument of its own (Gitlin, 1995) that can be used preemptively.

Ironically, in an age in which newspapers, TV, and radio stations have come under ever-greater corporate control (e.g., Fox Television and Clear Channel), pundits and politicians on the right have successfully branded the media as *liberal,* and attacked them for their supposed left-wing bias. Since the repeal of the Fairness Doctrine under Ronald Reagan there has been a growing preponderance of right-wing radio and TV pundits, and an absence of liberal response, culminating in the phenomenon of "fair and balanced" news reporting on the Fox News channel (*Outfoxed: Rupert Murdoch's War on Journalism,* 2004). As Eric Alterman (2003) argues, "the myth of the 'liberal media' [now] empowers conservatives to control debate in the U.S. to the point where liberals cannot even hope for a fair shake anymore" (p. 3) Accusations of liberal bias have made newspapers such as the *Washington Post* and *New York Times* bow to pressure from the right. Look at the triumphal and jingoistic way in which the Iraq war was initially reported across the broad spectrum of the media and one begins to wonder how liberal the media really are. Even the *New York Times,* one of the most liberal newspapers, was caught up in the rush to war, and dutifully embedded its reporters with the troops. But in the brutal realities of postwar Iraq the *Times* was forced to reevaluate its position and publish a *mea culpa* denouncing its own errors in reporting the war (May 26, 2004). Given the conservative hegemony over the reporting and commenting on the news, in retrospect one can see that it was impossible to hold an intelligent and open democratic debate over the rush to war, either in the print media or over the airwaves. In fact, the reporting looks with hindsight very much like an uncritical parroting of the government line. Here one is compelled to note that the Fourth Estate signally failed to perform its function, which is to inform public opinion and question government pronouncements. And without this vigorous questioning, democracy cannot flourish—or even function.

Hermann Goering's testimony during the Nuremburg War Trials describes how easy it is for the government to manipulate the public in this way:

Why of course the people don't want war.... That is understood. But after all, it is the leaders of the country who determine the policy and it is always a simple matter to drag the people along, whether it is a democracy, a fascist dictatorship, or a parliament, or a communist dictatorship. Voice or no voice, the people can always be brought to the bidding of the leaders. That is easy. All you have to do is tell them they are being attacked, and denounce the peacemakers for lack of patriotism and exposing the country to danger. It works the same in any country. (Hermann Goering, March 18, 1946, Nuremberg War Crimes Trial)

This is especially true when the press plays its part in doing the politicians' bidding.

Simultaneous with the right-wing takeover of the media in the 1980s was the rapid proliferation of neoconservative think tanks. This development too would have a profound impact on the debate over the teaching of history and social studies. These organizations were founded in response to a growing perception on the part of conservatives that the liberal elite controlled universities and government bureaucracies, and was stifling conservative thought. Privately funded foundations such as the John F. Olin Foundation, the Hudson Institute, the Heritage Foundation, the American Enterprise Institute, the Cato Institute, the Hoover Institution, and the Free Congress Foundation, to cite only a few, have had a remarkable influence on public opinion because they can feed a stream of articles, books, research studies, policy pieces, and opinion pieces directly to their contacts in the press.

In *Soldiers of Misfortune*, Valerie Scatamburlo (1998) observes that the American Enterprise Institute (AEI) was one of the first of the conservative think tanks to figure out how to gain access to the mainstream media in order to market their ideas. For example, according to Scatamburlo, AEI, founded in 1943, has systematically hired ghostwriters to write opinion pieces in the names of well-known scholars and distribute them to sympathetic newspapers such as the *Wall Street Journal* and the *Washington Times*. In fact, the American Enterprise Institute would serve as the launching pad for Lynne Cheney's 1994 preemptive strike against the *National Standards for History*, published in the friendly columns of the *Wall Street Journal*.

Given this symbiotic relationship between the conservative think tanks and large sections of the media, it has not been difficult for conservative reformists and politicians to dominate the educational reform discourse, especially in the field of social studies and history. Conservative policy makers such as William Bennett (1986, 1992, 1994), Lynne Cheney (1994, 2004), Chester Finn, (1984, 1987), and E.D. Hirsch Jr. (1987) make a very simple and persuasive argument that the nation is losing the common cultural glue that holds it together, and that its very survival depends on creating and maintaining a common culture in the schools. However, their concept of a common American culture is essentially backward-looking. From their point of view, our common culture is defined by principles like democracy, freedom, goodness, economic promise, and social advancement. But they do not examine these complex principles too closely. For them, the inherent contradictions among these principles, -- e.g., economic and social advancement vs. democratic equality—are masked by an unconditional reverence for the Founding Fathers, the Constitution, the flag, and the capitalist system, all legitimized by reference to early American history.

They believe that too much emphasis on cultural plurality and historical change challenges our sense of national identity, which for them is somehow immutable and outside history. (But, as Perry Anderson, 1992, has shown, national identity is a very slippery concept). They see American history as a fulfillment of the potentialities inherent in the early American republic, which they believe established these principles in their purest form and handed them down for successive generations to venerate. They see all historical evolution since that time as linear progress deriving directly from the founding principles. Their view is thus in a sense static: the essence of American identity was created in the early, formative years of the new Republic, and any divergence from their view of that defining moment represents a threat, or worse, a betrayal.

Traditionalists thus reify and fetishize the nation-state, believing its political and cultural identity is fixed for all time. I will label this worldview *fundamentalist nationalism*. It is grounded in sacred texts (the Declaration of Independence, the Constitution, etc.) and should, according to its proponents, be taught as a sacralized, linear narrative, leading ever onward and upward to the present. As many commentators have observed, this type of nationalism is in effect a secular religion. Their opponents, whom I shall call *evolutionary nationalists*, believe on the other hand that the nation-state is a work in progress, that it evolves by trial and error over time, and that it is perhaps perfectible, but certainly not yet perfect. This is the perspective that I espouse. The culture wars now being fought over the teaching of history and social studies, and trumpeted in the press, are a struggle between these two worldviews, one essentially static, the other dynamic.

To understand better how these views differ, take for instance the hallowed motto *e pluribus unum* on the nation's currency. For fundamentalist nationalists, it is the *unum* that counts; for evolutionary nationalists, it is the *pluribus*. Here there is a clear-cut divergence: a vision of social, political, and cultural unity is challenged by one of diversity. Or take the Declaration of Independence and the Constitution. For fundamentalist nationalists these are immutable texts whose meaning is to be understood through *strict construction*. For evolutionary nationalists, they function as the starting point for the construction and reconstruction of the nation's identity over time.

This divergence of views is of course part of a wider debate about the nature of American democracy and its cultural foundations. The fundamentalists want to tidy it up via the acceptance of prepackaged solutions grounded in the texts they revere. But this is actually a denial of what democracy means, for democracy is in fact a messy and often contentious business. Its lifeblood is the give-and-take of debate in what Habermas (1962/1989) classically defined as the public sphere, where shibboleths and sacred cows are subjected to free and open criticism. This is how it worked in fifth-century Athens or in seventeenth-century England, (two of the conservatives' cherished exemplars): people got together, and argued, often bitterly. As Milton argued in the *Areopagitica*, written in the midst of England's constitutional crisis in 1644, "Let truth and falsehood grapple: who ever knew truth put to the worse in a free and open encounter." This principle should guide discussion in the print and television media in a truly democratic society.

Conservative reformists have always insisted on the centrality of texts like Milton's as the foundation of American democratic values. Yet their reading of these texts often seems to be rather selective. Thus E. D. Hirsch, in *Cultural Literacy* (1987), gives a list of terms that students should master to become culturally-literate citizens. He mentions the Greek historian, Thucydides, under the letter *T*. But one wonders how many of our current political leaders have passed his test of cultural literacy and have actually read Thucydides' *History of the Peloponnesian War*. It makes very instructive reading for citizens and leaders of a democracy. In it Thucydides describes how an imperialist power, Athens, overly confident of its own strength, falls victim to the belief that might makes right exemplified dramatically in the Athenian envoys' dialogue with the citizens of Melos. But in the end, as Thucydides shows, Athens's hubris leads to resounding defeat in the Peloponnesian War.

Careful reading of the *Melian Dialogue* might perhaps have counseled against our rush to war with Iraq. This example suggests that the great texts of the Western canon, like Thucydides, must be read critically; their message is not univocal, but rich, complex, and often contradictory. Their lessons are not simple, cut-and-dried validations of present-day patriotic sentiment, as conservative reformists like Hirsch or Bloom and their followers would have us believe, invoking the great western canon in order to validate a simplified ideology of cultural nationalism that purveys feel-good and unifying mantras, rather than provoking critical reflection. They use the canon to feed and flatter patriotic sentiment: they gloss over the critical elements it contains, just as the fundamentalist nationalists gloss over the tensions and contradictions built into the American republic since its foundation.

The conservative view of American culture is grounded in an implicit notion of the nation-state as at once the origin and the product of that culture. But I would argue that this thinking is increasingly out of date and out of touch in today's globalizing world: a world of multinational corporations, instantaneous communications, and porous frontiers. Many historians are problematizing the very concept of the nation state, and now consider it obsolete in what we can call the dawning *post-national* era. They observe that the nation-state is in fact a relatively recent construction; that by the mid-nineteeth century scholars and laymen had come to accept it as the natural order of things, and that it reached the apogee of its development in the twentieth century. But they point out that globalization and micro-nationalism are eroding the nation-state from above and below. For example: the Basques, Bretons, Scots, Québecois, and ethnic groups in America are seen to be undermining the nation-state from below. At the same time the nation-state is threatened from above by global capitalism, by supranational organizations such as the World Trade Organization, the United Nations, or the European Union and NAFTA. All this has led many historians to theorize the decline of the nation state as we have known it for nearly 2 centuries (Anderson, 1983; Gellner, 1983; Hobsbawm, 1990; Kohn, 1955; Smith, 2000). In fact, we now live in a post national world. But conservative reformers and the general public still cling to the paradigm of the nation-state. In Thomas Kuhn's terms (1962), the nation-state is "normal science," and the "Copernican" model that will better fit the data of the globalizing, post-national world is only beginning to be constructed. Here is the real issue at stake in the culture wars. Liberal or evolutionary nationalists and educators are seeking to formulate a concept of national identity and culture adapted to what they perceive as a post-national era, while fundamentalist nationalists and conservative educational theorists seek to reaffirm an ideal of national culture rooted in the nation-state.

This leads to a contradiction, neatly illustrated by Lynne Cheney's 1994 attack on the Standards. In a recent article entitled "Dead Souls: The Denationalization of the American Elite," Samuel P. Huntington (2004) defined a new cosmopolitan class that transcends national boundaries. It consists of elite public intellectuals, politicians, and corporate millionaires who think and operate globally rather than nationally. Their interests lie not with the nation-state and its citizen body but with their global economic and corporate partners. Let us take the current president and vice-president (and Mrs. Cheney) as exemplars of this postnational class at work. Bush and Cheney happen to belong to this cosmopolitan class through their involvement in the oil industry, although Bush has done his best to avoid foreign travel and *foie gras* in favor of Texas barbe-cues; they profit handsomely from the new global environment. And while their policies advance the process of globalization, they urge the minimum-wage American worker to remain patriotically attached to the nation-state whose foundations they themselves are helping to sap. They use nationalist rhetoric and appeals for loyalty to the nation-state to head off the discontent brought on by globalization. They know very well that playing the patriotic card is a guaranteed way to mobilize support, and that the press and the media—with a few notable exceptions—will happily follow their lead.

Lynne Cheney showed them the way in 1994. Her attack on the U.S. *Standards* employed a shrill form of nationalist rhetoric—"where is Robert E. Lee?"—to rouse the public, the media, and Congress in support of her denunciation. With the help of a compliant press, led by the *Wall Street Journal*, and the 24-hour news media eager for a story, she carried all before her. No matter that her rhetoric was misleading and unfounded: it worked. No matter, either, that by then her rhetoric was in fact obsolete – or obsolescent. Mrs. Cheney argued her case in what I have called funda-mentalist nationalist terms. She appealed to the deeply-rooted popular idea of national values and a national culture that derived from an ideal-ized foundation and remains immutable over time, that is the product of a traditionalist vision of history, and that strikes a deep chord in public discourse. In this way she routed the evolutionary nationalists and liberal educators arrayed against her, and won that round in the culture wars. But in this emerging post-national era, how much longer will this type of argument trump the opposition? And how much longer can the paladins of traditional values count on the complaisant support of the media in the culture wars, in an era when the public is increasingly multicultural and diverse (Garcia, 2004; Glazer, 1997)?

NOTE

1. The *National Standards for History*, funded jointly by the National Endow-ment for the Humanities under the direction of Lynne V. Cheney and the U.S. Department of Education Office of Educational Research and Improvement under the direction of Diane Ravitch, were developed as a collaboration among public school teachers, state social studies specialists, school superintendents, university historians, professional and scholarly organizations, public interest groups, and parents' and teachers' organiza-tions. Under development for 32 months, by October 1994 the Standards books were in press, with a general feeling of consensus throughout the educational community. I served as the assistant director for the project.

REFERENCES

Alterman, E. (2003). *What liberal media? The truth about bias and the news.* New York: Basic Books.

Anderson, B. (1983). *Imagined communities: Reflections on the origin and spread of nationalism.* London: Verso.

Anderson, P. (1992). Fernand Braudel and national identity. In P. Anderson (Ed.), *A zone of engagement* (pp. 251-278). London: Verso.

Armstrong, O. K. (1940, September). Treason in textbooks. *The American Legion Magazine,* pp. 70-72.

Bennett, W. J. (1986). *Completing the Reagan revolution. Heritage lecture # 62.* Washington, DC: The Heritage Foundation.

Bennett, W. J. (1992). *The devaluing of America: The fight for our culture and our children.* New York: Summit Books.

Bennett, W. J. (1994). *To reclaim a legacy: A report on the humanities in higher education.* Washington, DC: National Endowment for the Humanities.

Bloom, A. (1987). *The closing of the American mind: How higher education has failed democracy and impoverished the souls of today's students.* New York: Simon & Schuster.

Cheney, L. V. (1994, October 20). The end of history. *Wall Street Journal,* pp. A22, A26.

Dow, P. (1991). *Schoolhouse politics: Lessons from the Sputnik era.* Cambridge, MA: Harvard University Press.

From the editors. (2004, May 26). *New York Times,* p. A10.

Garcia, G. (2004). *The new mainstream: How the multicultural consumer is transforming American business.* New York: Rayo.

Gellner, E. (1983). *Nations and nationalism.* Ithaca, NY: Cornell University Press.

Gitlin, T. (1995). *The twilight of common dreams: Why America is wracked by culture wars.* New York: Henry Holt.

Glazer, N. (1997). *We are all multiculturalists now.* Cambridge, MA: Harvard University Press.

Habermas, J. (1962/1989). *The structural transformation of the public sphere: An inquiry into a category of bourgeois society.* Thomas Burger. Cambridge, MA: MIT Press.

Hirsch, E. D., Jr. (1987). *Cultural literacy: What every American needs to know.* Boston: Houghton Mifflin.

Huntington, S. P. (2004, Spring). *Dead souls: The denationalizaton of the American elite.* Retrieved April 4, 2004, from http://www.nationalinterest.org

Hobsbawm, E. J. (1990). *Nations and nationalism since 1780: Programme, myth, reality.* Cambridge, England: Cambridge University Press.

Jacoby, M. (2004, August). *Madame Cheney's cultural revolution.* Retrieved August 26, 2004, from http://www.salon.com/news/feature/2004/08/26/lynne_cheney/index2.html

Kliebard, H. M. (1986). *The struggle for the American curriculum: 1893-1958.* New York: Routledge.

Kohn, H. (1955). *Nationalism.* Princeton: D. Van Nostrand.

Kuhn, T. (1962). *The structure of scientific revolutions* (3rd ed.). Chicago: University of Chicago Press.

Nash, G. C. C., & Ross, E. D. (1997). *History on trial: Culture wars and the teaching of the past.* New York: Alfred A. Knopf.

National standards for United States history: Exploring the American experience. (1994). Los Angeles: Regents, University of California.

Scatamburlo, V. L. (1998). *Soldiers of misfortune: The new right's culture war and the politics of political correctness.* New York: Peter Lang.

Smith, A. D. (2000). *The nation in history: Historiographical debates about ethnicity and nationalism.* Hanover, NH: University Press of New England.

Symcox, L. (2002). *Whose history? The struggle for national standards in American classrooms.* New York: Teachers College Press.

Trial of the Major War Criminals before the International Military Tribunal. Volume IX. Proceedings: 3/18/1946–3/23/1946. (1947). Nuremberg, Germany: IMT. (Cross-examination of Hermann Goering.)

CHAPTER 7

THE ILLUSION OF KNOWLEDGE

Editorial Perspectives on the Teaching and Learning of History

Richard J. Paxton

Daniel Boorstin once wrote that the greatest obstacle to discovery is not ignorance, but the illusion of knowledge (Boorstin, 1985). The popular historian was referring to the generations of humans who struggled to ascertain the shape of the earth, the continents and the oceans. He might just as well have been writing about generations of editorial writers laboring to understand students' knowledge of history (or lack thereof).

Among an apparent majority of the nation's columnist class, it is common wisdom (almost an article of faith) that when it comes to history, most American students know very little indeed, especially when compared with past generations. History teachers do not fare any better. They are frequently portrayed as poorly trained (Ravitch, 2003a), antithetical to the teaching of facts (Jacobs, 2000), dim witted (Miller, 1988), or all of the above.

Social Studies and the Press: Keeping the Beast at Bay?, 79–90
Copyright © 2005 by Information Age Publishing
All rights of reproduction in any form reserved.

These are just a few of the vogue ideas that pose as editorial analysis in this country when it comes to the teaching of history. It is as if there is a computer search engine for the commenting caste: Google the appropriate key words (i.e., history survey results *and* vituperative; history test scores *and* scabrous) and out pops a convenient list of condemnatory talking points. Repeated over and over again, these soon become accepted as common truths, even if there is little empirical support to back them up.

The purpose of this chapter is not to categorically rebut every one of these familiar assertions, for some hold at least a kernel of truth. Rather, the objective is to examine these claims in greater detail than is common in the pages of our country's op-ed pages (undoubtedly due to a shortage of space), and to raise objections when merited.

Before beginning this process, a note about my own biases. I am an advocate of history education who believes our schools need more, but even more critically better, history teaching. That said, in general I am a defender of history teachers—because I used to be one and I know how difficult the job is, especially given the constraints imposed by states and outside interest groups (cf. Nash, Crabtree, & Dunn, 1997; Ravitch, 2003b). Should our students' historical education be expanded and enhanced? In my opinion, there is only one answer to this question: Yes. However, trotting out half truths and falsehoods about history education does not serve to advance the cause, or even as a suitable starting point for reform.

With this preamble, the remainder of the chapter will be devoted to providing examples of common "truths" about K-12 history education in the United States that frequently appear on the editorial pages of newspapers, news magazines and, nowadays Web sites. Analysis will follow.

Common Truth #1:   Today's students know less about history than students of past generations.

The claim that history education was better in the past is often left implicit in stories about the students of today: an unstated detail, so obvious it is not worth mentioning. You do not have to read far to get the drift--headlines hint that there was once a golden age of yore when students knew much, much more than today's slackers.

Some example headlines: "Decline and Fall of Teaching History," (Ravitch, 1985), "Time was when school was all about knowing," (Jacobs, 2000), and "Restore prestige to teaching American history," (Will, 2001). Get the spin? This type of headline immediately places a rhetorical blanket over the problem-space: the reader's fogy schema is cued, and the test scores/survey results that follow are placed in an unspoken yet unambiguous context.

Not that the perceived inferiority of today's students is always left unspoken. "We are in danger of having our view of the future obscured by our ignorance of the past. We cannot see clearly ahead if we are blind to history. Unfortunately, most indicators point to a worsening of our case of American amnesia," wrote Bruce Cole, chairman of the National Endowment for the Humanities, in a *Wall Street Journal* op-ed piece (Cole, 2002).

James J. Kilpatrick explains the problem this way. "Fifty years ago, the humanities shared equal billing with mathematics and the natural sciences.... But 25 years ago, when the Soviets' Sputnik shocked the Western world, the balance abruptly shifted. The importance of literacy became computer literacy." Kilpatrick goes on to call students of the latter 1980s, "dimwitted" and "cultural numbskulls" (Kilpatrick, 1987).

A sure sign of old age is the unsupported belief that young people are not learning as much *these days* as *back when we were in school*. This kind of codger-speak goes right along with stories about walking to school and back ... in the snow ... up hill both ways.

It may well be that American students do not know history as well as they should, but there is little evidence that they are any worse, historically speaking, than their ancestors. This is the case whether one is talking about test scores (Bracey, 1997; Whittington, 1991) or survey results (Paxton, 2003; Wineburg, 2004).

In a metaanalysis of test scores entitled "What Have 17-Year-Olds Known in the Past?," Dale Whittington, concluded that "students of the 1980s are evidently not demonstrably different from students in their parents' or grandparents' generation in terms of their knowledge of American history." Whittington goes on to note that, "given the reduced dropout rate and less elitist composition of the 17-year-old student body today, one could argue that students today know more American history than did their age peers of the past."

More recently, the 2001 National Assessment of Educational Progress (NAEP) test of U.S. history (which mysteriously bills itself as the "Nation's Report Card," even though it is a test) reveals that, "Students at grades 4 and 8 had higher average scale scores in 2001 than in 1994, the first year in which the current U.S. history framework was used;" and "The average scale score for twelfth-graders in 2001 was not statistically different from 1994."

Oh, by the way, although there was no *statistically significant* difference for the twelfth grade scores, the raw scores were slightly higher.

Gerald Bracey contends that we adults engage in "Knowledge Nostalgia" (Bracey, 1997). That is, we often recollect our youthful erudition somewhat like we do our school ground romances: with considerable exaggeration. If this is true, then it explains the line of reasoning of the next common truth.

Common Truth #2:   Because of truth #1, democracy and ultimately our freedom are at risk.

This fashionable (if alarmist) spin on history education became popular in the year 2000, when the American Council of Trustees and alumni released a survey in which seniors from 55 elite colleges and universities were asked 34 multiple-choice questions over the telephone. The average score was 53%.

A great deal of hysterical language blotted editorial pages in the days and weeks that followed release of the survey. For example, an editorial in the *Philadelphia Inquirer* was entitled "The basis of freedom." It begins metaphorically, noting that fireworks are cheap fun, demanding nothing more than a blanket and some grass to spread it upon. The conclusion is rather more ominous: "To citizens so clueless, democracy will seem like just a bunch of firecrackers, showy bursts of noise and color that evaporate abruptly into silence and darkness" ("The basis of freedom," 2000).

A column on the CATO Institute's Web site, under the headline "Civic Ignorance Threatens American Liberty," notes the following: "As America celebrates 224 years of independence, one wonders if this nation's citizens are equipped to defend their freedoms against the state's natural penchant for mischief. The evidence would make you drop your hamburger" (Murdock, 2000).

An editorial in the *Seattle Times*, commenting on the results of the 2001 NAEP history test, begins as follows: "If we do not know where we have been, we do not know where we are. We are lost" ("Don't know much," 2002).

These kinds of quotations are common indeed, but rarely is there an editorial retort. One exception concludes as follows:

> Craig, who routinely quizzed his students on history and current affairs and despaired over their inadequacies, a few years ago posed this question: ' If our most promising young people have no appreciation for why democracy is worth preserving, how will they know when it is threatened?' Allow me to respond on behalf of all of us who could readily be embarrassed by what we do now know. Just because we may fail to recognize the name of a dead tyrant does not mean that we would be any slower in recognizing his successor. (Gup, 2000)

All the handwringing about the potential downfall of our system of government might make sense, except for one inconvenient fact: The bulk of evidence suggests that students today know at least as much—and possibly more—about history as their parents or grandparents (Bracey, 1997; Paxton, 2003; Whittington, 1991). Recall that according to the U.S. Census Bureau, only about half of students actually graduated from high school during the 1940s, and yet miraculously, democracy survived that challenging decade more or less in one piece.

Common Truth #3:   Dim/lazy/unqualified history teachers are to blame.

Almost a century of test/survey results that are widely perceived to be anemic at best has led to many an editorial blunderbuss aimed at the nation's history teachers. Common themes include the charge that these teachers are poorly trained, slow on the uptake, and that too many have more passion for sports than academics.

For example, Alan Miller, an editorial writer for *The San Diego Union*, opined as follows:

> All too often, students are taught by slugs who barely manage to stay a page or two ahead of the class. Sadly, there is a disproportionate percentage of such instructors in the social studies, inasmuch as most athletic coaches have a minor in the subject and thus are "qualified" to teach the panorama of mankind.

In conclusion, he asks, "Come to think of it, a much more useful book might be 'What do our English and Social Studies Teachers Know?'" (Miller, 1988).

A more recent commentary in *Education Week* made similar points while quoting Diane Ravitch: "'The two fields taught in school with the highest percentage of out-of-field teachers are history and physics,' said Ravitch. A history teacher herself, Ms Ravitch maintained that there is no excuse for teachers of U.S. history not to be required to study the subject extensively in college. She suggested that many districts overlook the lack of preparation of many history teachers because they also tend to coach athletic teams"(Manzo, 2002).

Of course, it would be nice and, in my opinion, helpful if all history teachers had their bachelor's degree in the subject. It would also not be possible under our current educational set up. That is because most history teachers teach more than one subject—they are in fact social studies teachers.

Social studies is a broad field that encompasses as its principal subject areas not only history, but also economics, geography and political science. The Social studies teacher requires, in order to be certified in most states, a wide range of college classes.

Furthermore, even if all history teachers had university degrees in history, it would not necessarily improve instruction. Content knowledge and pedagogical skills do not go hand-in-hand, and the latter is not the focus of most history courses. As many a university student will attest, it is quite possible to be a content expert and still be a lousy teacher.

Common Truth #4:   Students know more about modern culture than about history—and there is something wrong with this.

In the 1980s, *A Nation at Risk* (1983) made huge waves by suggesting that the perceived lack of knowledge of American students placed our democratic institutions in jeopardy. Clever survey writers in the 1990s took the bait and came up with the idea of sprinkling questions about modern culture amongst multiple-choice queries targeting the past. The idea, it seems, is to make the shocking discovery that today's students know more about their own society than they do about ancient civilizations. Editorial writers and other journalists responded with glee.

One writer launched his column as follows: "The future of American liberty rests in the hands of young people more familiar with the Three Stooges than the three branches of government" (Murdock, 2000).

Commenting on NAEP 2001 history test, another columnist quipped, "One of the problems, of course, is the test itself. It doesn't ask the right questions. Instead of arcane questions about such ancient history as World War II, if it had asked: 'Buffy is the slayer of: A) Dragons; B) Mosquitoes; C) UPN; D) Vampires,' a majority might have done better" (Kitman, 2002).

These kinds of quotations are plentiful. Here's another: "Students were much more knowledgeable about popular culture. For example, 99% of seniors could identify profane adolescents 'Beavis and Butt-head' as 'television cartoon characters.' But only 23% identified James Madison as the principal framer of the Constitution" ("Ignorance of things past," 2000).

The purpose of this adept wordplay is apparently to skew the younger generation; as if some idealized past generation knew more about James Madison than James Dean, or more about Benjamin Franklin than Frank Sinatra. In short, this line of reasoning makes great copy, but absolutely no sense.

Common Truth #5:   Surveys are good indicators of historical knowledge.

Rarely a year goes by without the release of some survey of student historical knowledge followed by a prompt echo of press derision (Paxton, 2003). The idea that out-of-the-blue surveys are a good way to assess historical knowledge is questionable, to say the least. As far back as 1917, educational researchers pointed out that the most important aspects of historical thought are poorly suited to swift and simple assessments, and that surveys are particularly inappropriate for this purpose (Bell & McCollum, 1917; Myers, 1917).

Yet the pages of our newspapers seem ever eager to report on the latest survey results, often finding in them cause to forecast dire consequences for the future of the country. Whether surveys (today mainly taking place over a telephone) are a good indicator of historical knowledge is more seldom examined.

As Ted Gup pointed out in a column in the *Washington Post*, the incessant cycle of academic surveys followed by anguished cries may say more about the American psyche then it does about the achievement of our students:

> If there's one thing Americans do excel at, it is self-flagellation. These perennial reports of intellectual inadequacy have become a kind of national sport. We seem to take perverse pleasure in putting ourselves down before the world, demonstrating once more how woefully illiterate we are, how bankrupt our schools, how unworthy our citizenry," he wrote under the headline "Life is an Essay, Not Multiple Choice." (Gup, 2000)

This is not to say that all history surveys are bad, but rather that they must be viewed in proper context. For a history survey that sheds light on what Americans actually know (as opposed to what they do not know) the reader should check out Roy Rosenzweig and David Thelen's 1998 book, *The Presence of the Past: Popular Uses of History in American Life*. Their survey did not feature quickie multiple-choice/fill-in-the-blank questions. Instead, it took the form of interviews lasting half an hour. The findings from this survey of some 1,500 Americans are complex; difficult to sum up in a sentence or two. Suffice to say that Rosenzweig and Thelen found average Americans to be deeply engaged with history, pursuing the past in a wide variety of manners and modes. Many were less concerned about the official version of history taught in most public schools.

Common Truth #6: Today's teachers think students do not need to know facts.

There are some in the media that believe there is a vast conspiracy in the educational establishment whose main purpose is to remove facts from the history classroom. A few examples of this literature:

- "Many educators fear memorizing facts will prevent students from thinking, so they teach students to acquire knowledge on an as-needed basis," writes Jacobs of the *San Jose Mercury News*, later referring to a cohort of "anti-factualists" (Jacobs, 2000).
- "The educational establishment scorned the teaching of mere facts and dates. If a high-school graduate could not say when Columbus discovered the New World, no matter. 'He will know how to look it up'" according to Kilpatrick (1987).

This begs the question: Where are these antifactualists? Who are they? Well, actually many of them are historians at our finest universities and colleges, although it is difficult to find any scorning facts.

Instead, some argue that facts, while important, are not enough; that facts should serve as the beginning of instruction, not its end (Sellers, 1969). There are also those who make the point that focusing exclusively on facts while putting off higher-order thinking skills, is contrary to what we know about human learning, and that doing so is a killer to students' desire to learn and even their ability to think like a historian (Holt, 1990; Wilson & Wineburg, 1993).

The results of history surveys taken over the past 90 years provides no evidence that students have ever been capable of remembering large volumes of decontextualized facts. In a story about the 2001 NAEP history test, UCLA history professor Gary B. Nash made the point: "I'm not sure we should even expect 18-year-olds to remember dates and facts and names and places if there's no practical use for that knowledge" (Colvin, 2002).

Common Truth #7:   NCLB will help.

The 2001 NAEP history test prompted a news release from Secretary of Education Rod Paige. The remarks were widely quoted in editorial pages around the country (cf. Manzo, 2002; "Class struggles," 2002). Paige called the test scores (which, again, had gone *up* in all three categories) "unacceptable."

"What this report card is telling us is that too many of our public school children are still struggling in this critical core subject area—history," Paige said. He went on: "Yes, we've got a lot more work to do. But we've got just the tool to do it—the sweeping new education reforms of the No Child Left Behind Act of 2001 [NCLB]."

However, many believe that NCLB, which targets mathematical and language literacy, is undermining history education in the United States. The obsession with math and language, and the pressure to raise test scores in these areas, appears to be putting the curricular squeeze on other subject areas, history among them.

Kay Knowles, a U.S. history teacher from Virginia and a board member of the National Council on the social studies, was quoted making this point. She said that students may be more poorly prepared in history because the subject is being overlooked on standardized tests targeting elementary and middle school students ("Class Struggles," 2002; Manzo, 2002).

Princeton historian Theodore Rabb views NCLB as an educational mistake. "By multiplying the distractions that already cause schools and students to play down the transmittal of information—once considered the heart of education and a prerequisite for intelligent thought and values—No Child Left Behind is draining academic substance out of the classroom," he wrote in the *Chronicle of Higher Education*:

> Here, I would argue, is the most insidious effect of the law: not its financial, pedagogic, or constitutional shortcomings, but its devastation of subjects other than reading and math in the first eight grades. The outcome is clear and widespread. (Rabb, 2004)

A central tenet of NCLB is for states to set standards, and to hold schools accountable for meeting them. However, an editorial in the *Seattle Times* noted of the 2001 NAEP history test: "The disappointing results came after many states around the country have developed content standards intended to closely guide how history is taught to students in the classroom" ("Tests show youths", 2002).

Of course, no one knows at this date what NCLB's ultimate effect will be on history education, but at this point the auspices are far from positive.

CONCLUSION

I have learned silence from the talkative, toleration from the intolerant, and kindness from the unkind; yet strange, I am ungrateful to those teachers.

—Kahlil Gibran (1926)

The teaching and learning of history has been the target of a great deal of editorial commentary in recent years. However, much of the analysis by the various writers and omnibus public intellectuals who chip in on the subject has tended toward the reflexive, as opposed to the reflective. Specifically, the observations are long on criticism and short on remediation. For ideas about how to improve history education, one would have to turn away from part-time education pundits and turn to the literature of full-time educators.

It seems clear that many critics are ungrateful to K-12 history teachers, but what have they learned? If there is little agreement on what excellent history teaching looks like, there is at least some concurrence regarding its opposite; and here the critique does not revolve around a dearth of facts or the extent to which teachers are accredited.

In "What do our 17-year-olds know?" Diane Ravitch and Chester E. Finn ask readers to take the students' perspective.

> In the eyes of the students, the typical history classroom is one in which they listen to the teacher explain the day's lesson, use the textbook and take tests. Occasionally they watch a movie. Sometimes they memorize information and read stories about events and people. They seldom work with other students, use original documents, write term papers, or discuss the significance of what they are studying.(Ravitch & Finn, 1987, p. 194)

Marvin Kitman, in a 2002 *Newsday* column entitled "Failure of Historical Proportions," notes that the fault does not lie with students: "The U.S. Department of Education also blames history teachers.... But even more of a problem is the way the qualified teach history. It is taught as a musty, dusty collection of facts from the wastebasket of time without relevance to what's happening today, baby."

It is not the subject itself that bores students, Kitman argues, but the way it is all too often pitched to them in the classroom: "Time and again they watch something on the History Channel or A&E and they are amazed. It's fascinating. But they didn't learn the details in high school" (Kitman, 2002).

George Will writes that,

> When history is taught at all nowadays, often it is taught as the unfolding of inevitabilities—of vast, impersonal forces. The role of contingency in history is disparaged, so students are inoculated against the 'undemocratic' notion that history can be turned in course by great individuals. (Will, 2001)

Teaching facts is essential, and having history teachers who know content is indeed important, but these things alone will not necessarily improve history education in the United States.

I, for one, have never run across an undergraduate who did not know what year Columbus sailed for the New World. Likewise, I have never met a student who could not tell me the names of the three ships under his command. On the other hand, it is the rare and precocious student who can critically examine whether Columbus and his shipmates *discovered* the New World.

Retention of historical facts is one thing. Thinking historically is another, and by far the more challenging (and interesting) aspect of learning history. How to teach this latter skill is a difficult and complex task, and one that is in many ways still relatively poorly understood, even by historians (Holt, 1990; Wineburg, 2001).

Perhaps this is a good place to return to Daniel Boorstin. Like many who write about the past, Boorstin had no advanced degree in the field (his doctorate was in law), yet he managed to become one of America's most prolific and popular historians. He was, however, fascinated and obsessed with the field. Fundamentally understanding how to instill these characteristics in our students would be a good place for our nation's editorial writers to turn their quest for knowledge. As Boorstin once wrote, "Education is learning what you didn't even know you didn't know."

REFERENCES

Bell, J. C., & McCollum, D. F. (1917). A study of the attainments of pupils in United States history. *Journal of Educational Psychology, 8*(5), 257-274.

Boorstin, D. (1985). *The discoverers*. New York: Vintage Books.

Bracey, G. W. (1997). *Setting the record straight: Responses to misconceptions about public education in the United States*. Alexandria, VA: Association for Supervision and Curriculum Development.

Class struggles: Tests show youths lack grasp of U.S. history (2002, May 10). *The Seattle Times*, p A3.

Cole, B. (2002, June 11). Our American amnesia. *The Wall Street Journal*, p. D7.

Colvin, R. L. (2002, May 10). High school seniors can't say what happened when: Earlier grades fare little better. *The Los Angeles Times*, p. A16.

Don't know much about history ... (2002, May 13). *The Seattle Times*, p. B4.

Gup, T. (2000, August 6). Life is an essay, not multiple choice. *The Washington Post*, p. B2.

Holt, T. (1990). *Thinking historically: Narrative, imagination and understanding*. New York: College Entrance Examination Board.

Ignorance of things past: U.S. history isn't students' forte. (2000, June 29). Retrieved June 22, 2001, from http://www.cnn.com/2000/fyi/teacher.resources/education.news/06/29/history.ap/

Jacobs, J. (2000, July 12). Time was when school was all about knowing. *Akron Beacon Journal*. Available: http://www.ohio.com/bj/editorial/com/2000/July/12/docs/001159.htm

Kilpatrick, J. J. (1987). Bring back the humanities. *Bergen Record Corp*, p. B13.

Kitman, M. (2002, May 19). Failure of historical proportions. *Newsday*, p. D39.

Manzo, K. K. (2002, May 15). US history again stumps senior class. *Education Week on the Web*. Available: http://www.edweek.org/ew/newstory.cfm?slug=naep.h21

Miller, A. (1988, February 21). Sad truth of rampant ignorance among teens. *San Diego Union-Tribune*.

Murdock, D. (2000, June 30). Civic ignorance threatens American liberty. *Cato Institute*. Retrieved June 22, 2001, from www.cato.org/dailys/6-30-00.html

Myers, G. C. (1917). Delayed recall in history. *Journal of Educational Psychology, 8*(4), 275-283.

Nash, G. B., Crabtree, C., & Dunn, R. E. (1997). *History on trial: Culture wars and the teaching of the past*. New York: Alfred A Knopf.

National Commission on Excellence in Education. (1983). *A nation at risk: The imperative for educational reform. A report to the nation, the Secretary of Education, and the United States Department of Education*. Washington, DC: U.S. Department of Education.

Paxton, R. J. (2003). Don't know much about history—never did. *Phi Delta Kappan, 85*(4), 264-273.

Rabb, T. K. (2004). What happened to historical literacy? *The Chronicle of Higher Education, 50*, B24.

Ravitch, D. (1985, November 17). Decline and fall of teaching history. *New York Times Magazine*, pp. 50, 52, 54, 56, 101, 117.

Ravitch, D., & Finn, C. E. (1987). *What do our 17-year-olds know? A report in the first national assessment of history and literature*. New York: Harper and Row.

Ravitch, D. (2003a). A brief history of social studies. In J. Leming, L. Ellington, & K. Porter(Eds.), *Where did social studies go wrong?* Daytonm OH: Thomas B. Fordham Foundation.

Ravitch, D. (2003b). *The language police: How pressure groups restrict what students learn*. New York: Alfred A. Knopf.

Rosenzweig, R., & Thelen, D. (1998). *The presence of the past: Popular uses of history in American life*. New York: Columbia University Press.

Sellers, C. G. (1969, May). Is history on the way out of the schools and do historians care? *Social Education*, 509-515.

The basis of freedom. (2000, July 4). *The Philadelphia Inquirer.* Retrieved May 24, 2001, from http://www.freerepublic.com/forum/a396267275264.htm

Will, G. (2001, December 23). The importance of teaching and learning history. *Tulsa World*, p. 11.

Wilson, S. M., & Wineburg, S. S. (1993). Wrinkles in time: Using performance assessments to understand the knowledge of history teachers. *American Educational Research Journal, 30*, 729-769.

Wineburg, S. (2001). *Historical thinking and other unnatural acts: Charting the future of teaching the past*. Philadelphia, PA: Temple University Press.

Wineburg, S. (2004). Crazy for history. *The Journal of American History. 90*(4), 1401-1414.

Whittington, D. (1991). What have 17-year-olds known in the past? *American Educational Research Journal, 28*(4), 759-780.

PART III

THE LESSONS FROM THE FIELD

CHAPTER 8

THE PRESS AND
GLOBAL EDUCATION

Merry M. Merryfield

In its short history global education has entered the media spotlight when its content and pedagogy have provoked heated controversies, reasoned debates, and, at times, support for the ways in which American students learn about their world (Schukar, 1993). Unlike other approaches to teaching about the world, global education is characterized by the study of multiple perspectives, cross-cultural experiential learning, and global interconnectedness—cultural, economic, political, environmental and technological (Anderson, 1979; Becker, 1979; Case, 1993; Hanvey, 1975; Pike & Selby, 1995; Wilson, 1993). Recognizing global education as an emerging trend, the Association of Supervision and Curriculum Development noted in 1989 that 23 states required that global or world studies be taught in K-12 schools (O'Neil, 1989). After the attacks of 9/11 global education took on a new immediacy as reporters first sought out stories of how schools were responding to terrorism and later how they were teaching about ongoing events in Afghanistan and Iraq.

Given the critical role of the United States in the world today, this is an especially significant time to examine how media depict the role of global education in the education of young Americans. This chapter begins by examining the meaning of global education so that we can compare its

Social Studies and the Press: Keeping the Beast at Bay?, 93–108

goals and content as set forth by educators with the way it is portrayed in the press. Then I examine a number of themes in press articles over the years that have challenged and illuminated different elements and views of global education. Finally I share some of my own experiences with the press on this topic in the last few years.

GLOBAL EDUCATION AS PRACTICED IN AMERICAN SCHOOLS

Although global education has been conceptualized by many scholars, the most common rationale for its implementation in schools is summed up in the 2001 position statement of the National Council for the Social Studies:

> The human experience is an increasingly globalized phenomenon in which people are constantly being influenced by transnational, cross-cultural, multi-cultural and multi-ethnic interactions. The goods we buy, the work we do, the cross-cultural links we have in our own communities and outside them, and increased worldwide communication capabilities all contribute to an imperative that responsible citizens understand global and international issues. The increasing globalization in the human condition has created additional opportunities and responsibilities for individuals and groups to take personal, social, and political action in the international arena.

The statement goes on to explain that:

> A global perspective is attentive to the interconnectedness of the human and natural environment and the interrelated nature of events, problems or ideas. An important characteristic of global studies is the analysis of problems, issues, or ideas from a perspective that deals with the nature of change and interdependence.[1]

In a 2004 review of the global education literature, these elements were identified as characterizing global education in K-12 schools in North America:

- Students come to understand economic, political, cultural, environmental, technological and historical *interconnectedness* between their own communities, their nation and the larger world.
- They examine *multiple perspectives* of events and issues both past and present.
- They study *other cultures* and recognize that people in other cultures often have experiences, beliefs and knowledge that create a worldview that differs from their own.

- They develop *cross-cultural understanding* through study and experiences online and face to face with people different from themselves that reduce stereotypes and ethnocentrism.
- They study *global issues, current events,* and the actions of *non-state actors* (individuals, multinational corporations, and nongovernmental organizations such as the International Monetary Fund, labor unions, Greenpeace, terrorist groups).
- They learn to *participate and make decisions* in local and global communities.

Other elements of global education include the study of globalization through history, anticipation of complexity, resistance to stereotyping, critical thinking skills and thematic and interdisciplinary instruction (Diaz, Massialas, & Xanthopoulos, 1999; Gaudelli, 2003; Merryfield, 2001; Merryfield & Wilson, 2005; Pike & Selby, 1995). Unlike traditional ways of teaching about the world that have centered K-12 students within their local community, state or province, nation, or region (European, for example), global education centers students within the world, its peoples, its systems and issues.

GLOBAL EDUCATION IN THE PRESS

In general, press coverage on global education falls into three categories. First are the articles that address the *threat of global education.* Often precipitated by statements or publications of well-known conservatives, these tend to be opinion pieces that attack ideas or curriculum materials purported to exemplify global education (Clifford, 1991; Finn, 2001; Hunter, 1991; Hymowitz, 2002; Schlafly, 1986; Sorokin, 2002). The source of information about global education is usually a curriculum document, a national organization, or a scholar. Second are articles that aim for balance by portraying multiple points of view about some element of global education or its application in the schools (Alfano, 2003; Draper, 2003; Manzo, 2003, September 3; O'Neil, 1989; Shanker, 1989; Vail, 2003). These articles are usually authored by education reporters for newspapers or writers for education journals or organizations, such as *Education Week,* The National School Board, and the Association for Supervision and Curriculum Development. Finally there are the reality-based articles that draw upon teachers' practices, frequently from schools in the community that the newspaper serves (Fiely, 2003; Hunter, 2003, Keller, 2003; Lane, 2003; Maines, 2003; Marselas, 2003; Schoichet, 2003; Stern, 2002). These articles focus more on what teachers are thinking and doing than educational theories or political rhetoric. Like mushrooms popping up after a rain, these articles emerge when profound events take place and there is interest in how schools and teachers are addressing them.

One other contextual factor is important. Global education is often a sidebar to other issues—referenced to explain the death of history in the schools or the cultural relativism of multicultural education, general issues in school reform, or the ways in which teachers are teaching about Islam, terrorism or current events. Thus readers are much more likely to learn bits and pieces about global education than to read substantive articles. Such references are often opaque, shallow and frequently misleading. Given the ways in which it differs from the Eurocentric approach of past generations, it is not surprising that global education has been perceived as a controversial topic. Here are some different but related themes in articles about global education over the last 25 years.

Theme One: *Global education detracts from the study of Western civilization and seeks to de-exceptionalize the American experience.*

> Global education promotes "the falsehood that other nations, governments, legal systems, cultures and economic systems are essentially equivalent to us and entitled to equal respect." (Schlafly, 1986, p. 23)

Since global education includes the whole world—all world regions within world history, world geography, economics, comparative political systems, and so forth—it has been criticized for decreasing the study of western civilization (Western Europe and the U.S.) and contributing to the lack of knowledge young people have about their own country. But this is not simply an issue of class time. Some writers focus on the ways in which the United States and western civilization are positioned within the K-12 curriculum. There has been concern about what critics have called *the de-exceptionalizing* of the United States—the process of teaching about other countries and peoples as though they merit the same attention as do the United States and Americans (Buehrer, 1990; Hymowitz, 2002; Schlafly, 1986). This issue appears to take on a critical immediacy whenever the U.S. is threatened or at war (Burack, 2003).

The period following the 9/11 attacks exemplifies this debate. Some organizations, such as the National Education Association (NEA) and the National Council for the Social Studies (NCSS) quickly made materials available so that American teachers could teach about Islam, Afghanistan, terrorism, and events in the Middle East through many perspectives and primary sources. Web sites and e-mail created instant access to lesson plans, resources in other countries, and breaking information. At the same time other organizations, such as the Fordham Foundation, prepared their own materials on American documents and U.S. history.

Their strong objections to the responses of the NEA and the NCSS made the news (Burack, 2003; Manzo, 2003, September 3; Sorokin, 2002).

This ongoing debate is centered on a fundamental question: are American students better educated by focusing on the history of western civilization and the United States or by learning about the whole world with the U.S. as an integral part of it? Global educators argue that for the U.S. to survive in this century, its citizens must understand the workings of the global economic systems and global issues such as pollution and deforestation, the movement of people within and across borders, and the effects of new technologies in Latin America, Southeast Asia and Eastern Europe. Without an educational background that allows Americans to view their own country from the perspectives of a global historical context and through the cultural lenses of diverse world people—such as the Chinese, Japanese, Arabs, Indians—Americans will not know enough about the world to make sound political, economic, or military decisions.

Theme Two: *Global education undermines the teaching of patriotism.*

World-class/global education is used to undermine democracy and patriotism. It promotes fear of nuclear war, teaches animal rights, vegetarianism, pollution control, redistribution of wealth, feminism, and worship of goddess Earth/Gaia. (Hunter, 1991)

Perhaps no accusation against global education plays better in headlines than the charge that schools are teaching antiAmerican ideas or undermining American values. Some global educators teach students to examine how people in diverse regions perceive American decisions and interactions across the planet. How do Canadians perceive the effects of coal-burning power plants in the U.S.? What do people in Latin America or Asia think about American multinational companies situated in their home towns? Or why do some Europeans support and others object to the American invasion of Iraq?

Articles which criticize the teaching of multiple perspectives capture differences of opinion between those who want students to see events and issues through only mainstream American perspectives and interests and those who want students to examine the perspectives, experiences, and interests of diverse people across the world. The press has furthered the debate on whose perspectives, ideas, and experiences should be taught in the nation's schools (Alfano, 3003; Landrum, 2003; Manzo, 2003, January 23).

The center of this controversy often is the us/them debate, since global educators do not divide the world into black and white, first world/third world, good/evil, those like us and those not like us. Global educators examine how different countries construct patriots and democracy and view patriotism historically and in current settings. Who do the Israelis and Palestinians see as patriots? In U.S. government courses, global educators may ask such questions as "Do patriots always support their government's point of view?" "Is it disloyal to examine diverse points of view held by people within the U.S. and around the world towards an event or issue?" Patriotism is taught within global education as a cultural universal as patriotism is valued within many nations around the world and yet can have different meanings as it is constructed from diverse cultural norms.

Theme Three: Global education serves leftist agendas that include teaching moral and cultural relativism and promoting a one-world government and a new world order.

> [T]he theoreticians in the social studies establishment have a more radical agenda. They want children to think of themselves not as Americans, but as members of the "global community." (Hymowitz, 2002, p. 28)

In the 1980s and 1990s curriculum controversies in Colorado, Minnesota and Iowa catapulted global education into the public eye across the United States. Syndicated writers and national organizations responded to the controversies through articles in newspapers and other publications. Often the catalysts were single lesson plans or resources that were held up as unbalanced or indoctrinating students into a leftist agenda. In 1986 Gregg Cunningham's article, "Blowing the Whistle on Global Education," accused the Center for Teaching International Relations at the University of Denver of producing materials that seek "to ridicule our value system by suggesting that we relinquish our economic and political preeminence in the interest of some shadowy 'global justice'. Their worldview is utopian and pacifistic. They are redistributionists" (Cunningham, 1986, p. 21).

His arguments were taken up by Phyllis Schlafly (1986) in "What Is Wrong with Global Education" published in the *St Louis Globe Democrat*. She attacked global education as an attempt to censor content about American history, culture, and heroes, to promote moral equivalence and brainwash teachers to use techniques of indoctrination.

In 1988 the controversy spread to Minnesota when Katherine Kersten wrote "The Radicalization of Minnesota's Public Schools," an exposé of what she called the one-sided and inaccurate views on Central America that were being promoted and distributed to teachers by the Minnesota Global Education Coalition (Kersten, 1988). Although her target was the Central American Resource Center in Minneapolis which was associated with the Coalition, her critique of global education was reported nationally as it served to further political agendas (Schukar, 1993).

Al Shanker, then President of the American Federation of Teachers, expanded the debate in a series of national syndicated columns from 1989 to 1991. Referencing Kersten in his column titled "Which way global education? Propaganda or education?" published in the *New York Times*, February 19, 1989, he recognized that students "do need to know more about world history, geography, different forms of government and issues that cross national borders" while he agreed with Kersten that the instructional materials she identified provided "an oversimplified picture of Central America." Unlike Kersten, however, he concludes that it would be a shame for such materials to undermine or jeopardize the future of global education (Shanker, 1989, p. E7).[2]

"Farmers' groups are beefing about an Iowa Department of Education catalog on global education activities, charging it is biased against agriculture" charged the headlines in the *Des Moines Register* on March 18, 1991. All it took was one lesson plan to set off a major controversy in Iowa. The Iowa Department of Education developed approximately 1500 pages of lesson plans and resource materials in a major effort to infuse global perspectives across the K-12 curriculum. A math lesson that directed students to compare feeding people through grain versus grain-fed beef set off farmers who then questioned all of global education as promoting biased information. Soon conservative groups found other objectionable ideas.

"Under the banner of global education we can expect to see promotion of environmentalism, vegetarianism, pacifism, the unity of mankind, world population control evolution, Eastern religions, and worship of Gaia" (*Concerned Women*, February, 1991, p. 3). Since the late 1980s critiques of global education often included a litany of accusations. Global education is purported to divide the world between oppressors and the oppressed, promote one-worldism, one-world government, a new world order, and render the nation-state obsolete (Buehrer, 1990; Burack, 2003; Cunningham, 1986). Global education is said to be hostile to capitalism and encourage student activism (Cunningham, 1986). It is said to teach students to be comfortable with ambiguity and cultural relativism (Buehrer, 1990; Burack, 2003; Cunningham, 1986; Hunter, 1991; Shanker, 1991).

The most committed proponents of the global education ideology outlined here are activists with an agenda. They explicitly seek to wean American students from a "retrograde" loyalty to the nation-state and refocus them on a globalist agenda that is hostile to the West. (Burack, 2003)

Certainly global education does promote student participation in local and global communities (which can be called activism) and teaches students to look at the world in new ways, including through the perspectives of people in many nations and walks of life. Global educators teach about the United Nations and other multinational organizations from the World Bank to the Grameen Bank, from global environmental organizations to global religious organization. However, none of these topics threaten the nation-state or promote one-world government. It is the teaching of different perspectives that often upsets people who want students to learn only one point of view. Yet it is impossible for students to understand their world if they only study one point of view.

Theme Four: Global education prepares students to understand their world.

There is a quite different theme that has appeared in the press over the years. It often is seen in local news about schools and links them to world events. Writing of a local teacher, a *Sun* reporter noted: "Holley was one of many Thursday who sought ways to answer the questions of students confronting a changed world. Educators call the attack on Iraq a teachable moment when student interest soars and the lessons in textbooks come to life" (Maines, 2003).

Interconnectedness is one of the major elements of global education. Following 9/11 and the invasions of Afghanistan and Iraq, many teachers developed teaching strategies to help their students understand these difficult events and related issues such as foreign policy decisions, cultural and religious differences, and terrorism. Across the nation reporters sought out stories about what teachers were doing and how students were responding. Many of these stories provided insights into the teaching of global perspectives in local schools (Fiely, 2003; Hunter, 2003; Keller, 2003; Lane, 2003; Maines, 2003; Marselas, 2003; Schoichet, 2003; Stern, 2002). Here is an illustration from *The Greenville News*:

> War, not textbooks, has become the focus of lessons in some classrooms across the Upstate. Each day, Jamie Gestwicki opens her freshman World Geography class with discussion of the latest happenings in Iraq.
>
> They've tackled issues such as how U.S. foreign policy, the religion of the region and geography and history have influenced the conflict.
>
> On Thursday, about 12 hours after the United States unleashed cruise missiles and precision-guided bombs on Baghdad, the talk centered around students' fears that terrorists would retaliate for the strikes by hitting targets here. In middle and high school classrooms across Greenville County—and the Upstate—war has become the avenue teachers use teach economics, government, geography and history.

"Good social studies teachers can connect whatever is going on in the world with the curriculum," said Merry Merryfield, a professor of social studies and global education at Ohio State University.

In Maxie Preshia's seventh-grade social studies class at League Academy, students debated whether the war launched Wednesday night was justified.

In a point-counterpoint format, students argued the threat of terrorist was reason enough to attack. Others argued there was no proof that Iraq had done anything to the United States. Although the war to topple Saddam Hussein was a half a world away from Mauldin High, it was hard to get away from it Thursday morning. (Landrum, 2003)

These articles often demonstrate how teachers connect their students to the larger world as they teach mandated content in geography, history, or other subjects. These articles are often couched within local experiences, such as a teacher being called up or ways in which the students see the relevance of learning about global events and issues.

MY EXPERIENCES WITH THE PRESS

I had just arrived for a board of directors meeting of the NCSS in May 2002 when I was handed a copy of an article entitled "Anti-Social Studies." The article attacked NCSS, its journal, and several presenters at the NCSS national conference. And then I saw my name in the article:

Global studies works to de-exceptionalize both America and the Western world as a whole. "Globally-oriented teachers don't teach an 'us-them' dichotomy that only views events or issues from the norms of American foreign policy or Eurocentric tradition," explains Merry M. Merryfield, a teacher of education at Ohio State University. "Instead they focus on the commonalities of the human experience." (Hymowitz, 2002, p. 28)

As I read the article a second time, I was delighted to see that for once I had not been misquoted or had something I had said taken out of context. Although the author obviously disapproved of my ideas and made some rather harsh accusations about my field, she had accurately reported what I had said. Given other experiences with reporters over the years, I have come to the conclusion that the best I can hope for is accuracy in context.

I write this section based on being interviewed over 25 times in the last 3 years by print reporters, for television (CNN, MSNBC), and live on talk radio in Los Angeles, Cleveland, and Gainesville, Florida. I also draw from the experience of being an invited speaker to the Education Writers Association conference [EWA], "Beyond 9-11: What American Students Should Know about the World" that was held in Washington D.C. in

March 2003. Although I have been interviewed on other topics such as prejudice and online teaching, I am focusing here on my interaction with journalists concerning global education and how teachers teach about world events.

> Date: Tue, 20 Apr 2004 17:24:56 -0400
> From: "Woodall, Martha" <mwoodall@phillynews.com>
> Subject: Teaching Islam question
> To: merryfield.1@osu.edu
> Hi,
> I'm one of the education reporters at *The Philadelphia Inquirer*. Al Frascella recommended I e-mail you for an article I am working on about how—or if—schools are teaching students about Islam. It sounds as if the coverage may vary greatly. I was wondering what you have observed and what you think students should know about Islam by the time they graduate from high school.
>
> Thanks very much for your time.
>
> Martha Woodall, staff writer
> The Philadelphia Inquirer
> 215-854-2789

Most of my experiences can be characterized as follows. I receive a phone call or e-mail message asking for an interview. Some reporters assume I can stop what I am doing at that moment and talk to them immediately; most ask for a time when it would be convenient to talk. Some provide details on the story they are working on while others only offer a couple of words -"It's on the war and teachers"—which may or may not help me understand the story they are after.

The interviews themselves vary a great deal in both process and content as some reporters really know the topic and have done their homework in researching the issue and contextual factors. Others have no background knowledge to inform their questions. In my experience few reporters demonstrate substantive knowledge of global education, social studies curricula, or even K-12 schools. I have found myself defining *curriculum mandate* or explaining *supplementary materials* so that the reporters would understand a point I was making about teaching global perspectives. I am evidently fairly good at these explanations as I have had a few reporters call me back a second time for further explanations of the process of curriculum development or educational jargon.

Really good reporters make being interviewed easy. In October 2002 I was interviewed by Seth Stern of the *Christian Science Monitor* who was writing a story about how social studies teachers were incorporating the situation in Iraq into their instruction. He e-mailed me to find a good time to talk and explained what the article was about and what he wanted from me. In the 20 minute phone interview he asked me very specific questions on how teachers were responding to the war in Iraq which led into the effects of the Internet on teaching about current events and how students are learning about other parts of the world through Web-based materials and online connections. The article "History class puts current events on the map" had three short paragraphs from the interview, and my words were reported accurately.

> They really want kids to understand both the immediacy of this and the long-term American interests, and how this fits in with actions other countries may take," says Merry Merryfield, a professor at The Ohio State University in Columbus, who instructs social-studies teachers.
>
> That war, in fact, may have had a lasting impact on social-studies teachers. Over the past decade, Professor Merryfield has found that teachers are better informed about the Middle East and more interested in including non-American perspectives.
>
> And the Internet and e-mail allow for faster access to a broad range of primary sources and viewpoints. Merryfield says students in social-studies classes exchange e-mails with students in the Middle East and read local newspapers from Egypt and Turkey.

Mr. Stern also e-mailed me the URL for the article, a courtesy I very much appreciated. These best-case aspects were repeated in September 2003 when I was interviewed by G. Jeffrey MacDonald for another *Christian Science Monitor* article, "Try to make sense of 9/11" that was published in a special section on learning.

Contrast those experiences with a reporter who calls during office hours and must speak to me *NOW* to meet a deadline. Or another who wants me to tell her what questions to ask so she can write about the differences between social studies and history. Or the reporter who takes 50 minutes of my time but cannot tell me when the article will come out or e-mail me a copy of it. It does not take many such experiences to understand why people develop preferences for some reporters and newspapers over others.

There are some typical problems that can make a person want to throw up their hands and say, never again! First, there is what might be called the *Russian Roulette* nature of an interview. A reporter takes 45 minutes of one's time and then decides to (a) not use anything from the interview, (b) use one word, (Dr. Merryfield says "good") or (c) use a phrase out of context so I look like an idiot (this I am not repeating!) or miraculously (d) use something accurately from the interview that makes sense given the topic of the article. I have also been interviewed for articles that were never published. When I agree to be interviewed I usually have no idea what may result.

What have I learned? As Al Frascella of NCSS has pointed out to me, those of us being interviewed should give reporters short quotable statements. At times I have obviously forgotten this sage advice and made points in long sentences which are then edited into short quotes that either misconstrue what I meant or miss the point entirely. Following the EWA conference I was interviewed about a dozen times within a month. After reading a half dozen articles, I started taping the interviews since I was curious as to whether reporters were actually making up quotes attributed to me or just taking my words out of context. I found both problems.

One reporter for a large city newspaper literally did make up a quote as when I listened to the tape of the interview I found I had not said anything anywhere close to the words attributed to me. Two others took my words out of context so that the meaning was changed. What I did not know was why. Were these honest mistakes or were they writing what they wanted me to say? I understand why high profile scholars can become paranoid about the press.

The EWA conference, "Beyond 9-11: What American Students Should Know about the World," was my wake-up call to the realities of the press reporting on global education. Held March 14-15, 2003, in Washington, D.C., the conference aimed to educate the press who write on education topics for newspapers and other media in national, regional and local markets. There were seven sessions over 2 days on topics from "Foreign languages—How important?" to "What should students know about Islam and other religions?". I was an invited speaker for a panel entitled "Is global education necessary?"

As soon as I walked into the room where the presentations were to be held I knew that there were problems. Two long tables at the back were covered with colorful brochures, articles, and instructional materials but none promoted global education. There was nothing on display from the educational organizations that support global education until Al Frascella from NCSS added some copies of a recent issue of *Social Education* that featured articles on women of the world. The EWA staff had also prepared a notebook for each reporter of background information, yet nothing there represented the global education I knew from 30 years of work in the field—no conceptual works, no research, no position statements from the Chief State School Officers, or the various associations of teachers or principals.

After a rather frustrating panel discussion and questions from the audience of 60+ education reporters, I got into a discussion in the hallway with three journalists who took issue with a statement I had made during the panel on how negative press coverage shapes public opinion on schools and teachers. The reporters said they were objective, just reporting the news. When I asked why they did not report on the exciting things teachers were doing in global education, they told me that was not news. And they were serious. "So if there is a very effective teacher who is reducing anti-Muslim feelings among her students, that is not worth putting in the paper, but if some students attack a Muslim student in a classroom, then that would be a good story?" I asked. Yes, they agreed.

As the conference progressed I found that my reality of global education was barely visible. Dominating many of the sessions were speakers who felt that in light of 9/11, students should know more about American freedoms, the U.S. Constitution, U.S. History, U.S. Government, American heroes and American values. At times it was implied that teaching about other cultures, especially the Middle East and Islam, is unpatriotic and *giving comfort to the enemy*. Although I am situated in the middle of the field of global education, I was definitely on the margins of popular opinion expressed at the conference.

Since then I have experienced many interviews and gradually learned to take some actions to make the process more worthwhile for me. First, I make sure I know what the reporter is after and what he/she expects of me. Before the interview I write out the points I want the reporter to use and stick to them. I do not get off on tangents, share stories or divulge anything that does not meet my goals for the interview. I plan juicy quotes in advance and repeat them. I try to ensure that reporters do not lead me into topics I do not feel knowledgeable talking about. I have become comfortable saying, "If you want to talk about that, I suggest you call...." I make interviews much shorter than I used to as I find I can say everything that needs to be said (keeping in mind they probably will use 15-75 words) in 15 minutes. I have become much more businesslike and less friendly and obliging. I have also learned how to be active in generating press coverage. I know how to get press releases out, when to call journalists, and how to get my university's public relations people to help me. After years of research on intensive cross-cultural experiential learning, I shared some of my work with our college of education's communications person who then had me interviewed by an OSU reporter who sent the resulting story to a number of outlets. It was published in total or in part several places, including in the Indian newspaper, *The Hindu*, which led to some Indian teachers e-mailing me and the development of a collaborative project that is currently going on between 30 teachers in my online course on world cultures and a teacher in Chennai. Making the press work for us will always be a challenge, but informed engagement is critical. The good news is that we can learn how to work with the press so that all benefit.

As I have been working on this chapter, the U.S. continues to occupy Iraq and Afghanistan and Ohio has become increasingly important within the upcoming American elections. I have been asked by reporters about how teachers should be teaching about the war during a hotly-contested election. And that is one element of global education. The major problem, however, with press coverage of global education is that, by and large, it does not inform the public of the ways in which learning a global perspective and interacting with people from diverse world regions can affect individuals' opportunities and our society in an increasingly interdependent world. By centering their coverage on the controversies, reactions to current events, and other hot topics, the press has neglected the big picture of global education in the U.S. and other countries—the ways in which students are being educated to become global players with the skills and knowledge to effect changes on the planet.

NOTES

1. The entire NCSS position statement on global education can be viewed on the NCSS homepage http://www.socialstudies.org/positions/global/ retrieved September 6, 2004.
2. Shanker also included global education in columns debating multicultural education and the teaching of cultural relativism. See "Multicultural and global education; Value free?" in the *New York Times*, January 6, 1991, p. F1.

REFERENCES

Alfano, S. (2003, July 29). Bringing September 11 to history class. *MSNBC*. Retrieved August 1, 2003, from http://www.msnbc.com/modules/exports/ct_email.asp?/news/934052.asp

Anderson, L. (1979). *Schooling and citizenship in a global age: An exploration of the meaning and significance of global education*. Bloomington, IN: Social Studies Development Center.

Becker, J. M. (Ed.). (1979). *Schooling for a global age*. New York: McGraw Hill.

Buerhrer, Eric. (1990). *The new age masquerade*. Berentword, TN: Wolgemeith & Hyatt.

Burack, J. (2003). The student, the world and the global education ideology. In J. Leming, L. Ellington, & K. Porter (Eds.), *Where did social studies go wrong?* Washington DC: Fordham Foundation. Retrieved from http://www.edexcellence.net/foundation/publication/publication.cfm?id=317&pubsubid=907

Case, R. (1993). Key elements of a global perspective. *Social Education, 57*, 18-325.

Clifford, G. (1991, March 18). Farm groups charge bias in education. *Des Moines Register*, p. 22.

Cunningham, G. L. (1986). *Blowing the whistle on global education*. Denver, CO: United States Department of Education.

Diaz, C., Massialas, B. G., & Xanthopoulos, J. A. (1999). *Global perspectives for educators*. Boston: Allyn & Bacon.

Draper, N. (2003, September 15). New social studies standards to get citizen scrutiny this week. *Star Tribune*. Retrieved from http://www.startribune.com/stories/462/4097472.html

Fiely, D. (2003, April 18). Spontaneous learning: Teachable moments combine life with lessons in unforgettable ways. *The Columbus Dispatch*, pp. F1, F3.

Finn, C. E. (2001). Teachers, terrorists and tolerance. *Commentary, 112*(5), 54-57.

Gaudelli, W. (2003). *World class: Teaching and learning in global times*. Mahwah, NJ: Erlbaum.

Hanvey, R. G. (1975). *An attainable global perspective*. New York: Center for War/Peace Studies.

Hunter, H. (1991, February 14). Not world class. *Cedar Rapids Gazette*, p. 22.

Hunter, M. (2003, August 20). *No time to study timely events*. Retrieved August 21, 2003, from http://www.cnn.com/2003/EDUCATION/08/13/sprj.sch.current/

Hymowitz, K. S. (2002, May 6). Anti-social studies. *The Weekly Standard, 7*, 33. Retrieved September 5, 2004, from http://www.weeklystandard.com/Content/Public/Articles/000/000/001/188qolmw.asp

Keller, B. (2003, December 3). Teachers travel the globe for professional development. *Education Week, 23*(14), 8. Retrieved October 24, 2004, from http://www.edweek.org/ew/articles/2003/12/03/14devel.h23.html

Kersten, K. (1988). *The radicalization of Minnesota's public school curriculum*. Minneapolis, MN: Minnesota Association of Scholars.

Landrum, C. (2003, March 20). War replaces textbooks in classroom. *Greenville News*. Retrieved September 20, 2004, from http://greenvilleonline.com/news/2003/03/20/200303203227.htm

Lane, M. B. (2003, March 29). Teachers called up; students learning to pay attention to war. *Columbus Dispatch*. Retrieved March 29, 2003, from http://ee.dispatch.com/Repository/getFiles.asp?Style=OliveXlib:L

MacDonald, J. (2003, September 9). Try to make sense of 9/11. *The Christian Science Monitor*, pp. 13-15.

Maines, S. (2003, March 21). Learning history as it happens. *The Myrtle Beach Sun News*. Retrieved September 25, 2004 from http://www.myrtlebeachonline.com/mld/myrtlebeachonline/news/local/5445227.htm?temp

Manzo, K. K. (2003, September 3). Contrarians' launch salvo at social studies. *Education Week, 23*(1), 12. Retrieved September 5, 2003, from http://www.edweek.org/ew/articles/2003/09/03/01history.h23.html

Manzo, K. K. (2003, January 23) History invading social studies turf in schools, *Education Week, 22*(19), 1-12.

Marselas, K. (2003, March 21). War brings varied reactions in schools. *The Capital*. Retrieved March 21, 2003, from http://www.hometownannapolis.com/cgi-bin/read/2003/03_21-36/TOP

Merryfield, M. M. (2001). Moving the center of global education. In W. B. Stanley (Ed.), *Critical issues in social studies research for the 21st century* (pp. 179-207). Greenwich, CT: Information Age.

Merryfield, M. M., & Wilson, A. K. (2005). *Global perspectives in the social studies*. Silver Spring, MD: National Council for the Social Studies.

The new age and our children. (1991, February). *Concerned Women*, p. 3.

O'Neil, J. (1989, January). Global education: Controversy remains but support growing. *ASCD Curriculum Update*, pp. 1-8.

Pike, G., & Selby, D. (1995). *Reconnecting from national to global curriculum*. Toronto, Canada: International Institute for Global Education, University of Toronto.

Schlafly, P. (1986, March 6). What is wrong with global education. *St. Louis Globe Democrat*, p. 23.

Schlafly, P. (1995, August). The NEA proves itself extremist again. *The Phyllis Schlafly Report, 29*(1). Retrieved November 6, 2004, from http://www. eagleforum.org/psr/1995/psraug95.html

Schukar, R. (1993). Controversy in global education: Lessons for teacher educators. *Theory into Practice 32*(1), 52-57.

Shanker, A. (1989, February 19). Which way global education? Propaganda or education. *New York Times*, p. E7.

Shanker, A. (1991, January 6). Multicultural and global education: Value free? *New York Times*, p. E7.

Shoichet, C. E. (2003, August 13). Chalking up global lessons: Social studies educators try to keep world focus. *Atlanta Journal-Constitution*, p. F1.

Sorokin, E. (2002, August 20). NEA plan for 9/11 not backed by teachers. *Washington Times*. Retrieved August 21, 2002, from http://www.wash-times.com/national/

Stern, S. (2002, October 15). History class puts current events on the map. *The Christian Science Monitor*. Retrieved October 15, 2004, from http://www. csmonitor.com/2002/1015/p21s01-lecl.htm

Wilson, A. K. (1993). *The Meaning of International Experience for Schools*. Westport, CT: Praeger.

Vail, K. (February, 2003). Where in the world are we? Many students haven't a clue. *American School Board Journal*, 6-7.

CHAPTER 9

RIDING THE TIGER

The Press, Myra, and Me

David Sadker

Editor's note: Myra Sadker died from the treatment of her breast cancer in 1995.

Let us start with the "Today Show" in the 1980s, our first *big* media event. Myra and I were asked to talk about our article in *Psychology Today* (1985) describing how teachers gave males more instructional attention than females. Jane Pauley was excited to alert her audience to this subtle but persistent gender bias. Later, we would visit "Good Morning America," Phil Donahue, and even Oprah. What did we learn from this media ride? That is what this chapter is all about.

In the beginning, it was all very sweet. That "Today Show" interview went well, and our friends and family told us the show was terrific. True, our friends were far from objective, but it all added to the excitement. Our parents loved seeing us on television, a medium that bridged our world and theirs, a venue their friends could relate to (as opposed to an American Educational Research Association convention, for example). There seemed few joys grander for parents than sharing their children's behind-the-scenes stories: our elegant limousine ride to the studio at 6

Social Studies and the Press: Keeping the Beast at Bay?, 109–117
Copyright © 2005 by Information Age Publishing
All rights of reproduction in any form reserved.

a.m., the fancy hotel and outrageously expensive breakfast (have you seen those New York prices?!), and especially the *green room* encounters we had with the rich, famous and strange. It was all so exciting for us, our parents, our friends. But had we looked closer, we might have detected the seeds of media exploitation taking root. Perhaps the limousine-as-metaphor offers an example.

On the "Today Show," a very impressive limousine takes you to the studio early in the morning, and it all seems like harmless, self-indulgent fun as the hotel doorman helps you into the elegant limousine for your 15 minutes of fame. The trap is to believe that the limo symbolizes recognition; in reality, it is a device used by the producer to guarantee that you would arrive for the show on time. Once the show is done, the limousine is no where to be seen. Myra and I, a bit dazed and disoriented from our show biz premiere, walked in two wrong directions before we got our bearings and found our way to the hotel (another dizzying metaphor for the media events that would follow).

It all began innocently enough. Myra and I had researched gender bias in schools for a quarter of a century when the American Association of University Women (AAUW) came upon our work, and asked us to coauthor a chapter for their report on *How Schools Shortchange Girls* (1992). Although we had done a few media appearances, and there were some news stories about our research in the past, we were far from media savvy. The AAUW's report changed all that. The report hit a responsive chord that fascinated Jane Pauley's producer. She asked if we would be willing to be on a new show, not yet named, where we would show videos of our findings. Our research uncovered how subtle patterns of bias, a series of microinequities, create different learning climates for boys and girls. Teachers question boys more, praise them more, criticize them more, and give them more active and precise help with their work. Girls, on the other hand, are rewarded with good grades (but less instructional attention) for conforming to school norms.

The new show was "Dateline," and we were scheduled to be on the premiere (although we got bumped to the second show). We were excited and worked hard to insure that we would find a school willing to participate (after all, showing egregious sexism in the classroom offers little incentive for most educators). We were determined to create positive energy and inform the public, rather than join the all too popular teacher bashing craze. Myra and I had both taught in public schools, and we appreciated teachers' contributions and sacrifices more than most. We found a wonderful ally in this effort, Laurie Low, a teacher in Arlington, Virginia who agreed to let the cameras in her classroom to see if we could find sexism. Together we uncovered the sexist practices that were compromising the impact of this talented teacher. We focused not on pointing fingers, but on the need to provide gifted and dedicated teachers with the training and the resources they need to eliminate sexism. We had weeks to put the show together, and we loved the final product. That segment was entitled "Failing at Fairness," a positive show and a positive experience. Truth be told, it opened many doors.

So as I recall our media experiences, let me try to distill some lessons along the way. Let us start with the first, and I admit, pretty obvious lesson.

Lesson 1:   The impact of the media on an academic's professional life can be dramatically positive, or disastrously negative. Academics better be ready for that national peek behind the ivy curtain, because the media gleefully tears away that veil of academic obscurity.

Here is how "Dateline" helped us professionally. Several years earlier, Myra and I (OK, mostly Myra) had come up with the grand idea of writing a popular book on gender bias in school. We sent around a prospectus to a score of publishers, most of whom seemed remarkably unimpressed. While one publisher did express some interest, she wanted a major rewrite of the prospectus. That request came at a bad time as we were already working on the next edition of our textbook. So we took a pass and forgot about it, forgot about it that is until our "Dateline" appearance. We dusted off the prospectus and called the publishing company back, but the interested publisher was now gone, and no one else at the company seemed remotely attracted to our book idea. Fortunately, the company gave us her home number. We called to discover some amazing news: although she was no longer working for a publisher, she was now a literary agent. She immediately became *our* literary agent, passing our book prospectus around the publishing world, and being sure to include a tape of our "Dateline" show. The prospectus that 4 years earlier drew only yawns now went to auction. Publishers were bidding on it. Our advance was wonderful. So a book that we would have gladly written 4 years earlier for a pittance (when it would have really been groundbreaking), we were now writing for a mind-boggling monetary advance. Thank you "Dateline." The publisher decided she even liked the "Dateline" title for our segment, and so our book was called *Failing at Fairness* (1994).

Lesson 2:   Print and nonprint media if not siblings, are at least first cousins: If people watch it, publishers are convinced they will want to read it as well.

When the book came out in 1994, the media madness started in earnest. Our publisher, Charles Scribner's and Sons, treated us wonderfully, and even hired a publicist to promote the book. The publicist created a whirlwind of activity that soon engulfed us in a 10-city tour. A typical day included three or four radio shows, a few local television appearances, perhaps a book signing, one or two newspaper interviews, and whenever they popped up, a national television show. We revisited the "Today Show," "Dateline," "Good Morning America," lots of NPR [National Public Radio] and endless morning talk shows. Then we were booked on the "Oprah Winfrey Show," considered the best venue for book sales. But on the eve of the show, we learned that this show would be different.

Lesson 3:   Never fully trust the media, for they can turn on a dime. Today's celebrity riding the tiger can in a flash be eaten by that same tiger. The media has a term for this: ambush.

The difficulties began when a producer thought it would become a more exciting show if an outspoken critic would confront us on television and argue against the existence of sexism in schools. Lovely. Their nominee was Christina Hoff Sommers, a far right ideologue who had been on the phone when we did NPR's "Talk of the Nation" a few months earlier. On that show she took that opportunity to impugn our character and our motives. Believe it or not, we had never met this woman, but there was this voice making hurtful and baseless charges on a national show. Funny thing about unfounded charges, the audience has no way of judging if they are true or not. We were offended by the negative energy she brought and objected to her appearance with us on Oprah. Oprah's producer pleaded: "It will be a great show!" We stood firm.

But the story does not end there. Listening to Ms. Sommers accuse us of everything short of bombing Pearl Harbor was a university colleague who decided then and there to settle an old score. Myra and I were the key votes against this colleague's tenure, and he vowed publicly to "get us." Now, coming right over the radio was his golden opportunity. (This is beginning to sound like a mystery!) He called her up and he created some pretty awful stories about us and our research, all quickly dispelled if anyone cared to check them out. Rather than checking them out, Ms. Sommers preferred publishing these tales and simply attributing them to an unnamed source in her book, *Who Stole Feminism* (1994). Our former colleague and Ms. Sommers became a team.

Now back to Oprah. When we refused to be on the show with Ms. Sommers, she recommended another "gender equity expert-critic" as a replacement. (You saw this coming, didn't you?) The new gender expert was our former disgruntled employee. Never mind that he had never published in this arena and was publicly hostile to the notion that sexism existed; he was now a gender equity expert who disagreed with our findings. This time, the producer did not tell us that he was going to be on the show. He flew him to Chicago to *surprise* us. This is an ambush.

Students at our university called us at our hotel in Chicago hours before the show to say that our hostile colleague had just cancelled his classes announcing that he was going on the Oprah show. Once again, we refused to participate. Our publicist called to remind us that Oprah was critical for book sales. We said no. The producer called us "difficult." The audience was arriving. Oprah looked great. Everything was set to go, everything except us. The producer was distraught.

We did not give in, and with the show ready to be aired, they finally relented, but they did it in pure media style. When our newly anointed gender-expert got into his limousine that morning, he assumed he was on his way to be on the Oprah show. Instead, the limo took him back to O'Hare Airport, where he was flown out of town. (Remember the rule about not trusting those limos?) It was an awkward situation created by the show, but one rich with lessons.

Lesson 4:   The media often presents two sides of an issue. While sometimes this offers a balanced view, many times it is to create a conflict and attract viewers.

While some issues certainly have two sides, most have many sides, and a few have only one side. Consider the sacred ground of the Holocaust as an example, as television and radio shows invite deniers as guests, a quest for an audience at the expense of the horrific truth. The media can confuse, even incite, rather than inform. It is important to remember that you do not have to accept the role of combatant in a negative debate. You actually can just say no.

Before we get too pulled away into the media's short-comings, let me share one of our own. We had an error in one of our findings about classroom interactions. We said that boys were eight times more likely than girls to call out in class. Not so. While boys are certainly more likely than girls to call out or, for that matter, to be called upon, the eight to one figure was wrong. Ms. Sommers described our error in her writing, and when we checked, to our surprise, she was correct. So the one good thing that came out of the Christina Hoff Sommers' attacks was that we found and corrected an error. When the paperback edition of *Failing at Fairness* was published, the mistake was already corrected. People do make mistakes, but we sure wish we did not make that one. In her writings, Christina Hoff Sommers rarely fails to cite our error, but never corrects her errors.

***Lesson 5:   You will undoubtedly make mistakes; correct them as soon
as possible. But do not expect others to correct their mistakes.***

We believe that correcting mistakes is important, but it is frustrating
when those opposed to your view make many mistakes, are informed of
their error, and then choose to repeat the mistake. The cover story in *The
Atlantic Monthly* (Sommers, 2000) is a case in point. Rather than fact
checking, *The Atlantic Monthly* relied on Ms. Sommers in a cover story
declaring that "Girls Rule in School." Ms. Sommers charged in that *Atlantic* story and in her book, *The War Against Boys*, that the final report for
one of our studies was inexplicably missing. The not-so-subtle implication
was that we lacked evidence for our findings.

Of course, the report did exist (Sadker & Sadker, 1984). So how, you
ask, did such a misrepresentation get in print? A few years earlier, Judith
Kleinfeld, a professor from Alaska, was hired to do quick research for the
far-right Women's Freedom Network (1998). Ms. Kleinfeld called me
from Alaska. Although she had no money to pay to duplicate the few hundred pages of the report, or to pay for the mailing, she asked that I duplicate and mail it to her. I did not copy and send it, but luckily the report
was readily available in the Educational Resources Information Center
(ERIC) system. Thousands of university libraries, including I was certain,
her own, subscribe to ERIC. But rather than go to the library, she
declared the report "missing in action." Lovely. *The Weekly Standard* and a
number of conservative columnists repeated the charge that our final
report on gender bias in schools did not exist. The assumption was that if
the report did not exist, gender bias did not exist. (Seems like nobody
goes to the library anymore.) And so Ms. Sommers, not known for fact
checking, simply repeated the story of the *missing report* in her new book
and in *The Atlantic Monthly*. One columnist for a Canadian paper relished
the image of "the professor whose dog ate his homework." He ran the
story in his syndicated column in many newspapers in the U.S. and Canada. My messages on his answering machine documenting his error went
unreturned, his column uncorrected, but the snappy phrase remained.

It was an awful time to be us. In fact, only one conservative columnist,
John Leo, took the time and professional courtesy to check story. After I
faxed a few pages of the "missing" report to his researcher, he chose not
to use the "hot" story of the missing report.

Here is the clincher. In her first book, *Who Stole Feminism* (1994), Sommers explained in great detail how she went to the library, retrieved our
final report, and actually quotes from it in her book. A few years later, she
had a new book out claiming the report that she quoted from earlier
never existed. Frustrating, isn't it?

Lesson 6:   In the media, credentials are quickly submerged and one professor is seen as pretty much like another.

When the tobacco industry funded studies proving that smoking was not related to health problems, people rightly questioned the studies. Yet when right wing groups funded studies reporting there is no real bias against girls or women, few journalists question the validity of the studies or the source of the funding. Ms. Sommers is neither an educator nor a researcher; she was a philosophy professor paid by far right groups (the Bradley, Olin and Carthage Foundations, among others) to author attacks on the feminist movement. The missing report is an example of how *The Atlantic Monthly* and many others were taken in. But the strategy of attacking is very effective. I never heard of a single reporter asking for a copy of *her* final report. Nor in my literature reviews have I ever found so much as a single peer reviewed study written by her. But in media world, it was just a case of one professor disagreeing with another.

As I write this chapter in the summer of 2004, another professor contacted me about a book she was reviewing, *Scrutinizing Feminist Epistemology*, edited by Cassandra Pinnick, Noretta Koertge, and Robert Almeder (2003). The authors of the new anthology included Ms. Sommers' errors published in a column from a 1996 edition of *Education Week*, a typical *attack* column filled with errors. The anthology editors printed her column, but not the corrections published by myself and others shortly after (Lee, 1996; Sadker, 1996). So now the mistakes are recycled for a new generation.

Lesson 7:   Keep good records, notes and all documentation accessible. Finding the right information quickly can save you a lot of grief.

Record keeping is not my favorite thing, but it is often important. My ability to quickly fax those first few pages of my final report to John Leo mitigated the attack on gender equity, although it did not end it. Even old class lists can be important. When *Who Stole Feminism* received a bad book review in the *New York Times*, the reviewer drew a harsh rebuttal from the indefatigable Ms. Sommers. She accused the reviewer, Nina Auerbach of the University of Pennsylvania, of giving the book an unfair review because she was settling an old score. Ms. Sommers' charged that while her stepson was attending the University of Pennsylvanis (UPenn), she had complained about the marginal notes written on her son's paper in a course taught by Nina Auerbach, the *Times* reviewer. Choosing such a vengeful reviewer was the result of obvious bias at the *Times*. Howard Kurtz of *The Washington Post,* a rival of the *Times*, relished the growing dispute about sloppy journalism and gleefully featured the story of how badly Ms. Sommers was treated by the *Times*. So the reviewer and the *Times* were now the targets, and the critical review of an error filled polemic was not. (Auerbach, 1994)

There was only one problem: the well-respected Auerbach doubts she ever taught Sommers' stepson, nor did she ever write that infamous marginal note. By the way, that egregious note she was accused of writing simply said, "Even today women make only 59% of what men make!" far from the "political correctness" charged by Sommers. In fact, Sommers' never produced the paper nor the marginal comment for anyone to see. Auerbach remembers that Sommers' had charged another UPenn professor of political correctness, and perhaps she was confused. But Professor Auerbach could not retrieve her old class lists in time to check and see if she ever taught Ms. Sommers' stepson. For the world, it appeared that a biased professor in a liberal paper was unfair to Ms. Sommers. (If you have a choice reading the book or the review, I recommend the review.)

Myra and I were pleased that the reviews of our book, *Failing at Fairness*, were positive, but there was one notable exception: the conservative *Wall Street Journal* really panned it. Later, we discovered that the reviewer was a colleague of Ms. Sommers, and active in far right-wing groups. That reviewer's integrity was never questioned: I guess that bias at *The Wall Street Journal* is not news.

Lesson 8 (The most important one):   Seek the truth, and look for more sustaining and meaningful values than those offered by today's media.

I choose the title "Riding the Tiger" for several reasons, one of which is the ephemeral nature of media fame. The notion of a fleeting 15 minutes of fame has some truth to it. While the media can be intoxicating, offering financial and psychic rewards, it is important not to be seduced, not to be pulled from your principles. Myra and I always tried to use the media as a teaching tool, but we did not always succeed. Sometimes answering bogus charges became the center of our effort, and that is when the tiger began nibbling at us.

The media can be a wonderful teaching device, and perhaps thinking of it in that light is most helpful. If you have the opportunity to appear on a show, try to keep your ego out of the decision-making. Think of the media as a teaching opportunity. Will people gain insights, knowledge, and positive values from your appearance, or might your contribution be neutralized by the setting, the host, or the other guests?

Part of this decision making is to think carefully about which media outlets are appropriate, and avoid being pulled into what Deborah Tannen called *The Argument Culture* (1999). In the argument culture, hostile guests or hosts use combative tactics to create more heat than light, in part to increase the size of the audience. Although this has become common in our increasingly polarized nation, it is a good venue to avoid. Did you advance ideas, or were you sucked into an ill-conceived debate, a trick question, or an uncomfortable situation that corrupted or compromised your ideas or values?

Are you wearing a grin—or is the tiger?

REFERENCES

American association of university women. (1992). *The AAUW Report: How Schools Shortchange Girls*. Wellesley college center for research on women, Washington, DC: AAUW Education Foundation and National Education Association.

Auerbach, N. (1994, Fall). Christina's world. *Democratic Culture, 4*(2).

Kleinfield, J. (1998). *The myth that schools shortchange girls: Social science in the service of deception*. Retrieved from http://www.uaf.edu/northern/schools/myth.html

Lee. V. (1996, August 7). *Letter to the editor education week on the web*. Retrieved from http://www.edweek.org/ew/vol-15/41gender.h15

Sadker, M., & Sadker, D. (1984). *Promoting effectiveness in classroom instruction*. Educational research and information clearinghouse. Washington, DC: National Institute of Education.

Sadker, M., & Sadker, D. (1994). *Failing at Fairness*. New York: Charles Scribner's Sons

Sadker, M., & Sadker, D. (1985, March). Sexism in the schoolroom of the eighties. *Psychology Today*, pp. 54-57.

Sadker, D. (1996, September 4). Where the Girls are. *Education Week*. Retrieved from http://www.edweek.org/ew/vol-16/01sadker.h16

Sommers, C. H. (1994). *Who stole feminism?: How women wave betrayed women*. New York: Touchstone.

Sommers, C. H. (2000, May). The war against boys. *The Atlantic Monthly, 285*(50), 59-74.

Tannen, D. (1999). The argument culture: Stopping America's war of words. New York: Ballantine.

CHAPTER 10

WAITING FOR THE
OTHER SHOE TO DROP

Mark Sass

It was 7:20 a.m., and I was on the phone live with a local talk radio host being interviewed about a story that had appeared in *The Denver Post* the previous day. The story revealed that the Denver police department had kept secret files on some 3,200 Denver residents; I was one of those individuals. As I answered the radio host's questions, I was conscious of fellow teachers in my office listening in on my end of the conversation and looking at me with an expression that said, "Who are you talking to?" I thought I would get bombarded with questions when I hung up the phone, as well as throughout the day when news of my stint on the radio spread. I thought I was in the midst of one of those *teachable moments* where the media would hand me my lesson plan for the day. However, that was not to be the case.

I have been a local activist for years. The focus of one group of which I am a member, End the Politics of Cruelty (EPOC), is police accountability. We monitor the police at various rallies and gatherings throughout Denver to make sure that officers do not overstep their authority. For example, during the annual Cinco de Mayo celebrations in a Latino neighborhood, several EPOC members patrol the streets and videotape police interactions with Latino youth to document any unnecessary or

Social Studies and the Press: Keeping the Beast at Bay?, 119–124

improper harassment. In 1998, EPOC performed a play at a city park that parodied police accountability by reenacting media stories about police misconduct. What we did not know then, and did not discover until years later when the *Post* story broke, was that we were being spied on by undercover Denver police officers.

What the *Post* story revealed was that, since the 1950s, the Denver police department had secretly conducted surveillance on demonstrations, rallies, and marches throughout Denver and recorded and compiled the names of those who attended—often accompanied by photos. These *spy files*, as they came to be known, came to light in the spring of 2002 when a group of activists was charged with criminal activity. The district attorney provided the defense with several police intelligence files that the police had shared with the district attorney during investigation of the crime. After the story broke, and the city was sued by a myriad of organizations and individuals, anyone who suspected he or she had a spy file was able, through a court-ordered mandate, to receive a copy. My file contained a description of the play in which I acted, as well as a description of my car. More damaging, however, was that the file labeled me a "criminal extremist."

Because I am a high school social studies teacher, the local media pounced on me as an example of a regular person who unwittingly became the subject of a covert police investigation. I was interviewed for a story on the spy files in the *Post* and the other Denver daily, *The Rocky Mountain News*, as well as in the local Broomfield, Colorado, newspaper, the city where I teach. In addition to being a guest on a local talk radio station, I appeared on a local public TV show, where I had the opportunity to confront a former Denver police chief about the unlawfulness of the spy files and constitutionally-protected activities. (The producer has now pegged me as her "education" contact. When the state of Colorado passed a compulsory Pledge of Allegiance Law, which was eventually ruled unconstitutional, I participated on a panel debating the constitutionality of the law. The producer has also used me as a sounding board on other educational issues.)

In addition, I was interviewed by National Public Radio (NPR), during which the reporter accompanied me to my classes and recorded one of my class discussions on the Civil Rights Movement in the 1960s. In almost every one of my interviews with the media, the question arose as to how I would deal with students who were curious about my activism and—perhaps more importantly—how I would deal with parents who questioned whether a teacher who was also an activist could refrain from imposing his own views onto students.

Admittedly, this question troubled me. I have been a high school social studies teacher for 7 years, teaching mainly U.S. history and American government. Although I have been in the same district for all 7 years, I have been at Legacy High School in Broomfield for only 4 years. Broomfield is located approximately 10 miles north of Denver in a predominantly white, upper middle-income community; it is conservative and religious. Parents are very involved in nonacademic issues, such as school sports and the school's music program. They are also involved in the academic careers of their students, although many times their involvement surfaces only when their students have received an unacceptable grade for an assignment or course. Most households have two incomes.

In this community, parents have high expectations for both their children and the schools and see high school as a steppingstone for their children to gain entrance into good colleges. Until the *Post* story broke, few of my peers knew about my activism, and I was quite sure none of my students did, nor their parents. How would my exposure in the media affect my interaction with my students as well as the community? I prepared myself to deal with any questions or criticisms that might arise and to use the event as a teachable moment in the classroom. (It should be noted that I have a very positive and constructive relationship with the administration at my school. This is in part due to my involvement in school leadership activities, as well as giving them a heads up if I was going to be in the news.)

I love teachable moments—those rare times that occur in the classroom when something happens in the world or locally that relates directly to what is being discussed in class. I hope to take advantage of students' interest, even if it seems like a stretch. Teachable moments can often be found in current events, which sometimes deal with controversial issues. These controversial issues can be a dicey adventure for some teachers. Whenever curriculum is supported by resources that can be viewed as subjective—that is, they are not used consistently by all teachers teaching the same course or they have not been supplied by the textbook publisher—teachers need to be able to show how those resources fit or connect with the established outcomes or, in most cases, state or district standards. In my case, the NPR reporter made the connection for me: She used the discussion of the Civil Rights Movement she taped during my class in her finished story to show listeners the similarities between the activism happening then and what was happening to me today.

The story in the *Post* happened to fall on a Friday. This is the same day a weekly newspaper assignment is due in my American government class that gives students the opportunity to apply a topic or concept covered in class to a contemporary event or issue. Students can use any of the national newspapers, such as *The Chicago Tribune* or *The New York Times*, to complete the assignment. They can access the dailies via the Internet, or they can simply use the newspaper they get delivered at home or at the school library. (I have since stopped assuming that families subscribe to a newspaper or at least buy one on a consistent basis.) So, still going over my conversation with the radio host in my head, I went to class ready to continue the topic *du jour:* me.

I knew that most high school students were loathe to read a newspaper unsolicited, but I assumed that they would nevertheless scan the paper and complete the assignment with some ease. Instead, I discovered that students were more willing to use the Internet to access newspaper articles. But, instead of going to the various Web sites of large newspapers and scanning the day's stories, students were more apt to use a search engine, such as Yahoo or Google, to type in key words, topics and concepts from class. For example, if the topic of the assignment was to write about states' rights, students might Google the words *states' rights* to find an article. Sometimes this worked, but many times it did not. For example, the words *states' rights* might appear in the article they found, but only because they were used in a quote by a politician, for example. The story itself was not about states' rights; the words just happened to appear in the article.

Instead, what I wanted students to do was find an article dealing with states' rights (same-sex marriage, for example), and then make the connection. I wanted *students* to be the search engine, scanning the paper for relevant issues and bringing them up in class. Locating and critically consuming information from the media is a skill I want my students to understand and master. Because none of my students scanned the paper, not one of them saw the article about my spy file, which, in the case of both the *Post* and the Broomfield paper, also included a photo of me.

I was frustrated. Here I had an opportunity to take a current issue dealing with someone they knew—their American government teacher!—and apply it to class, but not one student brought it up. The question for me then became, should *I* bring it up? Should I expose myself and let students know about my activism? Should I show them the *Post* article unsolicited? I was hesitant, because I did not want to appear self-serving, nor did I want parents to think that I was imposing my views on their children. The issue of teachers' personal views affecting their teaching is not new. Indeed, just a few weeks before my interaction with the media, a teacher in another Denver metro school had been reprimanded for wearing an anti-Bush button on her coat during a school field trip. I am not in education to maintain the status quo, and because of this I am not afraid to share my opinions in the classroom when provoked by students' questions. I also believe it would be hypocritical of me to advocate active citizenship and not be an active citizen myself. But, because of my hesitations to bring the topic up myself, coupled with the fact that not one of my students saw me in the newspaper, I missed an exceptional opportunity not only to connect a real-life issue to the classroom, but also to show my students how to be an active citizen.

I also use newspapers in class to break the barrier that the media can place between subjects of news stories and the reader—the *us versus them* polemic that makes it easier for students, as well as the general public, to keep from acting (and which, eventually, breeds cynicism). When students can say that people who are being spied on by the police or who are protesting globalization are not like them, they absolve themselves from acting and, in many cases, from caring. But, here was their American government teacher being labeled a criminal extremist merely for exercising his right to free speech. How would carrying that label affect my life in a post-9/11 world? Is it wrong for the police to spy on peaceful, law-abiding citizens? What is the harm? All great questions that would not only make connections to what we were studying in class, but that would put the student face-to-face with the subject and break the us versus them barrier.

During my interviews with reporters, each one questioned me about how I handled my activism with my students. Each time I responded that I was hesitant to bring my activism up on my own, but that if a student brought it up, it would make for a great class discussion and, more importantly, help make connections for students. I was prepared not only to connect my exposure in the press to what we were studying in class, but also to deal with parents and guardians who might have a problem with a teacher who is also an activist. I had hoped that my interview in the *Post* and the local Broomfield paper might open this door for me. The *Post* article said:

> Realizing that police ran the tag to his car because he exercised his right to free speech unsettles Sass and tempts him to impart his real-life lessons to his American Government students. He refrains he said, because he does not want to add to his students' cynicism, nor does he want to be accused of pushing his political views on them. "I can talk about the 'Red Scare' and McCarthyism, and they just shrug their shoulders and say, 'That was back in the day,'" said Sass, who teaches at Legacy High School in Broomfield. What he wants to say: But it's going on now. (Herdy, 2003, p. 1B)

I hoped that I was talking to my students through the press, giving them permission to broach the subject with me.

I took the same approach in the local Broomfield paper. The reporter went so far as to interview some of my students to ask them if I brought up my personal experiences in the classroom. One student said, "He doesn't use it at all"; another said, "He'll talk to you about it if you ask, but he doesn't bring it up in class." After both of these articles came out, I was prepared to deal with a barrage of questions, questions that I thought I had given my students permission to ask by telling reporters that, in effect, I was waiting for them to ask first. But nothing happened!

As I look back on what happened, or more accurately, what did not happen, it seems fairly obvious that I had assumed that by simply being in the media, I would become a news celebrity and, with this newfound status, I could stand back and respond to my students and mold what happened to me into a learning moment for them. I should have exploited my celebrity as a way to capture the students' attention and to make a connection to what we were studying in class.

Teachers should not be afraid to use personal connections to construct knowledge. In *Rethinking Globalization: Teaching for Justice in an Unjust World*, editors Bill Bigelow and Bob Peterson say:

> Neutrality [in producing curriculum] is neither possible nor desirable. Teaching—regardless of grade level or discipline—always takes place against the backdrop of certain global realities. The teacher who takes pride in never revealing his or her 'opinions' to students models for them moral apathy. (p. 5)

I missed the moment because of personal hesitations, as well as my presumption that the news media plays a big role in the lives of my students. I can only hope that next time, I—and all teachers—will not be seduced by the news media.

REFERENCES

Bigelow, B., & Peterson, B. (Eds.). (2002). *Rethinking globalization: Searching for justice in an unjust world*. Milwaukee, WI: Rethinking Schools Press.

Herdy, A. (2003, January 6). Spy file scrutiny unsettles targets, cop say citizens' worries unfounded. *Denver Post*, p. 1B.

CHAPTER 11

WHAT COUNTS AS A (NEWS/HIS) STORY?

Whose (News/His) Story?

Catherine Cornbleth

While it has been commonplace for social studies and other educators and researchers to complain about media treatment, and I have done my share, I have come to consider that we have more in common than might be apparent. In this essay, my intent is to explore two key issues that I see as germane both to the news media and to history and its teaching as well as the tensions between them. One is "What counts as a story as in news story and history?" The second, "Whose news/his story?" probes questions of access or whose/which story gets told. A third might well examine the impact of consolidation in its various forms, but that is a story for another time. I end with some reflections on these issues in terms of improving communication with the press and, consequently, the general public.

WHAT COUNTS AS A STORY?

In the recurring debates about the nature and amount of history that should be taught in the nation's public schools (and to some extent in aca-

Social Studies and the Press: Keeping the Beast at Bay?, 125–134
Copyright © 2005 by Information Age Publishing
All rights of reproduction in any form reserved.

demic debates about history), one persistent issue is often oversimplified as a dichotomous choice between chronological and thematic history. Usually, chronological history is considered traditional and favored by conservatives along with the conception of history as story or narrative— grand, master, or otherwise. Thematic history, in contrast, is usually portrayed as newer or more modern and favored by progressives and social historians along with a conception of history as multilayered or consisting of multiple, intertwined perspectives.

Chronological history is event oriented, what some students reportedly have described as "one damn thing after another," and might be more politely described as a chronicle or chronological record. U.S. history, presidential administration-by-presidential administration, is a common example. Thematic history sacrifices broad linear chronological sequence for a larger block of time in order to follow a movement, trend, or longer-term *event* such as industrialization (instead of an Industrial Revolution), (sub-)urbanization, or imperialism. A striking example is provided by S. G. Grant's study (2001) of two eleventh grade U.S. history teachers' treatment of civil rights. One dealt with civil rights *events* (e.g., protests, legislation) as they occurred during the presidencies of Eisenhower, Kennedy, and Johnson, while the other offered a 2-week unit on the civil rights movement in which the students became immersed in the activities of the period and more briefly considered subsequent civil rights history. One teacher highlighted the civil rights movement, using it as her organizer, while the other highlighted the presidents, using the administration as his organizer.

Insofar as history texts (if not lived or recorded history) present history as stories or narratives, a crucial question is what counts as a story? What does it matter if the story is of a president's administration or of a civil rights movement? In either case, much more than just the facts is involved. Which facts are selected, and how they are organized and interpreted, affects the story being told. The media parallel is evident in its overwhelming focus on events rather than themes, movements, or processes. My journalist coauthor of *The Great Speckled Bird*, Dexter Waugh, explained it this way, first with reference to the controversial 1989 New York state task force report and then the 1990 California textbook adoption controversy.[1]

In New York, only a few people, including historian Arthur Schlesinger Jr., were able to have their voices magnified by the media and to stall a 1989 minority task force effort to steer New York's social studies curriculum away from its traditional Eurocentric perspective. Schlesinger and education historian Diane Ravitch railed against people who were disturbed by the move toward a sanctioned national history that downplayed the more challenging aspects of diversity, calling them "ethnic cheerleaders" and "tribalists" out to "balkanize" the country. Their catch-phrases were catnip to the main-stream media. There was hardly a liberal, moderate, mainstream or conser-vative publication that did not pick up and endorse their views. (Cornbleth & Waugh, 1995/1999, p. 19)

The issues raised by the 1989 *Curriculum of Inclusion* report in New York and the 1990 history textbook adoption process in California were com-plex and difficult for the media to cover. In New York, attention was focused on a few instances of so-called inflammatory language and con-troversial metaphors such as King Arthur's round table. In California, questions about historical perspective and whether California would move beyond a modest form of multiculturalism did not receive serious atten-tion; the media dealt mainly with some of the more gripping citations which critics said demonstrated "distortions, stereotypes and inaccura-cies" in the only K-8 textbook series to be approved by the state curricu-lum commission.

Newspapers, seeking concrete examples, seized on these in an attempt to convey to readers what the dispute was all about. Very few reporters or editors had the opportunity, time or inclination to give careful readings to the textbooks. The underlying problem with the textbooks' immigrant narrative perspective was difficult to convey and usually got lost as sup-porters and opponents quarreled over various passages.

A second factor is that the textbooks did represent an improvement over past textbooks in their increased inclusion of literature and stories of ethnic and racial minorities. As the debate got increasingly hot over the summer and early fall of 1990, it seemed that many in the media simply became impatient with the critics, agreeing with Superintendent of Public Instruction Bill Honig's caustic assessment of them as mere "special inter-est groups."

Textbook adoption in California usually is a mundane proceeding, unless there is a controversy—there had been one, for instance, a few years earlier over the treatment of creationism vs. evolutionism in new science textbooks. And the focus for the media usually is an "event," in this case the public hearing in July before the state's Curriculum Commission which recom-mended the textbooks, and another before the state board in September. Newspaper coverage prior to September was minimal, and only started building as the September hearing neared. However, one newspaper, the *San Francisco Examiner*, followed the entire adoption process from beginning to end; it is our belief ... that this [critical] coverage probably stimulated coverage by other media, and brought more attention to the on-going pro-cess than otherwise might have occurred, given its esoteric nature. (p. 20)[2]

In contrast to the *Examiner*, nearly all of the large newspapers in Califor-nia which had anything to say about the events approved of, and thus legitimated, the state board's adoption of the texts. The media continue to play a significant role as their attention switches from one flashpoint in the debate over America's schools to another. It tends not, however, to help the public understand connections among events, complex issues, or longer term trends.[3]

What I had hoped would be a good example of keeping track of a story by my local *Buffalo News* has turned out not to be. Instead, there's a January 2004 feature about racial desegregation (or not) at a local magnet high school "50 years after Brown" (Simon, January 18, 2004) occasioned by the presence of documentary film-makers Marco Williams and Whitney Dow (of *Two Towns of Jasper* note). Their documentary has been completed (following a return visit to the school in early spring 2004), and it has been shown on a cable channel, but I have not received any response from Simon to my inquiries about a possible follow-up to his initial story. Did the school district deny access for another news story; was another story not written; or was it written but shelved by an editor?

If multipart stories, or series, are too much to expect of the news media on a more frequent basis, perhaps some attention to change and to historical perspective on events might be feasible. (Note that the same might be said of history texts and teaching.) A positive example from the same local journalist and paper is a feature in the Sunday "Viewpoints" section titled "Eager Minds, Poorer Kids: Buffalo School Officials Face a New, Tougher Challenge as Students Increasingly Come from Low-Income Homes" (Simon, March 28, 2004). This piece takes a 35-40 year perspective and documents the demographic changes over time, the current challenges, different points of view on the situation, and the school district's responses. While photos and their captions provide the attention-getting human interest appeal, the text takes a broader, deeper view.

To what extent are school history textbooks providing similar perspectives on changing U.S. demographics or the terrorist attacks of September 11, 2001 and subsequent events? Or any other event or trend-movement-process deemed worthy of mention? It is at least ironic when history texts or teaching lack historical perspective(s). When such perspective or points of view are included, which ones or whose are selected? Omitted? What difference does it make?

WHOSE STORY?

Who has access to historians (or others) who write the books or to the media? Once there is access, whose or which story gets told? Those who wish to be heard, by contemporaries and/or future generations, not only have to have something to *say* but also a way of leaving their mark so that their voices can be noted and heard. Familiar examples include elaborate burial grounds, written records, and protest demonstrations captured on film. But not all voices are heard, or listened to, by either historians or journalists. Once there is potential access, whose or which story gets told? This is a more complicated matter.

Raymond Williams, in *The Long Revolution* (1961), distinguishes among lived, recorded, and selective cultures or traditions. The "lived culture of a particular time and place [is] only fully accessible to those living in that time and place" (p. 49). The recorded culture of a period is that subset preserved and available to others, while the selective tradition consists of contemporary selections from the recorded culture. Representations of an event, history, or culture will change over time to reflect contemporary values and special interests. Whose or which story gets told is akin to Williams' selective tradition.

Until the second half of the twentieth century, there was very little attention to social history or the experiences and perspectives of ordinary people in academic or school history books. Political-military-diplomatic history predominated. Not surprisingly, it was largely the story of relatively affluent, usually Christian, white men who were the presidents, generals, statesmen, and historians. More attention was given to written records than to artifacts or oral traditions, thus further limiting the stories that were told. At the present time, change is both ongoing and resisted (see, e.g., Cornbleth, 1997). The historical stage is now broader, hosting a wider range of characters and more complex story lines.

And the media? Who is asked for their perspective or opinion? Which heads are invited to talk, to be quoted in the newspapers and appear on radio and TV for example? There appears to be a slowly changing lineup of regulars or usual suspects who are contacted and quoted, whose letters or op-ed pieces are printed in newspapers, who appear on radio and television, who publish magazine articles-monographs-books, and who also serve on each others' advisory boards/boards of directors, and become regular foundation grant recipients. This observation, based on my experiences in the 1990s with *The Great Speckled Bird: Multicultural Politics and Education Policymaking* (Cornbleth & Waugh, 1995/1999 is echoed by Hutcheson, Domke, Billeaudeaux, and Garland (2004). They note that "journalists wield great power in choosing who gets to speak in news coverage" (p. 44). Moreover:

> Journalists have become increasingly sensitive to their too-great reliance upon government sources, so they often look elsewhere for "expert" viewpoints; as a result, the *same* non-government opinion leaders—particularly those with a flair for public communication—often are regularly approached by news media. (p. 48)

The usual suspects resemble an interlocking directorate, what in *The Great Speckled Bird* and the context of the America debate, 1985-1995, we (Cornbleth & Waugh, 1995/1999) called a neo-nativist network.[4] Included were Lynne Cheney, Chester Finn, Diane Ravitch, and Arthur Schlesinger, Jr. among others.[5]

A brief account of my experience of not getting through by telephone to anyone responsible for selecting guests for the PBS *MacNeil/Lehrer Newshour* (now the *Newshour with Jim Lehrer*) serves as illustration. A bit of background: the national history standards project, based at University of California at Los Angeles (UCLA) in the early 1990s, was cofunded by Diane Ravitch, then at the Department of Education, and Lynne Cheney, then director of the National Endowment for the Humanities. The project was scheduled to release its standards documents in the fall of 1994. Approximately 2 weeks ahead of the release date, Cheney published a scathing critique of the forthcoming standards in *The Wall Street Journal* and the next evening (October 26, 1994) appeared in a solo interview on the *Newshour* where she denounced the standards documents as a politically correct social history that ignored prominent historical figures such as Robert E. Lee and included previously obscure individuals. Note the timing of her attack, approximately a week before the midterm elections that brought Newt Gingrich et al. to power.

I was furious with the one-sidedness of the *Newshour* segment and called to express my disappointment with the seeming bias. Simply put, I could not get through. The unidentified young man's voice that answered said that I could write, and he gave me a fax number, but I could not speak to a producer or anyone else in charge. I then was inspired to ask whether Lynne Cheney could get through if she called. "Of course," he replied, "she's at the top of everyone's rolodex." I thanked him and turned to writing my comment, which I faxed that evening. There has been no reply. Within a few weeks, the *Newshour* did offer a procon segment on the standards, but there was no critique from the left, only the right.

As Cheney's break with her former allies at UCLA indicates, political networks are shifting coalitions that may fragment, reappear, and change over time. I wondered about contemporary incarnations of such a network involving the conservative activities of the Thomas B. Fordham Foundation, which has been highly critical of social studies education (especially the Foundation's self-created social studies strawpersons). Consequently, I examined the Foundation's recent history, its February 2004 publication of *A Consumer's Guide to High School History Textbooks*, and most importantly here, the nature and extent of press response to this damning report.

In 1995, following the death of Thelma Fordham Pruett, the Foundation made education reform its sole focus.[6] The next year, Chester E. Finn, Jr. was made President and chief executive officer (CEO) of the Foundation. Recall that "Checker" Finn is a former assistant secretary of education, heading the former Office of Educational Research and Improvement (OERI) and, with Diane Ravitch (an education historian and also former assistant secretary of education, heading OERI), cofounder in 1982 of the Educational Excellence Network (EEN) funded largely by conservative foundations and active in the America debate, aka culture wars. The EEN's activities were folded into Fordham. The foundation's board of trustees has included C. E. Finn Esq. (Checker's father) and Diane Ravitch.

The *Consumer's Guide to High School History Textbooks* (Ravitch, 2004), the report of a project led by Diane Ravitch, is described by Finn in his forward to the report as

> the fourth in a series of reports published by the Thomas B. Fordham Foundation and Institute as part of "Back to Basics: Reclaiming Social Studies," which aims to revitalize the subject with renewed focus on serious content, high standards, effective teaching, and sound instructional materials. (p. 4)

He also notes its funding by the Lynde and Harry Bradley Foundation, a long-time supporter of Finn-Ravitch-EEN activities.

The *Consumer's Guide* was announced in a February 25, 2004 press release, describing "the most widely used [U.S. and world] history texts" as "shallow, bland, and bulky" (p. 1). Finn says the reviewed texts "range from the serviceable to the abysmal," and he blames textbook publishers for "bend[ing] over backward not to offend anybody or upset special interest groups" (p. 1).

In the 1980s and 90s, such a Finn-Ravitch report would have been more media catnip. What has happened in the 5 months since the report's release? A Lexis-Nexis search revealed only five hits, including a modest, descriptive mention in the "Teaching and Learning Update" section of the March 10, 2004 *Education Week* online, with a photo of Diane Ravitch, and a March 25, 2004 piece by Finn in *USA TODAY* (p. 15A) titled "Today's Textbooks Offer an Unhealthy Diet of History." The other three were relatively brief pieces in the Jacksonville *Florida Times-Union* (February 29, 457 words, Insight section), the Denver *Rocky Mountain News* (March 14, 418 words, Op-Ed), and the District of Columbia's *The Washington Times* (March 22, 1069 words, Life section). The mention in *The Washington Times* was very brief, embedded in a story about differences of opinion on the teaching of history.

A subsequent Fordham Foundation news release reported a study of supplementary (to textbooks) social studies materials and teacher workshops entitled "The Stealth Curriculum: Manipulating America's History Teachers," authored by Sandra Stotsky. The language used here is of "twisting history," "fabricating facts," "underhanded intentions," and "often inject[ing] bias and political manipulation into the minds of teachers and, subsequently, their students" (p. 1). These rather incendiary claims generated only one Lexis-Nexis hit as of July 21, 2004 (3 months later), a 341-word piece in the Insight section of the April 18 Jacksonville *Florida Times-Union* that begins "In regard to their education in the important subject of history, the plight of children in public schools may be even worse than previously thought" (p. D-2).

If these Lexis-Nexis search results are indicative, the media nationwide are much less interested in Finn-Ravitch-Fordham diatribes against history-social studies curriculum, texts, and teaching than they were awhile back. Perhaps journalists and editors have tired of the same old, same old messages, no longer finding them newsworthy. Alternatively, the sources may have become suspect as a special interest group not unlike those against whom they rail, or other education topics and issues may have garnered more interest and higher priority over the past decade. I would like to believe that, as a whole, today's press is more knowledgeable and sophisticated.

If there is some semblance of a neo-nativist network today, it does not seem very potent. Older networks may not have the media access they once enjoyed, at least on some issues. It does not necessarily follow, however, that a greater range of less well-known people, or perhaps even dissidents, will have greater access. Without major changes in media habits, it seems likely that a new cast of favored characters will emerge.

REFLECTIONS

I have advocated giving more attention and time/space to historical perspective and multiple perspectives past and present—not only in media accounts of history-social studies education but also in history texts and teaching. Moreover, I would like to see more attention and time/space to complex and continuing stories, not merely isolated and (over-) simplified events. Beyond wishful thinking, social studies educators-researchers might try communicating with the media in understandable language, using events as entry points. While doing my best to be brief and directly to the point, I would highlight the local, personalized, or human-interest aspects of my story. If we can interest journalists and pull them toward our stories, then we may have opportunities to say more. It becomes a win-win situation more than an adversarial encounter.

In addition, and with recognition of the obstacles, we might aim to set more positive models in our own work—in history-social studies materials, teaching, and teacher education. We ought not ask of others what we have not endeavored to do well in our own arenas.

NOTES

1. Dexter Waugh, 1941-1999, was a reporter and occasional editor at the *San Francisco Examiner.*

2. How the *San Francisco Examiner* (now incorporated into the *San Francisco Chronicle*) became involved in the textbook controversy is described in Chapter 1 of *The Great Speckled Bird.* The account provides insight into how media coverage can exert some influence on education policymaking, and how reporters who have the opportunity to follow a process can develop deeper understanding of both the process and the issues -- and come to conclusions that journalists who cover an issue on only an occasional or event basis might not.

3. A notable and too rare exception beyond the *Examiner* is Karen Diegmueller and Debra Viadero's (1995) "Playing Games with History," appearing in *Education Week.*

4. In this version of nativism, "others" are welcome as long as they believe and behave like those of "us" who have been here awhile and dominate the culture at the time.

5. For more information about the cast of characters, see Cornbleth and Waugh (1995/1999, ch. 1).

6. See the Fordham Foundation's Website www.edexcellence.net and its 5-year Report, 1997-2001, available on its Web site. All of the documents referred to in this section can be found at this Web site or through Lexis-Nexis.

REFERENCES

Cornbleth, C. (1997). Birds of a feather: People(s), culture(s), and school history. *Theory and Research in Social Education, 25*(3), 357-362.

Cornbleth, C., & Waugh, D. (1995/1999). *The great speckled bird: Multicultural politics and education policy making.* New York: St. Martin's.

Diegmueller, K., & Viadero, D. (1995, November 15). Playing games with history. *Education Week, 15*(11), 29-34.

Grant, S. G. (2001). It's just the facts, or is it? The relationship between teachers' practices and students' understandings of history. *Theory and Research in Social Education, 29*(1), 65-108.

Hutcheson, J., Domke, D., Billeaudeaux, A., & Garland, P. (2004). U.S. national identity, political elites, and a patriotic press following September 11. *Political Communication, 21*, 27-50.

Ravitch, D. (2004). *A consumer's guide to high school history textbooks.* Washington, DC: Thomas B. Fordham Foundation Institute.
Available: www.edexcellence.net/institute

Simon, P. (2004, January 18). The living legacy. *Buffalo News*, E1, E3.

Simon, P. (2004, March 28). Eager minds, poorer kids: Buffalo school officials face a new, tougher challenge   as students increasingly come from low-income homes. *Buffalo News*, H1.

Williams, R. (1961). *The long revolution*. New York: Columbia University Press.

CHAPTER 12

WHEN YOUR LESSON PLANS END UP ON THE FRONT PAGE

James McGrath Morris

Like thousands of high school teachers I had to teach a lesson to bewildered adolescents only hours after the terrorists brought down the World Trade Center and destroyed a portion of the Pentagon a few miles from my suburban high school in northern Virginia. The planned lesson on Locke and Hobbes would wait for another day.

I also had a new guest in the class that afternoon—a reporter from *USA TODAY*. The next day would bring another reporter, this time from *The Washington Post*. Within a year I ended up on television and radio shows and quoted in newspapers across the country. As is traditional in the pack nature of journalism, my name ended up in many reporters' Rolodexes.

As a result I became the target of praise and criticism, both usually inaccurately directed at me. In some sense, I became a poster child for the efforts by educators to create lesson plans commemorating 9/11.

From the experience I learned a great deal about how groups use the media to try to shape lesson plans, especially in social studies. I may have been more keenly aware of these dynamics, having spent a decade as a reporter myself, but I was caught by surprise at the ferociousness of the fight.

Social Studies and the Press: Keeping the Beast at Bay?, 135–138
Copyright © 2005 by Information Age Publishing

I already knew that deciding what is taught to public school students regarding the history of an event that touches on issues related to ethnicity, religion, and nationalism is a highly contentious affair. But what I learned firsthand is that one of the main battlefields on which this fight is waged is the media.

Marc Bloch is often quoted for having said, "history is written by the light of victor's campfire." When it comes to writing lesson plans, I discovered one can easily be scorched by the flames of politics.

Before I explain what happened, let me explain the events that led to my being in this position. I had been asked to serve on an advisory panel to develop a unit of study for a national project called *9/11 as History*, launched by the Families and Work Institute (http://www.911AsHistory. org/) with funding from the Bank One Foundation. At the same time, I was also hired to develop lesson plans relating to 9/11 for WNET, in New York, and *Now with Bill Moyers*.

The most extensive work I did was with the *9/11 as History* project. Kathleen Steeves, of George Washington University's Graduate School of Education and Human Developments, and I developed two comprehensive sets of lesson plans for high school students. The work put me in touch with educators, teachers, and administrators from around the country that caused me to reflect extensively on how public school instruction should cope with teaching this event.

It seemed to us that, to many students, the collapse of the World Trade Center was like the sinking of the *Titanic*, a tragic event that occurred with the same randomness as the damage caused by a meandering iceberg. While it is true we are too close to the attack, chronologically speaking, to properly judge its place in history, we do know that it will be a central event in the formative years of young students in today's public schools. Like the actions of Neville Chamberlain, the bombing of Pearl Harbor, the building of the Berlin Wall, or the Cuban Missile Crisis, the events of September 11 will have a profound effect in shaping this generation's worldview. A solid grounding in history can help them see how the attacks are part of a bigger, unfolding story that dates back hundreds, if not thousands, of years.

On September 11, 2002, many high school teachers used lessons we developed and similar ones by teachers around the nation. Over time, one presumes that they will become an integral part of the curriculum rather than merely special lesson plans brought out on a day of remembrance.

Our lessons were published on the Web at the same time the National Education Association (NEA) was attacked for listing links to lessons that conservatives saw as unpatriotic.

As I had been extensively promoted to the media as a spokesperson on the how to teach the lessons of 9/11, I ended up being swept up in the debate over how best to teach the meaning of the event. One group accused me of being unpatriotic, another of being anti-Muslim. One might suggest that such criticism was evidence that I had succeeded in creating a balanced lesson plan. And, it may also be that many well-intentioned people feel teaching both sides of this issue is inappropriate when the horror of the attack is so fresh, which is understandable.

The issue of how to teach ceased to become one confined to educators and it spilled over into the media. Typical of the debate's new incarnation were the remarks made by Chester Finn, president of the Thomas B. Fordham Foundation, a conservative education reform group, to the Associated Press, when the news service did a story on how I was teaching about the potential Iraq war. Finn said teachers have an obligation to do more than elicit debate among students. Teachers, he said, must also help them understand why American values are worth defending even in war.

"There's a fine line between helping kids understand and telling them what to think, and good teachers do a good job on that line," Finn said. "But on matters of profound national interest, I don't think it's a sin to slip a little over the line, to tell them this is a better country than most and democracy is better than anything most people have tried."

Finn's comments as the Iraq war neared, as well as the media stir created by the attack on the NEA's Web posting of 9/11 lesson plans, including the ones I had been involved with, revealed that the ideological disputes of politics are never far from the classroom and the media is the choicest grounds on which the battle is waged. This choice of trying to use the media to select and devise a curriculum closes rather than opens a debate. Each side tries to score points and satisfy their own constituencies. As the struggle becomes more vitriolic compromise becomes more unreachable.

The destructiveness of this approach could be seen in the tactic taken by *The Washington Times*. A reporter called and asked to interview me about the 9/11 lesson plans. She asked me to compare ours to those developed by other teachers. Then she asked a few general questions such as would I include in my teaching that those who hijacked the planes were Muslim? Sure, I replied, thinking to myself I could make a wisecrack that they were also male as opposed to old female, but I let the temptation past.

The next day *The Washington Times* ran a front-page story attacking the NEA for the lesson plans it listed on its Web site. It was an unfair attack to begin with because the NEA was simply serving as a clearinghouse linking hundreds of lesson plans on its Web site.

I was quoted in the story and portrayed as a hero for teaching the "truth." This in turn spawned countless repetitions of my "courage" and "patriotism" on conservative Web sites around the country. Typical was this one posted on Concerned Women for America's site:

> "My lesson plans will not skirt the issues," James McGrath Morris, a high-school teacher from Virginia, told *The Washington Times*. Morris said he will try to explain the 9/11 attacks by tracing the rivalry among Islam, Judaism and Christianity—noting that the terrorists were Muslim. "These are all aspects of the facts."

The irony, lost on this vanguard of the right, was that I was actually an apostle of the left, and that I hoped my lesson plans would increase tolerance, empathy, and thus peace rather than war.

I ended up being interviewed by the local television station, which permitted me to restore my good graces with the large Muslim population in the suburbs of Washington and eased the pressure on my school district to cancel my speaking engagement before the county's social studies teachers.

But while I was misportrayed by the right in its efforts to discredit lesson plans they wanted barred from the classroom, the forum they chose is the same as that chosen by the left—the media.

Increasingly the media has been used to set the agenda of what should or should not be taught in school. Educators have failed to stem this tide of "front page lesson planning" because they continue to lack the power of other professions. Today's mass media is the worst possible forum for making educational decisions. It is as if we are to determine what is the most appropriate form of surgery through the pages of a newspaper, or what is the most appropriate form of therapy through a television talk show.

In the end, if lessons about 9/11 are going to be added in a meaningful fashion to the curricula of high schools in coming years, educators will not only have to convince the public of *what* ought to be taught but *how* it should be taught. The lesson I drew from my experience is that the media will be a key battleground on this curriculum issue as well as other issues--*whether we want to be or not*. If we choose, as teachers, to be absent from debate because it is distasteful and rankles our sense of professionalism, then our students will lose.

In my case, I came to believe that I had an imperative to remain a player in the media game because I felt we must convince the public that the point of history-based lessons is to empower students to make up their own minds about the meaning of the events. After all, creating citizens who are skilled in democratic decision-making is what differentiates us from our attackers.

PART IV

TEACHING ABOUT/WITH THE MEDIA

CHAPTER 13

GIVE US 8 SECONDS AND WE'LL GIVE YOU ... THE BUSINESS

Doug Selwyn

Think of something you know well or about which you feel strongly; a hobby, your work, your family, government policy, or a movie. Your task is to communicate as much as you can about it in 8 seconds. Take as much time as you would like to prepare, but you have only 8 seconds to tell your story. Why 8 seconds? Because when we heard from a candidate on the evening news during the last presidential campaign that was the length of the average sound bite we heard. Did you have to leave anything out in your 8 second soliloquy? How much complexity could you work into 8 seconds? How much history, or context, or subtlety? Eight seconds, the time a rider has to stay on a bucking horse at the rodeo, and the time a candidate has to stay on message without putting his or her foot in their mouth, or leaving an opening for ruthless editors or political opponents. This is now what passes for presidential eloquence.

If we move beyond the presidential sound bite to the nightly news, the length of the average story increases to around 45 seconds. So if you tried the previous exercise but allowed yourself the additional luxury of 37 seconds, what would that added time allow? Would it push you beyond a sur-

Social Studies and the Press: Keeping the Beast at Bay?, 141–158

face introduction or conclusion into depth, or understanding? Would it enable you to help to appreciate the context and history that situate your marriage, your love affair with golf or karaoke, your concern about tax policy, or your passion for travel to Thailand? This is a crucial question, for this slight allotment of time is one of the defining features of what news is, as defined by television, and it has had a significant impact on our lives in the social studies classroom.

TV NEWS AND THE HARM THAT IT DOES

The impact that television news is playing in our social studies classrooms is so complete that we do not notice it any more than we notice the air we breathe. It affects how long students can attend to lessons, the ways in which they expect their social studies to be delivered, and the ways in which they (and we) pay attention. It affects what we know about the world, and guides us in knowing how to feel about it. It has changed the definition of what it means to be informed, and has clearly changed the ways in which we must teach if we are to be effective in preparing our students for meaningful and productive (and joyous) lives. This chapter explores some of the ways in which media (especially television) have changed the world in which we live, and then presents some of the ways I work with my students to help them move beyond the restrictions and limits of the lenses they have been offered by the media.

Lenses and Point of View

An artist friend of mine developed an exercise with his middle school students; he gave them each the assignment of drawing a still life that he had arranged in the center of the room; the only catch was that they had to look through cardboard tubes (like personal telescopes) in order to view the objects. He had created a different shape across the end of each tube so that the viewer could only see what the shape allowed/determined, leading to a varied set of drawings, much to the surprise of the students who assumed that all had the same shaped lens through which to look (or more accurately had not really considered what the others saw at all). It was an elegant and simple exercise that made clear to his students that the lenses through which we view the world have a significant impact on what we see and what we do not see. We each have our own set of lenses and filters, based on our particular experiences, knowledge, training, racial and ethnic background, culture, economics, and history. We see and understand what we see based on who we are, where we stand, and where we have come from.

This is a crucial social studies point for three reasons:

- What we see of the world is not all there is to see; it is not the whole truth, but instead is based on what we are able to see, at this point in time.
- What others see of the world is based on their own set of factors, and they are no more correct than we are, but no less correct when they see the world differently than we do.
- The lenses that overlay our view of reality tend to convince us that the world actually exists in that particular form, especially if they are the only, or predominant lenses through which we look. We tend to believe the world really does look and behave the way we see it to the extent that we lose the ability to see the frames and lenses through which we are looking.

The media serve as the principle frames and lenses through which we view the rest of the world. They take us to events, to places, to people we would otherwise not see. When our son was traveling somewhere in China during the student democracy movement of 1989, we were glued to the television, watching the events unfolding in Tiananmen Square under the crosshairs of Chinese tanks and guns. We had the deluded notion that we would suddenly see Josh walk across the screen, or more rationally, that we would at least have some idea of what was happening in that square, thousands of miles away. CNN televised its negotiations with Chinese officials up to the moment when the plug was literally pulled from the wall and our screen went dark.

We, of course, could only see what the cameras were showing us, and could only understand what the translators and analysts led us to understand; this was obvious, and we were under few illusions about how little information we actually brought to the viewing. We found out later that there were tanks and troops lurking off camera, and that they moved in murderously after the lights went out. And that Josh had been a thousand miles away, on the other side of China while the Tiananmen Square massacre was carried out.

The ways in which the media shape and define what we will know about issues on the local, state, and national levels are less obvious but no less profound. The views they offer us, the choices they make about what we see and do not see, and the ways we are lead to understand the events in our own neighborhoods and nation are as carefully shaped as the tubes manufactured for Don's middle school students. No matter how unique our individual lenses may be, there is, via the media, an additional overlay that reflects both our national narrative, our sense of who we are in the world, and the world as structured by the format of Western storytelling.

This mix of national narrative and western storytelling mode, when joined with the constraints and dictates of television technology have conspired to produce the news we have ingested for our entire lives, and contributes to our worldly ignorance, arrogance, and impatience with history. If we want our students to develop what Bill Bigelow and Bob Peterson (2002) refer to as "global literacy," we must assist them to move beyond the limits described above. We can help our students to bring critical and informed analysis to that which they are viewing and reading and help them to develop strategies and resources for coming in contact with other voices and viewpoints—to look through other lenses so that they can understand stories and issues as completely as possible.

The News as Defined by Television

The major tenets or *truths* that shape the lenses through which we learn about the world (via media) may be summed up as follows:

- Television stations are owned by private corporations who are in business to make money for their investors; informing the public is secondary to their primary responsibility as for-profit businesses. Programs on television are designed to sell viewers to advertisers. The networks make more money from advertisers if they have a large audience of viewers to watch those ads. Network executives make decisions designed to keep people watching their programs. The news is as much a part of the entertainment offered on television as any sitcom, variety show, or sporting event, complete with theme music and logo, attractive anchors who engage in mindless banter between stories, and advertisements.

- If it bleeds it leads. This somewhat cynical newsroom cliché is shorthand for recognizing that television is a visual medium, and is a medium dominated by images. The stories deemed worthy of coverage are those that can best be told with pictures: natural disasters such as fires, floods, and earthquakes; news conferences featuring leaders or celebrities; crime scenes with high speed chases and criminals being led away in handcuffs; and cute pet or animal stories to leave the viewers feeling upbeat and ready for the next show.

- Television news is compiled of short stories, stories that can carry an emotional punch to viewers in under a minute. Neil Postman (1985) quotes Robert McNeil, former host of the "McNeil/Lehrer News Hour," on the process of presenting news on television.

"The idea," McNeil writes, "is to keep everything brief, not to strain the attention of anyone but instead to provide constant stimulation through variety, novelty, action, and movement. You are required.... to pay attention to no concept, no character, and no problem for more than a few seconds at a time." (1985, p. 105)

Charles Campbell notes that this approach to the news leads to myth-making, to stereotyping, for finding simple explanations for the images that race across our screens. The brevity of the stories calls for "the most simple explanations of events, ignoring the complexities that tend to surround many of the stories" (Campbell, 1995, pp. 12-13).

- The stories take place now, with no sense of context or history, much like the once upon a time fairy tales of our youth. We know little or nothing about what went on before the story began, we have no idea what has caused the problem or issue that forms the core of the story, and we are encouraged to realize that that really does not matter. Television has the ability to get to the scene quickly, and to bring the pictures, sounds, and emotions of events into our homes in an instant. It is the medium of the image, and especially because of the budget tightening cuts in staff, it does not have the ability to help us to analyze or to think critically about what we are seeing.

Television newsman Garrick Utley calls this approach to news reporting "broadcasting," to distinguish it from "journalism." On television and in the printed media, the increasing separation between *broadcasting* and *journalism* reflects the increasing power of emotion over thought or reason. *Journalism* traditionally occurred in the past tense. A reporter got the story, wrote the story, checked the facts, and presented it to the public via newspaper, radio, or television. *Broadcasting* has moved us to present tense. Reporters can show you what is happening while it is happening though they may not be able to explain it (http://www.loc.gov/loc/brain/emotion/Utley.html).

- Newscasts feature a laundry list of the news, presented in a succession of short, de-contextualized, disconnected accounts of the day's events. Each story is essentially complete and self-contained, and has little or nothing to do with story that precedes it or follows after.
- Stories are often built or structured around a fundamental battle between good and evil. They are rarely if ever presented as being either complicated or ambiguous.

- It almost goes without saying that we (the viewers in the country that produces the newscast) are the good guys, and the people with whom we are having conflict are portrayed as the bad guys. It is startling how coverage of the same events as seen in other countries differs from what we see here at home. Citizens around the world saw very different coverage of the U.S. war in Afghanistan, and the U.S. invasion of Iraq than did the citizens of the United States.
- There is a shelf life attached to each story, determined by the network's sense of how long people are interested in hearing about it. These stories, to repeat, are geared toward attracting and holding viewers, and they are discontinued, like any product that stops selling, when the public loses interest. When news directors realized that the public was sick of images from the abuses at Abu Ghraib prison, the story disappeared from the news, from "all Abu Ghraib all the time" to no coverage in an instant.

The War in Afghanistan

Let us take a blatant example of this shelf life phenomenon, a look at news coverage following the attacks of 9/11. When the U.S. administration decided to invade Afghanistan in pursuit of Osama bin Laden, the cameras were there. According to studies cited by Rampton and Stauber (2003), the amount of network coverage of the U.S. war in Afghanistan reached a high point of 306 minutes of coverage while the war raged in November, 2001, much of that repetitious screenings of the same video footage, either of Osama in a cave, speaking, or walking down a hillside carrying a weapon, of computer models of smart bombs going where they were supposed to go, or of images of the horrors of 9/11, reminding us of why the U.S. attacks on Afghanistan were taking place.

Audiences have been trained to have short attention spans; within 3 months, coverage of the U.S. war in Afghanistan fell to a total of 28 minutes, and by March, 2003 there was just one minute of coverage devoted to the pursuit of the world's number one bad guy. Bin Laden was old (and unsuccessful) news, and a new product (Iraq) loomed on the horizon. Viewers came away from the coverage knowing virtually nothing about the people of Afghanistan, about the impact the war was having on them, or the understanding that the bombings and deaths were continuing even after the cameras left. As far as the public was concerned the "War in Afghanistan" show was over, and it was time for the next show, tentatively titled "War in Iraq."

Why Does This Matter?

This approach to the news does great harm to those who watch. Viewers become trained to look at world events as if they occur the way they are reported on television, either on the news or in movies. They look for the good and bad guys, the de-contextualized problem, a quick fix that can be completed before the last commercial, and then the next situation, ready to forget the last one in a matter of moments.

We learn not to seek out a real historical understanding of the situation, we learn virtually nothing about the people involved, who are rarely if ever allowed to speak for themselves, and we understand that there is no room for subtlety, for nuance, or for points of view outside of the good/bad dichotomy shaping the main story line. We also learn that visual images, presented often enough, become true representations of what has happened whether there is supporting evidence or not; seeing becomes believing. As Postman says:

> Television is our culture's principal mode of knowing about itself. There-fore—and this is the critical point—how television stages the world becomes the model for how the world is properly to be staged. It is not merely that on the television screen entertainment is the metaphor for all discourse. It is that off the screen the same metaphor prevails (1985, p. 92).

And then there are those advertisements, the fundamental currency of the medium. In between the news stories come the essential elements of the television experience, the advertisements, tightly wound bits of media meaning designed to override critical judgment, to reach for the emotional jugular, and to cause viewers to want to purchase whatever product is being sold. These mini-morality plays follow the basic European fairy tale structure and deliver complete, persuasive packages in under a minute.

Their stories inevitably resolve into happily-ever-after endings due to the use of (or purchase of) a product. The moral is simple; if we are smart, we can be like the hero in the ad and be a winner, get the girl (or guy), drive to freedom, close the deal, or throw that football through the tire.

THROUGH THE CLASSROOM DOORS

Doing the Laundry

Newscasts have formed the shape, structure, and pacing of what many of our students now expect from social studies classrooms. Teachers quickly learn that their students respond to instruction that is quick paced and

entertaining. They want history that is delivered in the format of short stories without significant contextual demands (you do not have to remember
last week's lessons to know what is going on), and they want these stories to
resolve neatly, without complications in time for the last commercial, or a
bit of closing banter from the instructor. The combination of these student
expectations, when added to unreasonable district and state expectations
often lead to dysfunctional behavior in the classrooms.

Many teachers work to meet their students' expectations, hoping that
they will not change the channel, or turn their program off entirely. As a
result, many social studies classes are, in effect a succession of 180 daily
news shows. The teacher offers a series of simple stories, essentially self-
contained events featuring good guys, bad guys, a conflict, a resolution,
and, if not a happy ending, at least a resolution to the problem, usually
through heroic and moral action, and courage.

The students know that the problem or event is gone for ever, to make
way for the next item on the impossibly long laundry list that turns the
social studies or history curriculum into a yearly race against the clock. It
is a race, in U.S. history, for example, to get from pre contact to current
day by June, a race that is always lost. Making it to the Vietnam War these
days is somewhat par for the course; sadly, that leaves out the lives of all of
the students. Oh well.

And those teachers and students only make it as far as Vietnam by
steaming through that laundry list of facts, dates, wars, presidents, and
state capitols, offering what Walter Parker calls the mentioning approach
to social studies and history. Make sure you have mentioned everything
on the list, checking off each item before moving on. It is why so many
students have such an abiding hatred for the subject, and why so few of us
think critically about the world around us; we have been trained away
from it because there is not time for thought. We have too much to cover.

This state of affairs has had a significant impact on my work in the
social studies classroom, and has led me to approach the classroom with
the full intention of helping students to find meaning and relevance in
the material being studied, to make strong connection to the rest of the
world, and to come to an understanding of why the world is the way it is.

This approach requires that we pass through three integrated, insepa-
rable stages: unlearning/relearning; building skills, knowledge and awareness; and becoming makers of history. I will discuss these stages in the
following sections as if they can be separated from each other and as if I
teach them in a succession; first unlearning, then building skills, and then
makers of history, but that is not really how it works. It all actually happens all the time, some lessons offering a bit more of one (unlearning, for
example) than the others. My efforts represent a significant investment in

time and attention each year, but I view this teaching as the heart and essence of what we do in the room.

Unlearning and Relearning

As mentioned in the previous section, many students come to the social studies classroom expecting to learn historical stories told in that fairy tale/news show format, so I must help them to realize the limiting effect of looking through only one lens or structure. Through a variety of approaches and experiences, I encourage the students to begin to look beyond the limits of the simplistic fairy tale lens, and to realize that the world does not actually exist in that shape.

We look to understand the context in which events and issues have happened and look for historical antecedents to what we are witnessing. We explore the ways in which bias and point of view affect the things we know and the ways we know them, and then develop strategies for expanding and testing our knowledge. We learn to identify the ways in which certain voices and points of view have dominated and controlled the knowledge we have about events historical and current, and to recognize those voices that have been shut out or overpowered. We begin to make connections between and among events, and to continue to follow stories even after they have been pulled away from our attention. Finally, students learn to place themselves in the historical and current story as actors and researchers, as people who are connected to the events and issues being studied, and as citizens responsible and able to act on their own behalf and on behalf of others.

Once the students have begun to recognize the need to unlearn and to expand the ways in which they see and understand the world we can move towards building skills and awareness. We begin by bringing context back to our approach to the world. I use guiding questions such as these:

How do we know about the world? How do we know what we do not know? Who is telling the story? In what context does the story take place? How long has it been this way and what factors may have caused it to be this way? What do we not know? Who have we not we heard from, which voices are missing from the telling? What questions do we have? What evidence is presented on behalf of the statements made? What seems to line up and what seems to contradict? How can we make sense of what we are encountering? Are there other versions or accounts of the events we are learning about and why have we not heard them? Who makes the decisions about what we hear, and why is that so?

How does this make a difference in our lives? How can we find ourselves in history, in social studies so this is something real?

We most certainly do not ask all of those questions each time we approach a topic or issue, but we become aware of them, through practice, and they become habitual, unvoiced questions that we bring to everything we do.

We also apply those questions to ourselves (here in the United States) through the eyes of the other:

> What do students in other classrooms, citizens in other countries know about us in the United States? How do they know it? In what ways are they likely to see us clearly, and in what ways are they wrong? How has that happened? How could they know us more accurately? Are there some who benefit by the mistaken notions of who we are? How similar is this to what happens in our country, in our schools, in our own classroom?

These questions are themselves the topics of discussions we have throughout the year, but also become questions students learn to bring to all of the work we do throughout the year. We always ask how those who write the texts and articles know what they know, what other points of view might be relevant, and how we could find evidence to help us know more. This critical thinking becomes an integral feature of our work as historians, as social scientists, and as citizens learning about the world.

What follows are five brief descriptions of units or activities I bring to students to help them with the process of unlearning, relearning, skill building and acting. More complete accounts of these activities can be found in *History in the Present Tense* (Selwyn, 2003) and *Living History in the Classroom* (Selwyn, 1993).

History of the Class

I want the students to consider the limits to the evidence on which we base our theories and understandings of the world, and to recognize the role that point of view and bias play in those accounts. I also want them to understand the people through history who have never gotten to tell their stories, or have only had their stories told through the voices and lenses of their conquerors. This exercise helps to facilitate that discussion.

After several weeks of school I ask students to anonymously write a history of our class, including whatever they think is important. They have approximately 20 minutes to carry out this activity, without notes, remembering what they can. After collecting their writing we brainstorm a list of the natural and human caused events that might happen in the next 300 years. The board fills up: floods, wars, cures for cancer, overpopulation, loss of healthy water, cloning, global warming, earthquakes, the elimination of national borders, the Cubs winning the World Series, and so on.

I then announce that it is the year 2304, and historians of that time are seeking to understand what they can about those who came before (meaning us). Then, one by one, I discard the students' accounts (without reading them) due to one or another of the events on the board; this one was lost in the flood of 2200, that one became material for a rat's nest in an abandoned attic, that one traveled to space with the first Mars colonists, and so on until there is only one account left. I present it, with great excitement, as the official history of some unknown event from several hundred years in the past.

We discuss the "primary source document" as a class; what do we know from this account? What statements are made by the author? What evidence is provided for any of the statements? What facts and what opinions? Do we know anything at all about the subject of the account?

Then, miraculously, another story appears (I pull one at random from the discarded pile). We read it. Is there any reason to assume it is dealing with the same topic? Do facts agree or contradict? Are there more questions now, or fewer? We repeat the process four or five times, and then try to compile a definitive, historical account of the class from those five bits of primary source documents. What seems accurate? What was missed? How was it for those writers whose accounts were not included? Do they resent having their voices excluded from history, from the official account of what happened? Does that ever happen in *real world* history? Or from current events?

Textbook Analysis

The next activity is to investigate the textbook. Textbooks are not often recognized as media but they are; their publishers produce them in order to make money for their corporate parents and stockholders. The goal for publishers, as is true for television stations, is to reach as many consumers as possible so there is a strong drive to produce books that will satisfy as many as possible and offend as few as possible.

This approach tends to produce inoffensive, bland material that will enable large states and districts such as Texas, California, and New York, to purchase large quantities of books without offending anyone. There are significant consequences to this media and profit dominated strategy because telling the truth of historical events is trumped by marketing considerations, and material that causes people to rethink what they comfortably know, or that causes the nation's students to look critically at the actions of the United States may not survive the production or marketing meetings. The following activity helps students to understand more about this.

Students work in pairs or in small groups (no more than four) to analyze the textbooks we are using (or that we have been assigned), to try and understand the point of view, bias, and orientation of those who have written and published the books. I am assuming that we are looking at a U.S. history text in this example. There are several organizations, especially coming out of communities of color who have developed analysis protocols to bring to this exercise. I propose the following questions for my students:

1. What is the title of the book? Does it give clues as to who is included and who is excluded, or to the point of view taken by the author(s)?

2. What are the chapter titles? If a chapter title is "Westward Expansion," does that provide a clue as to where the authors' sympathies and point of view align?

3. How is the book organized? Is there any connection between one section and the next, or is it simply chronological in nature? Is there any analysis of information or simply a presentation of fact? Is there any evidence provided for the facts included, or any discussion about alternative understandings or interpretations of historical events?

4. What vocabulary or terms are used to describe people or classes of people in the book? Are there loaded terms used (savages and settlers, for example)? Whose language and labels are used?

5. Are there stories of others beside the wealthy, white men who are best known in traditional history? What roles do women play? What roles do working class whites play? What role do people of color play in the story of our nation's history? Who is included and who excluded?

6. How do accounts of events in our text compare with accounts offered in other texts, or in books written by historians? How often do people other than European Americans get to offer their own accounts of historical events?

7. What evidence do the authors give for their point of view, for their choices of what to include or exclude, and for their overall approach to the work? Texts often present their material as if they are value neutral and simply factual, as if there is no need to question what appears on those pages. It is important to remind students that these books are written by fallible humans and should be questioned, and read as products intended for sales first.

This question of voices included and left out is a crucial aspect of the unlearning/ relearning work that guides my work. Students learn to identify the voices who are defining the world for them (through media), and whose voices are omitted from the conversation. As Amy Goodman writes in *The Exception to the Rulers*, "the lack of diversity *behind* the news helps to explain the lack of diversity *in* the news. In 2001, the media watchers Fairness and Accuracy in Reporting (FAIR) looked at who appeared on the evening news on ABC, CBS, and NBC. Ninety-two percent of all U.S. sources interviewed were white, 85% were male, and where party affiliation was identifiable, 75% were Republican" (2004, p. 153).

Ms. Goodman also cites a FAIR study on *experts* who appeared on network news programs the week before Colin Powell made his arguments for invading Iraq to the UN Security Council, in February 2003. Of the 393 sources interviewed during the week before Powell's speech, three were associated with anti-war activism. The rest were government officials, retired generals who were now consulting with networks, arms experts, military strategists, and politicians brought in to gauge political reaction. She wonders what public reactions to the proposed invasion would have been if those numbers had been equalized, if more voices opposed to the proposed invasion had been allowed airtime?

LEARNING ABOUT THE WORLD THROUGH ORDINARY OBJECTS

A third approach I use with students has multiple objectives and takes multiple weeks, but it is an involving unit that pays great dividends throughout the year. The task seems simple enough: students are to research the manufacturing process for an item of their choice that is produced in another country and sold in their home town. They are to find out as much as they can about the materials used in producing the product, the manufacturing process, the people who do the work and what their lives are like, the transporting of the product from its point of origin to the stores in which they have purchased it, the decision making related to design, pricing, marketing, and production, and whatever else they can find. The students work in groups of approximately four and the group chooses the product based on their own interests; it could be a favorite item of clothing, a soccer ball, a cosmetic product, or bicycle part. I present them with a list of my guiding questions with instructions to focus on those questions that seem most relevant and of interest (though I identify certain ones they must research in order to meet my requirements). They do not need to cover all questions on the list.

My objectives with this assignment are several, including helping the students:

- To gain research skills that they can use in their lives, in school and out. How do they pose real questions about things in their world and then pursue those questions? This is far different than what is practiced in many schools, where students are often trained to fetch known information much like a dog fetches a stick (what is the capitol city of Nebraska?), and discouraged from pursuing their own real questions and interests. This kind of research is often messy and inexact as a process since students are traveling into new territory, which often leads to occasional dead ends, unexpected curves and crossroads. It also leads to the joy and excitement of discovery and offers the students the powerful ability to independently pursue their own interests and questions.

- To learn about the ways in which they are connected to people and places around the world through the objects they wear or use every day. This means that what happens around the world does matter to them, and that their choices as consumers have an impact on people around the world. When my class researched the production of soccer balls they found that most were sewn by children and women in Pakistan. This was at a time when there was a high tension alert on the border between Pakistan and India, and an ongoing manhunt for bin Laden; suddenly we were connected to those events.

- To understand in real terms the link between geography, economics, history, and civics. There is little connection made between underlying economics and political or historical decisions in most history and in virtually all newscasts. Energy interests are rarely mentioned as underlying reason for what is going on in the Middle East, nor is water, though they play significant roles. Through their research, students come to see that companies move their production operations to locations around the world for economic reasons, which have an obvious and enormous impact on those people and places left behind. There are also political repercussions, and students come to understand why the U.S. military has been sent to Nicaragua and other Central American locations as often as it has, and why U.S. interest in the Middle East is as great as it is. It is not just political dominoes; there are big dollars at stake, and the students learn to connect more dots than they are shown in their texts or on television.

- To connect their interests and lives to the rest of the world. Their favorite CDs, shoes, or shirts become an entryway into the larger world, and literal connections to it.

There's More to the Story

I work with current events to highlight the need for a complex strategy for gathering information, and the danger of relying on any one source of information.

I select a significant current event such as the March, 2004 coup in Haiti, the torture and prisoner abuse scandal at Abu Ghraib in Iraq, or the release of the preliminary report of the 9/11 commission. The assignment is a simple one: students, working in groups of three or four are to find articles in the media that represent very different points of views about the event in question. For example, regarding the ouster of President Aristide from Haiti, we had accounts from "Fox News", from common dreams (a progressive online digest of news), editorials from residents in Haiti, accounts from the White House, from the leaders of Central American nations (Caricom), from the very left journal Counter-Punch, from the far right National Review, from the International Herald Tribune, from The Economist, and so on. Each team of four is responsible for finding at least four articles, articulating a spectrum of viewpoints about the coup. The students are asked to respond to the following questions regarding each of their articles:

- What did you know about the topic (did you have prior knowledge and or bias about it)?
- What does the author say in his or her article?
- What evidence does he or she provide for what is said?
- What evidence is there of author bias or point of view?
- What do you think about what he or she said? What questions are raised? What seems to be left out? What do you want to know more about?

Each group shares their articles and analysis and then we reflect on what we now know as a group, what contradictions have arisen, and how accounts and interpretations differ from article to article. It becomes obvious that no one article has the whole story, that the bias or point of view of the writer plays a large role in what is communicated, and that any one article leaves an impression that is, at best, incomplete. And we realize that we have a tendency to put most trust in those articles that reflect our own points of view so that we have to bring an extra level of vigilance to them.

We carry out this exercise on a weekly basis so that students gain skills at researching the range of available resources, practice a critical analysis of what they are reading, and develop strategies for becoming well informed about their world by identifying multiple sources on which they come to rely. They also follow the news going on around them.

We apply this process to the historical events we encounter in the classroom as well, recognizing that any one source or account about a time, place, or event is vulnerable to the same limitations we discovered in our look at current events. We then strategize how to locate additional sources and other resources that may help us understand what we are studying more fully.

Making History

A fifth strategy I bring to my social studies classroom is based on the first four presented here; helping students to become makers of history in the world. I want students to make history, in every sense of that phrase. We analyze the media, to understand the ways in which it works. We watch newscasts, sitcoms, commercials, interview programs, teen oriented programming, and even sports. We then create newscasts and newspapers. We write straight journalistic pieces, editorials, create political cartoons, movie reviews, sports articles and weather reports, and advertisements. Students learn how to create various forms of media both as a way of understanding how they work (and how others are using it to work on them), and to gain skills that will enable them to join conversations about issues that matter to them. They turn research they have undertaken (about their products, for example) into editorials, letters, or presentations to relevant audiences. They use their new or heightened skills to communicate their new or heightened knowledge to building administrators, chambers of commerce, state or national congress members, or other, authentic audiences. They learn that knowing something affords them the power to act in the world, to bring what they know to others.

In Conclusion

I began this chapter by presenting a critique of television news. Television stations are in business to make money, and the news (and every other kind of programming) is structured to help them achieve that goal. Neil Postman quotes former news anchor Robert McNeil as saying that the assumptions controlling a news show are "that bite-sized is best, that complexity must be avoided, that nuances are dispensable, that qualifications impede the simple message, that visual stimulation is a substitute for thought, and that verbal precision is an anachronism" (1985, p. 105).

This approach targets us emotionally at the expense of our critical thinking and keeps us watching newscasts full of affecting images, of car crashes, crime, late inning home runs, and rescued pets. It also leads to an appalling ignorance and a sense of powerlessness and disconnect to those who watch a world growing evermore distant, dangerous and out of our control.

The lessons and units presented in this chapter are designed to reverse the damage done by exposure to television news, to textbooks designed to sell rather than to teach, and by classroom teaching ruled by impossible and conflicting expectations. I work to reconnect students to the world such that what happens in it matters to them. If they do not realize that their lives are linked to the lives of those working to make their sneakers in China, or to harvest their coffee on plantations in Colombia, they will not move beyond being spectators in their own lives. As they become aware of their inter-dependence and inter-connectedness with others across the globe they are ready to develop the skills, power, and knowledge that enables them to act, and they begin to see themselves as responsible actors who can make a difference in their own lives and in the lives of others.

I hope that these brief examples of how I approach my work in the classroom will suggest a more thorough and extensive curricula for the social studies classroom. It is crucial to help our students to become wise and skilled consumers of the information aimed at them, able to critically analyze what they are reading or viewing and to identify the voices not heard, the questions not asked or answered.

I would like to close with a final thought, taken from the pages of *The New Yorker*. Nick Paumgarten, writing in the "Talk of the Town" section of the magazine tells the story of Igor Larianov's trip to see the movie *Miracle*, a dramatic re-telling of the U.S. hockey team's upset victory over the Soviet Union in the 1980 winter Olympics held in Lake Placid, New York.

> The Soviets at that time were recognized as the strongest team in the world, a team of professionals playing against the amateurs of other nations, men against boys. It was the height of the cold war, so that the games were far more than games, and a match between the United States and the Soviet Union was as much a political event as it was an athletic contest. The win of the Americans was punctuated by the announcer asking rhetorically, "Do you believe in *miracles*?!" and the game itself has been referred to as the "*miracle* on ice."
>
> Igor Larionov, is a professional hockey player with the New Jersey Devils of the National Hockey League, and was one of the first Russians to come to North America to play hockey. Larianov was a long time member of the Soviet team, though he was too young to make the 1980 team that is charac-

terized on film. He knew and trained with many of the players on that team, and many are still his friends.

Larianov viewed the film alone, at a mall in New Jersey. Paumgarten says, "[He] (Larianov) saw his compatriots depicted, as usual, as talented but humorless automatons. He was caught up in the movie, riding the emotion. He liked the story.

"At the end of the movie, there was a standing ovation in the theatre." Larionov said. "I just left. To be honest, I felt like I'd lost. My friends played there—Krutov, Makarov, Fetisov, Kasatonov. I wish the guys in Hollywood had spent more time, maybe even just 5 minutes, to show the Russian side of the story. They should have showed a little bit of what happened inside the Soviet camp. But I know American movies are always like that." (March 15, 2004, p. 66)

It is our charge as social studies educators to keep our classes from being "like that." It is not enough to keep our students from turning the channel. We must encourage them to move beyond accepting eight second presidential sound bites and newscasts full of disconnected images and bits of information, and to become skilled and active consumers of information and responsible actors in their world. We can support them to care enough about the events of the world to develop their own questions, to engage in their own research, and to come to their own points of view about what is happening in the world so that they are then able to act responsibly and effectively, alone and with others, to make the world a better place.

REFERENCES

Bigelow, B., & Peterson, B. (2002). *Rethinking globalization*. Milwaukee, WI: Rethinking Schools.

Campbell, C. (1995). *Race, myth and the news*. Thousand Oaks, CA: Sage.

Goodman, A., & Goodman, D. (2004). *The exception to the rulers*. New York: Hyperion.

Paumgarten, N. (2004, March 15). Third period: Puck flick. *The New Yorker*, p. 66.

Postman, N. (1985). *Amusing ourselves to death*. New York: Penguin

Rampton, S., & Stauber, J. (2003). *Weapons of mass deception*. New York: Tarcher/ Penguin.

Selwyn, D., & Maher, J. (2003). *History in the present tense*. Portsmouth, NH: Heinemann.

Selwyn, D. (1993). *Living history in the classroom*. Tucson, AZ: Zephyr.

Utley, G. (2004). *Pressing our buttons: The media and emotions*. Retrieved May 23, 2004, from http://www.loc.gov/loc/brain/emotion/Utley.html

CHAPTER 14

CHILDREN'S EXPOSURE TO TRAUMA AND VIOLENCE IN THE MEDIA

Evolving Literacy Skills to Counter Hype and Foster Hope

Michael J. Berson and Ilene R. Berson

Children today are raised in a media-centric culture, and their exposure to various news media serves as a conduit to the larger social world. During difficult events, such as times of war and other crises, information on tragic issues may permeate their young lives and can influence their understanding of the world as well as their beliefs. Children's natural curiosity engages them as captive witnesses to the media images and messages which bombard them.

This influence is especially pertinent for children's development, since television news not only reflects the events of our society but also mirrors the values of our market driven culture, where content decisions are often based on what stories can attract the largest audience of viewers (Potter, 2004). Although many people will espouse the desire for a family-friendly

Social Studies and the Press: Keeping the Beast at Bay?, 159–169
Copyright © 2005 by Information Age Publishing
All rights of reproduction in any form reserved.

news media, news programs that project sensational and stereotypical images tend to attract more people than objective and representative accounts of our daily lives.

Nonetheless, watching the evening news has become a family activity in many homes, where dinnertime is accompanied by the drone of the news anchor and the flash of images across the screen. Some parents view this opportunity for their children to catch up on the day's news as a sort of rite of passage for becoming an educated and informed citizen. Knowledge of world events as well as national, state, and local happenings demonstrates an investment in the well being of America, and this immersion of the youth of the family into news media can even be equated with an act of patriotism, which serves as a concrete representation of the importance placed on caring about the country and faithfully staying abreast of new developments.

Children's exposure to breaking news, of course, may not be limited to those times in which they are surrounded by family. Whereas news during olden times was disseminated by word of mouth through the town criers, tribal runners, or community messengers, nowadays the mass media have assumed the role of relaying information. Coverage of crime, tragedy, and victimization has changed drastically as live footage of traumatic events has become commonplace, resulting in collective desensitization on the part of youth and adults to violence and adversity.

We live in the age of 24-hour news programming, and the quest for higher ratings can skew coverage to shock viewers and sensationalize events in order to appeal to an entertainment-oriented audience. Messages are crafted to appeal to some viewers' fascination with violence. Although we may abhor the acts themselves, many people are mesmerized by graphic images, which contribute to the perpetuation of sensationalized news coverage. Such stories feature eyewitness pictures of tragic disasters, photos of missing children, reenactments of crimes, close-ups of the effects of natural disasters, and explicit war footage. As a result, viewing the news can become an intense experience for the senses, eliciting feelings of fear, shock, and dread. To manage terror, people sometimes seek out more information; therefore, times of crisis often intensify exposure to traumatic events. Some people may find it difficult to resist this type of news coverage, hoping that information will increase their preparedness for future occurrences. Hamblen (2004) notes

> People are watching and reading in an effort to digest and process the event; still others say the media is intentionally creating seductive and addictive images almost like those seen in an action movie. Whatever the reason, it is important to understand the effects on the community that this type of exposure may have.

Given children's perpetual exposure to electronic mass media, social studies classrooms may play an important role in children's preparation to function as informed and responsible citizens as young people are immersed in the information age. This chapter explores how these issues affect young children, K-6, and how the social studies can equip students with the knowledge and skills to assess situations and make thoughtful decisions based on an informed understanding of the world around them.

THE ROLE OF THE MEDIA

Journalists have a historic role within democratic societies of serving as the watchdog of truthfulness and fairness. In the United States, the legal and judicial systems have provided special protections to the press in order to safeguard freedom and credibility as truth seekers. This role has necessitated adherence to standards of responsible reporting. News media provide this critical service, in part, by relaying up-to-date information on crises, tragedies, and disasters. In the aftermath of such events, many journalists have supplemented their news coverage with helpful guidance on how to recognize traumatic responses and provide access to resources for assistance. The media provide much-needed information, broadcast critical announcements, and offer information concerning victim services (Hamblen, 2004). They support the community with resources and hope.

The merging of news reporting with entertainment, however, has diminished the capacity of the media to maintain their credibility as impartial reporters of events. When the news is filled with clips featuring terrorism and political violence, an intense sense of national threat becomes pervasive. Explicit media accounts can contribute to anxiety, posttraumatic stress disorder, and other mental health problems.

Another potential casualty associated with media coverage of trauma and tragedy can be the victims' right to privacy. Of course, this right always stands in some tension with the public's right to know. Personal aspects of loss and tragedy can become the feature of a news story with gory and sensational details flagrantly overshadowing the trauma victim's right to privacy. Names and addresses of the victim may be disclosed. Complex experiences may be encapsulated in sound bites that overlook the emotional vulnerability of victims and survivors. News coverage may shape the public's perception of the event, color their view of the victim, and minimize courageous efforts to overcome trauma. Moreover, the portrayal may glamorize the violence or the offender.

Nonetheless, coverage of issues also can have a positive effect on public policy by drawing attention to criminal acts. For example, the Amber alert system evolved out of the institutionalization of parental efforts to safeguard children from child abduction. Media attention to tragedies can sway public perception and have a powerful effect on the enhancement of programs and improvement of services. Promising practices and innovative policies can be promulgated through media coverage.

The dichotomous role of the media as both a source of comfort and strain in the aftermath of a disaster has been observed by professionals who provide services to families after a trauma (Cohen, 1997).

> The media helped to allay the feelings of powerlessness that frequently afflict those stricken by a tragedy. However, the presence of reporters and cameras also imposed a heavy burden on family members. The most personal aspects of mourning could too easily become the subject of a television news feature. (p. 462)

While the media can be a resource for communities and provide an important source of information, trauma-related television can have a negative impact on children and their families. This duality is even more apparent with the expansion of information sources on the web. The Internet has become the most rapidly growing form of media in the world today. Sources of information are diverse and have simplified the exchange of information and ideas, thrusting private individuals into the global limelight. Victims receive high profile coverage made ever more accessible by the web that often ignores the fact that these individuals, their surviving family members, and friends may all be experiencing tremendous pain and suffering as a result of the tragedy.

These new realities have important implications for children. In short, too much trauma-related viewing may have a negative impact on their development by creating a distorted, even fearful, sense of apprehension of the world and their place in it. In the long run, this chronic exposure may desensitize children to violence. Each of these consequences is potentially damaging to a child's healthy psychosocial development.

MEDIA AND THE CHILD CONSUMER

Depictions of real life violence in the media have a more profound effect on children than other forms of aggression which are viewed on television (Huesmann, 2001). Since children spend an average of 6½-7 hours a day engaged with media (DeFleur & Dennis 2002; Woodard, 2000), their exposure to news portraying both responsible and sensationalized accounts of traumatic and violent events has increased significantly. This chronic exposure to trauma and violence can have a detrimental effect on their well being.

Although we might presume that children would be fearful when viewing these images, instead they often become desensitized to acts of violence (Huesmann, 2001). Routine exposure to violence may include stories in which aggressive behavior appears to be rewarded, justified as a solution to a problem, or presented without negative consequences. Children may perceive that violence is a viable option to solve problems and an accepted means of functioning in our culture (Congressional Public Health Summit, 2000). Children's values may be skewed to idolize individuals who exhibit anti-social and aggressive behaviors, and children may have less empathy for those who are the victims of violent acts.

Moreover, children may view violence in the world as an omnipresent force and become fearful for their own safety and well being. Violence (i.e., homicide, suicide, or trauma) is a leading cause of death for children, adolescents, and young adults. These causes of death are, in fact, more prevalent than disease, cancer, or congenital disorders (American Academy of Pediatrics, 2001). Despite the frequency of such realities in children's lives, young children have a limited capacity to cope with disturbing feelings as well as to assess the difference between real and perceived threats. Although a child may readily observe the tense reactions to tragic events modeled by significant adults, a child's inexperience with such events may be exhibited in sudden shifts in focus from concerns about the upsetting news to more immediate and superficial issues, such as going out to play or eating lunch. Children's fluctuating reactions may be troubling to adults who perceive that it is inappropriate for a child to focus on playing games upon hearing of traumatic events. However, vacillating responses may reflect a child's rudimentary coping mechanism to manage stress. By briefly touching on their negative feelings and quickly shifting to safer topics, children may temporarily diffuse their pain or discomfort. Since children are less familiar with making sense of their emotions and may not have words to voice their feelings, significant adults need to attend to cues which track a child's stage of processing their distress.

Children also have a tendency to be more self-centered in their responses to threat or harm, resulting in highly personalized fears of danger. Therefore, stories on missing children or national threats may contribute to fantastical fears of impending personal tragedy or harm. Educators need to be aware of this common reaction in gauging the degree to which younger children are exposed to news of this sort.

INFUSING MEDIA LITERACY SKILLS INTO THE SOCIAL STUDIES

Teaching children to be critical consumers of information from all sources—media and otherwise—may provide them with skills to evaluate information which allow them to generate constructive coping mechanisms and proactive responses. Such skills can maintain children's sense of control when the news provokes strong emotional reactions. To optimize the educational benefits of media resources, educators need to understand the potential impact generated by exposure to traumatic news content. Social studies educators should refrain from glorifying violent acts or people and avoid exposing students to graphic images intended to shock. In making school assignments to watch television coverage of current events, for example, teachers should consider the potential graphic nature of the content and its potential effect on their students. By the age of five, many children will begin experiencing an interest in not only the events of their own lives but also the world around them. However, kindergarten and first graders will struggle to integrate their emotional response to information with the facts. Even intermediate age children may not be ready for full exposure to media coverage due to mature content. Therefore, teachers should prescreen prior to use in the classroom.

If children have already witnessed particularly dramatic coverage of events, teachers may play an important role in helping them discriminate between sensationalized reports versus accurate information. Teachers should discuss efforts aimed at preventing future occurrences of tragedies and safety mechanisms which have been implemented since the tragedy occurred. Even primary age children can appreciate talking about difficult events to clarify their confusion about mistaken information and simplify facts. Such measures can aid children in learning how to cope in the aftermath of a tragedy and minimize the tendency to intensify a sense of personal danger.

Children also need assistance in maintaining perspective on the relative infrequency of disasters and tragedies in everyday life despite their command of airtime on the news. Children may need to be reminded, therefore, that the news exaggerates the level of threat or danger in the world. News reports focus on adverse events, and stories of safe and happy children are not common topics. Teachers in elementary classrooms can introduce stories of hope or classroom activities that engage children in helping others that may mitigate the negative ramifications of adverse events. Intermediate grade students can even create and disseminate throughout their school media stories that highlight positive achievements and experiences.

Classroom discussions which explore news reports as one means to gather information while providing context for world events can also be used as an opportunity to teach children how to ask clarifying questions. Such questions and discussions can help students better understand the true implications of a news report. These skills can aid young people in navigating the massive flow of information and bombardment by intense images which may result in their confusion of opinions with facts. The capacity to be a critical media consumer requires careful viewing of news coverage and an informed understanding of the role the media plays in contemporary society. Even very young children begin to form stereotypes about people based on messages conveyed through television, movies, and magazines (Kubey, 2004). News media may be a dominant source of information about individuals from other countries, and the paucity of instruction to foster media literacy skills may hinder efforts to overcome bias and prejudice in a diverse and interconnected world.

GUIDELINES FOR EDUCATORS AND CHILD SERVING PROFESSIONALS

Based on guidelines that were developed by the National Center for Child Traumatic Stress for reporters and media journalists, the following tips offer educators a set of strategies to enhance responsible use of news stories with young children in school settings.

Safety First

- When discussing dangers with children, also include information on safety plans. The media can play an important role in strengthening a community's ability to prepare for and respond to traumatic events. By providing information about risks associated with an event and about safety plans, children can feel more adept at effectively responding to danger. Likewise, the more educators know about an event, the better they can address children's questions about personal, family, and community safety. Furthermore, when emphasis is placed on pro-active steps to educate communities about plans *prior* to an anticipated event, like a severe storm, children will feel more secure in the abilities of significant adults to respond to the event.
- Provide information that enhances trust. Just as children look to their parents to provide a protective shield against danger and harm, families look to their communities and government to provide similar security. The press is perhaps the greatest conduit of information from such sources. Traumatic events, particularly ter-

rorist acts, can threaten a basic sense of safety. Such events can weaken faith and trust in the effectiveness of official responses and social institutions. It is important for educators to emphasize examples of how news sources inform the public about specific steps that community and government leaders are taking to protect them.

- Help restore a predictable order. Families' and communities' sense of safety can be undermined when there is a breakdown in order. Traumatic events significantly impact such order. Children are particularly vulnerable to increased distress when their world is unpredictable. By providing information and increasing awareness, educators can enhance a child's general sense of control and predictability. When it is advisable, education about the importance of re-establishing routine, even in the smallest of ways, can increase a child's sense of safety. Stories that highlight the ways families, schools, and communities restore safety and predictability can help hasten the recovery process of traumatized people.

Managing Exposure

- Educate about media exposure. Selectivity in the media consumption of children, particularly young students, can provide a more balanced perspective on topics of interest. Research has shown that news stories can be reminders of an earlier tragic event, and reactions to the coverage may be similar to the original reactions. When media outlets include sidebar stories explaining potential reactions to coverage of a traumatic event, both children and adults may better understand their possible responses to difficult material as well as make informed decisions about how to manage their exposure. Educators should highlight rather than marginalize these important sources of supportive information which can detail efforts to prevent future occurrences, investigate the cause of the event, discuss safety measures that have been put in place, and provide stories of hope.
- Regulate children's exposure. Children may be especially vulnerable to strong images and reminders. News stories, particularly those with graphic details may have a deleterious impact on children and should not be promoted or suggested as part of the educational learning experience.

Engaging Children in Discussions on Traumatic Events

- Remember that recovery time varies. After a traumatic event, children vary in their healing and recovery. Adults should bear in mind that reliving painful events and details, with a focus on loss and suffering, may increase the likelihood of traumatic reactions months or years after the original events. Children should never be forced to share their feelings or emotions about a traumatic event. When a topic comes up in a classroom setting, teachers should use open-ended questions, such as "What have you heard?" to encourage children to share what they are thinking about the event. This will help clarify how children have interpreted a situation as well as expose issues that may confuse or frighten them.

- Consider children's expectations of participating in a discussion on a tragedy. Generally, children want to be perceived positively, and they may be concerned about doing a good job. As a result, intermediate age children may provide information they believe an adult or the group wants to hear, rather than their true thoughts.

- Gain permission. Be sure to obtain parental/caregiver permission before allowing a child to be interviewed about a tragic event.

Helping Educators Help Children

- Promote classroom discussion. Young children may overestimate their risk when they see pictures of frightening events. If children have been exposed to frightening images or news accounts, clearly describe the events taking place and put them in context. It is important to find out what children are worried about and discuss their concerns with them. Focusing on the fear and trauma caused by tragic events perpetuates the misperception that children are not coping. In fact, in most cases, the opposite is true and emphasizing this image can unnecessarily raise children's threat perception.

- Provide older elementary students with classroom practice in discriminating between fact and opinion, and between sensationalized accounts which speculate who, what, where or when versus fully verified information. Engage students in discussions of the quality of sources of information, the capacity of eye witnesses to engage in a meaningful discussion following a traumatic event, and the tendency of personal points of view to infiltrate news accounts. Explore trends in the amount of air time dedicated to tragic topics in relation to actual incident rates to determine if media coverage is proportionate.

• Be aware of children's traumatic stress reactions. As a general rule of thumb, if a child's traumatic stress reactions (e.g., recurrent thoughts or fears) get worse instead of better over time, teachers should inform parents and encourage them to seek the support of a qualified mental health professional. Educators should monitor children for the following reactions: withdrawal from friends; lack of participation in classroom activities; school refusal for a period of weeks or months; marked deterioration in ability to concentrate, leading to diminished grades; preoccupation with fear, grief, or guilt to the exclusion of talking or thinking about anything else; and isolation from peers.

CONCLUSION

Elementary social studies provide a foundation of skills to foster the role of students as responsible citizens in a democratic society. As the world becomes increasingly interdependent, media resources offer an important information source to aid children in evolving their understanding of their communities, the nation, and the world. Developing the means to evaluate information is an essential process for citizenship in an information age (Berson & Berson, 2004), and the integration of media literacy into social studies instruction can prepare future citizens to participate in a world which is progressively dominated by visual and electronic media (Berson & Berson, 2003).

The present provides a critical time to respond to the changing needs of students. At this juncture, social studies teachers must assume a leadership role in nurturing students' capacity to attend to, analyze, and influence the media driven culture in which they are immersed. In particular, the elementary years of school provide an extraordinary opportunity to cultivate, formulate, and affirm the foundational media literacy skills to counter hype and foster hope for a brighter future.

REFERENCES

American Academy of Pediatrics (2001, November). Media violence. *Pediatrics*, 108, 1222-1226.

Berson, I. R., & Berson, M. J. (2003). Digital literacy for cybersafety, digital awareness, and media literacy. *Social Education, 67*(3), 164-168.

Berson, M. J., & Berson, I. R. (2004). Developing thoughtful "cybercitizens." *Social Studies and the Young Learner, 16*(4), 5-8.

Cohen, N. (1997). Lessons learned from providing disaster counseling after TWA flight 800. *Psychiatric Services, 48*, 461-462.

Congressional Public Health Summit. (2000, July 26). *Joint statement on the impact of entertainment violence on children.* Retrieved May 30, 2004, from www.aap.org/advocacy/releases/jstmtevc.htm

DeFleur, M., & Dennis, E. (2002). *Understanding mass communication: A liberal arts perspective* (7th ed.). Boston: Houghton Mifflin.

Hamblen, J. (2004). *How communities may be affected by media coverage of terrorist attacks.* A National Center for PTSD Fact Sheet. Retrieved May 30, 2004, from http://www.ncptsd.org/facts/disasters/fs_media_disaster.html.

Huesmann, R. (2001, November 5). *The psychology of media violence: Why it has a lasting impact on children. Iowa State University: The impact of entertainment media and violence on children and families.* Retrieved May 30, 2004 from http://www.extension.iastate.edu/families/media/program.huesmann.html

Kubey, R. (2004). Media literacy and the teaching of civics and social studies at the dawn of the 21st century. *American Behavioral Scientist, 48*(1), 69-77.

Potter, W. J. (2004). Argument for the need for a cognitive theory of media literacy. *American Behavioral Scientist, 48*(2), 266-272.

Woodard, E. H., IV, & Gridina, N. (2000). *Media in the home 2000, The fifth annual survey of parents and children.* The Annenberg Public Policy Center of the University of Pennsylvania. Survey Series No. 7. Retrieved May 30, 2004, from www.appcpenn.org/mediainhome/survey/survey7.pdf

CHAPTER 15

READING THE "NEWS" AND READING THE "WORLD" IN HIGH SCHOOL SOCIAL STUDIES CLASSROOMS

Alan Singer and Michael Pezone

Michael Pezone and Alan Singer have had a 10 year collaboration as teachers, researchers and authors. Singer is a former New York City high school social studies teacher who is now a teacher educator at Hofstra University. Pezone, seeking a second career as a teacher while in his mid-thirties, was a student in the Hofstra program. He is currently a social studies teacher at Campus Magnet High School in Queens, New York, and an adjunct and cooperating teacher at Hofstra. Singer and Pezone share a commitment to critically interrogating the print media in high school classes to help students develop essential questions about society while also identifying underlying biases in coverage that shape our perception of the world.

A major part of their pedagogy is nurturing doubt, a healthy skepticism about received truths in social studies classrooms. In order to do this, they focus on developing the critical literacy of students—teaching students how to think, organize ideas and express them. Paulo Friere argues

Social Studies and the Press: Keeping the Beast at Bay?, 171–185

that literacy should not be viewed as a technical skill, but as a necessary action for freedom (Freire & Machedo, 1987). According to Freire, critical literacy requires reading and understanding both the *world* and the *word* so that people have the ability to use words to change the world. He feels that interest in and the ability to "read the world" naturally precedes the ability to "read the word." Based on his perspective, in order to enhance traditional "pen and paper" literacy, teachers must engage students as activists.

Pezone and Singer frequently start the school year by using newspapers to help secondary school students identify their own questions about world events. They distribute newspapers and news magazines to teams of students and ask them to select articles they believe report on important issues facing the United States in the contemporary world. Teams write down the headlines of the articles and their reasons for selecting them on poster paper. At the end of the class period, at least one group reports to the class on their deliberations (Singer, 2003; Singer & Murphy, 2001).

On the next day the rest of the groups report. After the presentations, students categorize the issues, identify underlying problems raised by the news articles, and discuss questions they wanted to answer during the year. Articles on racial discrimination, sexual harassment, and police brutality have led to questions such as, "Can the United States become a more just society?" Topics like welfare reform, health care, unemployment, tax breaks, and crime promoted students to ask, "What is the responsibility (or job) of government?" Other questions developed by students have included, "Should the United States be the world's police force?", and "Is technology making the world a better place?" These essential questions are printed on poster boards and hung prominently around the room. During the course of the school year student generated questions, especially about social justice and the responsibility of government, led to other big questions, and provided a focus for studying about the past, understanding the present, and deciding how to engage the future.

In the next section of this essay, "Where I Come From", Alan Singer describes the origins of his view of media in his experience as a youthful activist and his approach to teaching social studies. This is followed by a discussion by Michael Pezone of his view that "Knowledge Construction is a Radical Enterprise." In the final section of the essay, Singer and Pezone describe and evaluate a lesson in one of Pezone's high school classes where they put their experience and ideas into practice and involve students in applying a critical lens to the media as they read the *News* and read the *World* at Campus Magnet High School.

ALAN SINGER DESCRIBES "WHERE I COME FROM"

As a child in the 1950s, I was taught at home and in school to believe in the veracity of the leaders of the United States. As a teenager in the early 1960s, I learned from my teachers and parents that *The New York Times* accurately provided readers with "All the News That's Fit to Print." However, my confidence in teachers, government and media began to deteriorate during the War in Vietnam. The real blow to my trust occurred in December, 1967, during my freshman year in college.

On Tuesday, December 5, and Wednesday, December 6, I joined thousands of protesters in lower Manhattan in demonstrations against the war and the draft. My decision to participate in "Stop the Draft" week was a very contentious one in my family. My parents strongly objected, so I had to sneak out of the house before my father got up to go to work in the morning. My father told me that if I were arrested, I should not call him because he would not bail me out. The first day there were symbolic arrests at the Whitehall Street Draft Center but I was not involved. I left early to go to classes at the City College of New York and to distribute leaflets encouraging students to join marchers the next day.

I remember that when I arrived at Battery Park before dawn on Wednesday morning it was very cold and I was shivering. A small group of demonstrators, nearly all college students, gathered and waited for someone to give us some direction. Mostly we were frightened. There were barricades all over and the police's Tactical Patrol Force, armed with guns and nightsticks, mounted on horses, and wearing helmets and body armor, loomed over us. I held a hand-made sign, "The Draft Violates the 13th Amendment." I was supposed to meet two friends from school, but was unable to find them.

At some point the group moved into the street and the next thing I knew the mounted police launched a cavalry charge. In my memories, the horses were galloping but I can not attest to it. As the horses and riders maneuvered into the middle of the crowd, the officers began flailing out with their sticks trying to do as much damage to the demonstrators as possible. It was a police riot and the students broke and ran. I think I ran for hours.

As we escaped, we shouted anti-war slogans and blocked rush-hour traffic. I was with a group that headed uptown, but the mounted police force caught up with us about a half-mile away at Canal Street. When they turned their horses into the crowd, we scattered. I remember that there seemed to be some sense of order after that. We continued marching north in the street, blocking traffic, past 42nd Street. Drivers and construction workers cursed at us. Someone recommended that we head toward the Waldorf-Astoria Hotel on Park Avenue and 50th Street where Secretary of State Dean Rusk would be speaking.

I was with a small group of a couple dozen people when mounted police burst out of the doors of St. Bartholomew's Church on Park Avenue and attacked us again. We hustled to the hotel where we were penned in behind barricades but allowed to set up a picket line. At this point I met one of my friends for the first time that day. As we walked on the side of the hotel we were pelted with construction debris from a site across the street. I went up to a police officer (I was admittedly a bit naïve) and asked him to do something about the construction workers before one of us was hurt.

I was promptly arrested, handcuffed, thrown into a police car with two other protesters, and there we were beaten by two police officers with nightsticks. One of the protesters in the car actually wrestled a nightstick away from one of the officers. When the other police officer drew a gun, the protester agreed to surrender the nightstick if the police stopped hitting us. As I said, I was frightened before. Now I was terrified.

That afternoon I was processed through the courts. We were charged with "obstructing pedestrian traffic," which meant that we were accused of standing on the sidewalk. Everyone else was released on their own recognizance, but because I was under age eighteen, I had to wait for my mother to come and get me. My father made me swear not to tell anyone about my escapade, but one of my aunts saw me being arrested on television and a photograph of the arrest made the front page of the City College newspaper. I had to appear in court three times during the next six months but eventually all charges were dropped. As an interesting side note, when I applied for a license as a New York City taxi cab driver, they held up authorization for 6 months because of the arrest. However, it had no impact on my ability to become a teacher.

The main point of this story is really my reaction to the next day's *New York Times*. The demonstration made the front-page with the headline "Police Turn Back War Protesters." The opening line was that "Anti-draft protesters clashing with the police in the second day of massive demonstrations over the Vietnam War were thrown back again yesterday in attempts to paralyze the armed forces induction center at 39 Whitehall Street."

Later in the article, the *Times* declared "The aim to close the induction center was defeated, and the result of these sorties in the financial district and of later weaker demonstrations... was an occasional tie-up of traffic, some minor scuffling, 40 arrests and dissension among leaders of the coalition sponsoring the protest." Much of the article poked fun at the ineffectiveness of the demonstrators, nearly all college students, who turned out in such poor numbers, had gotten lost on their way to the draft induction center, and were largely "docile."

Although the article did acknowledge that "At Canal Street they [the demonstrators] were temporarily routed by eight mounted policemen," the repeated attacks by armed and mounted police on peaceful demonstrators who they outnumbered by as much as two to one, had apparently never happened. The dumping of debris from elevated construction sites had also never happened. And in the last paragraph of the article I learned that the demonstrator who had grabbed the nightstick from the police officer and spared us an extended beating while we were in the police car had been charged with felonious assault and held in jail.

The New York Times, THE NEW YORK TIMES, had gotten the story all wrong. I did not know what to do or to think.

During the next 3 years of college I attended countless demonstrations. Some were reported on in the media and some were not. However, there was one constant. The media always seemed to get it wrong. Blinded by the assumption that the police and government officials were telling the truth, they either never saw or chose not to report what was actually happening. It took many years and much political organizing until the police, politicians and the media accepted that in order to have organized and peaceful political protests they had to respect first amendment rights, cooperate with leaders in the planning of demonstrations and assist, rather than disrupt, marches and rallies. It was not until large numbers of middle-class parents joined the protests and *The New York Times* itself was targeted by the Nixon Administration in the Pentagon papers case and during Watergate, that the veil that blinded the press began to be lifted.

My experience as a political activist made it possible for me to become skeptical about the media, government officials and received truth in general. As a social studies teacher and teacher educator, one of my primary goals is to have students develop a similar healthy skepticism about the pronouncements of people in authority (without their having to experience the same personal trauma) and the desire to raise questions, find answers, and search for, formulate and test out underlying explanations. I routinely work doubt into historical document analysis and current events lessons. We tried to figure out why President McKinley justified the annexation of the Philippines at a press conference by claiming that God wanted America to Christianize Filipinos (perhaps God did not know that most were already Christian) and how the United States State Department knew the date and time of the Panamanian revolution in 1901 before it even happened. One of my biggest heroes is Abraham Lincoln, who in 1846 torpedoed (temporarily) his political career by demanding that President Polk, who wanted a war with Mexico, show Congress the spot on the map where American blood was supposedly shed on American soil by Mexican troops.

I have been fortunate to work with a number of teachers who appreciate the need to question media coverage and its underlying assumptions. As the United States prepared for and attempted to justify an invasion of Iraq in the spring of 2003, I was invited by alumni of my teacher education program to present an alternative view to classes in six public middle and high schools. Unlike the media, I always began by acknowledging that I have a point of view. And, unlike U.S. government officials, I welcomed questions, comments and open challenges to my ideas by both students and teachers. I usually focused on my questions about Secretary of State Colin Powell's presentation of the *evidence* to the United Nations about Iraq's support for terrorism and its weapons of mass destruction. Most students believed that Iraq had something to do with the attack on the United States on 9/11, even though the FBI and CIA declared there was no evidence of a connection. Part of the problem was that the media buried coverage of the disclaimers. *The New York Times* (2002) ran a 146-word article on the bottom of page A12.

I had the most fun discussing the satellite photographs presented by Powell at the United Nations (Miller & Preston, 2003, p. A10). One photo supposedly showed weapons of mass destruction being loaded onto truck beds. My question was, "If we have pictures of the Iraqis loading the trucks, where are the pictures of the trucks being unloaded?" As far as I could discover, the media, committed to the idea that Powell was telling the truth, never asked the question. Finally, on May 26, 2004, *The New York Times* issued a formal apology to its readers for its uncritical coverage of claims made by the Bush Administration to justify the invasion of Iraq.

MICHAEL PEZONE BELIEVES THAT "KNOWLEDGE CONSTRUCTION IS A RADICAL ENTERPRISE"

I believe that a teacher of social studies is obligated to construct lessons in which students compare and analyze conflicting viewpoints. This obligation ultimately derives from basic philosophical conditions of knowing. If one accepts, for instance, a definition of knowledge as "justified true belief," the first term of the definition demands exhaustive and systematic consideration of possible explanations. Such a pedagogical approach is necessarily a radical enterprise, one that requires constant interrogation of accepted texts, including textbooks, standardized testing material, and dominant media. A teacher who ignores this obligation, and uncritically presents an accepted canon, is, in essence, nothing other than a propagandist.

Prevailing pedagogical practices are, with their overarching emphasis on teaching to the test and reliance on textbook knowledge, inhospitable to a critical approach. The fact that teachers are often overwhelmed with teaching requirements, and function in school environments that do not provide the opportunity for collaborative sharing of ideas and resources, represent additional barriers to a genuinely critical pedagogy. When one considers, for example, the breadth of material encompassed within the Global History curriculum, it is not surprising that many teachers depend, in isolation, on textbook summaries for basic information, and thus accept textbook framing of issues and events.

The result of this is that students are presented a sanitized official version of the past that they are expected to accept uncritically. This official version becomes so embedded in the way we think that it takes on the status of received truth. In *Culture and Imperialism* (1994, p. 90), Edward Said explored the power and scope of the dominant ideas of capitalist industrial society. His study of nineteenth century European and American literature showed the ideas justifying European imperialism and global conquest were deeply embedded in the culture and shaped the world views of leading writers and thinkers, including John Stuart Mill, John Ruskin, and Joseph Conrad.

The dominant universe of discourse within the United States today is characterized and defined by the essentially total control of major media outlets by giant corporations (Chomsky, 1993; Herman & Chomsky, 2002; Bagdikian, 1997). To a large degree, the ideological positions of students and teachers alike are constructed and reinforced within the limited and limiting horizons of this dominant universe. There is no easy solution to the problems suggested above; no easy answer to the question, "how can a critical pedagogical approach become the norm?" A radical rethinking and restructuring of pedagogy will not occur as a result of pedagogical initiatives alone, but will depend on transformation of U.S. society at large. Although schools and universities will not and cannot be the prime engine of such societal transformation, they can be arenas of crucial ideological movement. In this regard, progressive, critical educators must commit to a praxis that involves: (1) a pedagogy characterized by fundamental criticism of accepted assumptions and beliefs, both about history, contemporary society, and pedagogy itself; (2) collaborative sharing of pedagogical materials and ideas—the creation of a community of educators committed to transformative practice; and (3) breaking free of reliance upon dominant media, which requires investigation, sharing, and use of alternative sources of information in classrooms.

Ideal teachers are political prisoners who resist bondage by continuing to educate themselves and others. They teach for one reason only: to create a world of equality and freedom. My role model as a teacher is

Prometheus as described in classical Greek mythology. Prometheus was "the teacher of all arts and the giver of all good to mortal men," who, as a result of his transgression, was severely and eternally punished by Zeus. When Zeus offered him freedom in exchange for betraying mankind, Prometheus responded, "There is no torment or contrivance in the power of Zeus to wring this utterance from me...; none of these things shall extort from me the knowledge that may ward off his overthrow." I believe teaching can be an act of resistance to an oppressive social order.

As a teacher-activist, I am committed to working with students from racial and ethnic minorities and working-class and poor communities. One of my goals is to empower them to read the word and the world (Freire & Machedo, 1987) so they can become active citizens engaged intellectually and politically in challenging hegemonic dominance and, thus, leaders in their communities in struggles to transform society (Casey, 1993, pp. 160-163; Gramsci, 1980, pp. 330-333).

READING THE "NEWS" AND READING THE "WORLD" AT CAMPUS MAGNET HIGH SCHOOL

Campus Magnet High School is located in a working-class community in Queens, New York, one of New York City's outlying boroughs. The school is a few minutes from John F. Kennedy International Airport. Although it is less than a mile from the highway that serves as a border with the city's largely White suburbs, the students in Pezone's classes are overwhelmingly Black and Latino. A majority of them have parents who immigrated to the United States from the Caribbean. The graduation rate from the school is only 56% (DOE, 2004).

In New York City, most high school classes are reorganized in September and February. This lesson was conducted in a United States history elective class at the start of the third month of the spring semester. Students were in the 10th and 11th grade. During the period, instruction was full class and group. When students entered the room, the class discussed how you can get information from a newspaper story and picture and whether there were also underlying messages and views being presented to readers; messages and views that are virtually *"unconscious,"* assumed by everyone to be true, and accepted without question (Foucault, 1971, p. xi).

Next, working in groups, students were asked to examine a picture, with a caption and article headline from that morning's *New York Times* (April 1, 2004). They had to:

1. Make a list of things you see in the picture.
2. Write a paragraph describing what you see in the picture.

3.   What story is being told by the picture, caption and headline?

4.   What problems or questions do you have with this *story*?

Groups were given different pictures to examine. That morning, the World Business section (W1) showed a color photograph of someone working in a field surrounded by bright red chilies. The headline was, "India's Economy Soared by 10% in Last Quarter of 2003." The caption read, "Growth in agricultural production, like these red chilies harvested on a farm near the western Indian city of Ahmedabad, led an economic surge last year. Farm output was aided by a heavy monsoon season."

The front page (A1) showed a picture of a bridge. Three burned bodies were visible hanging from the trestles. A crowd of about 10 men appear to be celebrating. The headline was, "4 From U.S. Killed in Ambush in Iraq; Mob Drags Bodies." The caption read, "Iraquis[sic] chant anti-American slogans in Falluja yesterday as burned bodies of Americans were suspended on a bridge over the Euphrates River."

This article continued on page A12 where two other pictures showed three men celebrating in front of a burning truck while holding up a sign and a group of approximately a dozen teenage boys shouting with arms raised over the ashes of a burned body. The headline was, "4 From U.S. Killed in Ambush in Iraq; Mob Drags Bodies." The caption reads, "Top, a leaflet with the phrase 'Falluja, the cemetery of Americans,' was held up yesterday near a burning vehicle in Falluja, Iraq. Above, children cheered while bodies burned after an attack on American civilians working for Blackwater Security Consulting of Moyock, N.C."

While students worked in their groups, Michael Pezone and Alan Singer circulated around the room, asked follow-up questions and took turns videotaping the conversations. Team teaching and the videotaping of student conversations are ways we use to observe what students are saying and learning and to reflect on our teaching practice.

Group 1 had four students (student names have been changed; statements have been minimally edited for grammar). They examined the photograph about India and brainstormed about what they were seeing. In a typical go-around, students focused on the images in the picture and information reported in the headline and caption. While they drew connections with prior knowledge, they initially refrained from making judgments about any underlying message in the photograph or text. For example:

Alexis: That's a lot of red chilies.

Anna: A lot of red chilies; its abundance. It was caused by the heavy monsoon season, rainstorms.

Shaniqua:	It's about the growth of agriculture in India.
Steven:	India's economy grew by 10.4%?
Alexis:	I think it has overproduced.

After more than five minutes of discussion, however, one of the students had a crucial insight that stimulated a much more open-ended conversation.

Alexis:	This is child labor. In this picture, that child working on the farm is child labor.
Shaniqua:	I'm saying that it's not child labor because he's helping out on his family's farm. How do you decide if that's child labor?
Steven:	This is in India and it looks like a boy surrounded by pounds of chili because their economy is growing 10% a year. Half of us basically think its child labor and the other half don't believe it's child labor. So that's what we're arguing about, whether or not it's child labor.
Shaniqua:	I think that it's not child labor if you're working your family's farm. Calling it child labor is a false statement and you could mess up somebody by saying that. If you work on a farm and you are doing chores like you would do in your house, it's not the same thing.
Alexis:	How do you know it's his farm? Is he getting paid?
Anna:	The problem with the newspaper article is they don't tell you all that so we don't know the answers. It never says.
Alexis:	If a child in New York in the middle of Manhattan is surrounded by pounds of chili peppers, what you think is going to happen? Don't you think they are going to call child welfare?
Shaniqua:	But this is a different culture. People have different cultures, so you can't just decide something. To him, these are his chores. Like down south, you work on your farm, you're supposed to help your family work. You cannot say it's child labor. That's false.
Steven:	Anybody ever handle chili peppers when you cook? What's it like to handle a chili pepper? It's hot. It burns. What happens to your throat if you work with a lot of chili peppers?
Anna:	The spores from the chili get into your throat and it burns. You start to cough and gasp. Your eyes burn, water, tear. If you rub your face you get a lot of burning.

Alexis: That's my point and why I call it child labor. If you want to get technical and in the law and all, then it is child labor.

Alan: Let me interrupt for a second, because what you're all arguing about is exactly the point of this lesson. I need someone from the group to read the headline, the caption, and the first paragraph. Why don't you do it, Shaniqua? What does the headline say?

Shaniqua: India's economy soars by 10.4% in the final quarter of 2003.

Alan: And what does the caption say?

Shaniqua: Growth and agriculture production like these red chilies harvested on a farm in the West Indian city of Amid Baz.

Alan: Someone read the first paragraph of the article.

Steven: India, March 31. India's economy soars 10.4 percent in the final quarter of 2003 making it one of the fastest growing in the world, even ahead of China.

Alan: What do you notice about this story?

Steven: The economy is soaring. It's the fastest soaring economy in the world. But they never tell us about the boy.

Alan: Why don't they tell us about him?

Steven: Because that's not what they worried about. They're not worried about the boy. They're worried about the economy.

Alexis: .... and money-making

Alan: This is what we mean by critical reading. If you just look at the article, you say this is a great thing. They're making all this money. But if you stop to look at the photograph carefully, what kinds of issues begin to emerge in your head?

Alexis: Child labor.

Group 2 had four students. They examined the front page photograph of the bodies suspended from the bridge in Iraq. Members of the group had a visceral reaction to what they saw and were angry with the perpetrators of what they called a "dehumanizing" act. Their anger at the act and image dominated discussion and they were unable to move past it to discuss the possible intent of the newspaper in printing the image.

Stacy: People are really happy that they killed all these people and they're burning and hung them on the bridge.

Roberto: Well, I see there are bodies hanging by a river and these people are really happy of what they just committed.

Tamika: It's degrading and dehumanizing, that's it. Why do you do this? Aren't you supposed to bury bodies instead of burning them and hanging them on the bridge?

Carlos:	Because they don't want the Americans in their country.
Tamika:	They're anti-Americans.
Stacy:	They're heartless, because why would you kill someone just because they're from a different culture.
Tamika:	That they're taking joy in taking other people lives. I don't think it's fair, I don't think it's right.
Robero:	They are taking others' lives and I just think that's wrong. It doesn't matter what you are, who you are.
Tamika:	They're just dehumanizing.

In group 3, Alan Singer joined the conversation, asking questions about the photograph and the message it was presenting to readers. This group examined the photograph captioned: "Above, children cheered while bodies burned after an attack on American civilians working for Blackwater Security Consulting of Moyock, N.C." His questioning started to help the conversation move beyond description towards analysis.

Monica:	They're rejoicing: the Iraq people. It makes them feel like they won the battle, the war.
Victor:	They burned bodies and they're rejoicing. They just feel that they interfere against America's agenda.
Alan:	Can you imagine people burning bodies and rejoicing? What is the message to us? What does the photo say to you about these people?
Laurence:	They don't care.
Tinetta:	They believe their victims don't deserve to be alive.
Alan:	What do you think about these people rejoicing over burned bodies?
Tinetta:	They're a danger.
Victor:	They got problems.
Alan:	Look at these people. I want you to describe those people who are jumping up and down.
Monica:	They're kids.
Alan:	Excuse me.
Monica:	They're kids.
Alan:	How old do you think they are?
Monica:	Like about 10 to 18? Maybe younger.
Alan:	Yes, some of them are your age. Here you have young men your age, celebrating at the death of others. What is the message of this picture about Iraq?
Laurence:	That they're having kids, you know, our age and they're engaging in war.
Alan:	But is this war?

Victor:	No, it's not war. It's like they are teaching their kids violence at some early age.
Laurence:	I wouldn't say they're teaching it, but it's like they allow it. They're allowing it.
Alan:	What would you say about a society that allows kids to be violent like that at an early age?
Tinetta:	It's showing them how to become more powerful when they grow up.
Alan:	What does the photograph say about this society?
Monica:	Parents don't care.
Tinetta:	It's their culture. They want this. They want this.
Alan:	Well, what does this say about their culture and religion?
Victor:	Their religion is Islam. It's crazy.
Alan:	You think it's just crazy? You think these people are just crazy?
Victor:	It's that they don't care. They're on a different level. They don't care about life. They're showing them how to be terrorists.
Alan:	Do you think this is a culture that doesn't care about life and is training its children to be terrorists or is that the message the newspaper wants us to take from this photograph?

After groups finished their discussions, students presented their findings to the full class and everyone discussed the reports. Michael Pezone asked: "What is the message to the American people in the pictures about Iraq? What words do they want to come into our minds when we see these pictures?"

Roy:	The Iraqi's are saying "Americans stay out".
Yvonne:	Terrorism. They're teaching the young kids to become terrorists.
Patrick:	They're not afraid to die.
Christina:	They're evil. Iraq and Islam are evil. They're terrorists. They're not afraid to die.
Mike:	Is this a true report about these people? Are they unafraid to die? Are they that different from us?
Laurence:	I'm not afraid to die, but I am scared of death.
Alexis:	We aren't evil. We're not terrorists.
Mike:	Are we that much different from them as human beings?
Shaniqua:	That's what the pictures and articles make it seem like. That's what they are telling us.
Mike:	What do you think?

Tinetta:	Maybe they aren't crazy. Maybe they are willing to die for their country, for a cause.
Mike:	What do we call someone who is prepared to die for a country or cause?
Tinetta:	Patriotic.
Mike:	Are these people crazy terrorists or are they patriots?
Anna:	In the eyes of Americans, they're terrorists, but in their eyes, they're patriotic. Americans tend to forget is that we are not the only ones that are patriotic and love our country, are willing to die for our country. Other people feel the same way about their country. You know what I mean? For them it's patriotic.
Victor:	They feel like they had some kind of victory over the Americans.
Theodora:	They act like Americans tried to invade their country and take it over.
Mike:	When we first look at the picture, they come across as inhuman, but as we begin to discuss the picture, what begins to come out about these people?
Lissette:	That they have a purpose.
Tamika:	I still think it's degrading hanging bodies on the bridge.
Dominique:	If people with armies and bombs came and destroyed here and then tried to take over here, our reaction would be just like theirs.
Lissette:	We'd have to send a message back to the invader, a strong message.

CONCLUSIONS

John Dewey (1933) believed that human beings have "an innate disposition to draw inferences, an inherent desire to experiment and test. The mind...entertains suggestions, tests them by observation of objects and events, reaches conclusions, tries them in action, finds them confirmed or in need of correction or rejection" (p. 9). In our experience, what Dewey called an *innate disposition* is better understood as a *potential*. Human beings have the capacity to reevaluate, draw connections, and learn, but that does not mean they always engage in reflective practice or critical thinking. It is a capacity that must be nurtured by teachers, especially in a world where government propaganda, supported by the corporate media, powerfully influence the way we think.

In these conversations, students tended to approach the analysis of the photographs as a classroom exercise, rather than as something of importance to their lives. Even as they performed the assigned tasks conscientiously, they resisted going beyond a superficial level of analysis until pressed through teacher questioning. However, sometimes as a result of the insight of one of their peers and sometimes as a result of prodding by teachers, they did begin to question the truths presented by these media images.

We believe the willingness of secondary school students to accept what they see or read in the media at face value possesses a significant threat to democratic values and institutions in the United States, especially as the media grows more consolidated and sophisticated in the construction and manipulation of images. This places a great responsibility on teachers to promote critical literacy and nurture doubt as they teach their students to read both the News and the World.

REFERENCES

Bagdikian, B. (1997). *The media monopoly.* Boston, MA: Beacon.

Casey, K. (1993). *I answer with my life.* New York: Routledge.

Chomsky, N. (1993, Fall). Media control. *Alternative Press Review.* Retrieved August 1, 2004, from http://www.zmag.org/chomsky/talks/9103-media-control.html

Dewey, J. (1933). *How we think: A restatement of the relation of reflective thinking to the educative process.* Boston: Heath.

Foucault, M. (1971). *The order of things.* New York: Vintage.

Four from U.S killed in ambush in Iraq; mob drags bodies. (2004, April 1). *New York Times,* p. A1.

Freire, P., & Macedo, D. (1987). *Literacy, reading the word and the world.* South Hadley, MA: Bergin and Garvey.

Gramsci, A. (1980). *Selections from the prison notebooks of Antonio Gramsci* (Q. Hoare & G. Smith, Ed. and Trans.). New York: International.

Herman, E., & Chomsky, N. (2002). *Manufacturing consent: The political economy of the mass media.* New York: Pantheon Books.

India's economy soared by 10% in last quarter of 2003. (2004, April 1). *New York Times,* p. W1.

Miller. J., & Preston, J. (2003, January 31). Blix says he saw nothing to prompt a war. *New York Times,* p. A10.

Said, E. (1994). *Culture and imperialism.* New York: Vintage.

Singer, A., & The Hofstra New Teachers Network. (2003) *Social studies for secondary schools* (2nd ed.). Mahwah, NJ: Erlbaum.

Singer, A., & Murphy, M. (2001, September). Asking the big questions: Teaching about the great Irish famine and world history, *Social Education, 65*(5), 286-291.

The Times and Iraq. (2004, May 26). *New York Times,* p. A10.

U.S. drops last link of Iraq to 9/11. (2002, May 2). *New York Times,* p. A12.

PART V

NEW MEDIA AND CITIZENSHIP EDUCATION

CHAPTER 16

DEMOCRATIC EDUCATION AND SELF-PUBLISHING ON THE WEB

Howard Budin

DEMOCRATIC EDUCATION

In the past, one's work has typically needed to be published by someone else. True, wealthy individuals would often pay to get their own work published, but the actual publishing activity was done elsewhere. Computers and networking, however, have changed this. Instead of disseminating material from a central publishing authority to a mass audience, any individual (who has a computer and is connected to the Web) can publish directly to whoever else is connected and chooses to read his or her work. In this chapter I am concerned with a set of tools—software applications that make it possible to perform a variety of tasks—on the Web for self-publishing, and how they can be used to promote democratic education. Youth are often described as *insiders* to the Web culture, because they grew up with it, as opposed to older *outsiders* who are not native to that culture, and it is young people who tend to make the heaviest use of Web tools and to create new innovations with them (Lankshear & Knobel, 2003). I maintain that the way youth use the Web is conducive in some ways to the prac-

Social Studies and the Press: Keeping the Beast at Bay?, 189–198

tice of democracy. Unfortunately, this type of use occurs nearly always at home and not school. Thus, to enhance democratic education in schools, and to do it in a way that resonates with youth, teachers should become knowledgeable about tools for self-publishing and how they can fit into a vision of democratic education.

Of all the claims we hear for the Web, one of the most common is that it is democratic. As one recent report on youth culture says, "From its earliest incarnation as a 'network of networks,' constantly bringing new voices into an ever-widening circle of discussion, the Internet has had a basic democratic thrust" (Center for Social Media, 2004). And Weblogs (or blogs) are democratic because they are made by amateurs, not professionals, and "information flows from the public to the press" instead of "from the press to the public" (Rosen, 2004). This kind of claim usually means that the Web provides opportunities: anyone can publish anything, anyone can communicate with anyone, and anyone can retrieve a vast amount of information. But, even laying aside the issue of the large percentage of the world's population that does not yet have access to these opportunities, questions remain about what democracy means, and what constitutes an education for being a democratic citizen. Does simply allowing access, simply being able to communicate, equal democracy? I will argue that providing these opportunities, while a necessary precondition for democratic education and action, is only a beginning; what matters is what we do with the opportunities.

To begin with, though, what do we mean by democracy, and by educating students for it? Throughout much of our recent history, attention has focused largely on the percentage of the electorate that votes. And traditional American schooling, for much of its history, has focused on teaching students about government and its functions. But in the past, citizenship has meant much more than voting and learning about democracy (Schudson, 2000). It also meant being involved in decisions that affected living in a democracy. Perhaps our greatest theorist of what democracy and democratic education means, for school and society, has been John Dewey. Following is a brief outline of what Dewey conceived of as the necessary ingredients in educating students for democracy:

1. Democratic action is not something that happens only occasionally or at certain times of the year. Rather, it is, or should be, continuous and ongoing. It is not concerned only with large-scale national events, but with all decisions that affect us. Thus, democratic action is an integral part of our everyday lives.

2. Schooling is not just practice for life. Traditional schooling has typically viewed school activities as practice for a later real life. But what happens in school cannot be divorced from real life.

This has a couple of implications: students should be engaged in activities that have real consequences, and they should use the same kinds of skills that they will need after they graduate.

3. Democratic action has at its heart collaborative decision-making. One of the key roles of a democratic citizen is to make decisions, along with her or his fellow citizens, to improve their lives and the well-being of the nation as a whole. Voting is one type of decision, but life is filled with situations that citizens need to address. In schools, too, students should address real problems—problems involved in life in school or outside of it—and make decisions that lead to some action.

4. Decision-making entails thinking—critical thinking and problem solving. This is an activity that takes place not in a vacuum, as an abstract exercise, but as part of real situations in which there are problems to be solved. Thinking, according to Dewey, requires "that the student have a genuine situation of experience—that there be a continuous activity in which he is interested for his own sake" (Dewey, 1966, p. 163).

5. In order to tackle real problems, students (and citizens) need to be imbued with a set of "thinking dispositions," such as curiosity about the world, the ability to try different ways to solve problems, and the patience to sift through alternative possible solutions (Tishman, Parkin, & Jay, 1994). In general, schools need to develop powers of inquiry in students through active investigation of problems (Schutz, 2001).

6. Problems are solved not by individuals in isolation, but through communication and collaboration with others. Thus, problem solving is a social activity fostered by communication between people. In solving problems, people communicate with one another, find and share information, and find ways to come together and make shared decisions.

7. Groups solve problems through the process of deliberation. Deliberation produces "a decision to take a particular course of action," and it involves "forging that decision together, reasoning together, generating and considering alternatives together" (Parker, 2002). Deliberation requires reflection on information and issues, the ability to listen to and respect others' opinions, and the patience to come to collective decisions.

8. Deliberative decision-making requires that all involved have access to all the information they need, and that they know how to analyze information to think through problems. But, as Dewey wrote, "information severed from thoughtful action is dead, a

mind-crushing load" (Dewey, 1966, p. 153). Thus, access to information is a prerequisite of democratic decision-making, but by itself is not sufficient. We need not only to ensure that all people have access to the information they need (not an easy task in itself), but also that they have the skills they need to use information in thinking and analysis (Wilhelm, 2000).

9.   To be truly effective, deliberation needs a diversity of viewpoints and opinions. Diversity is vital in helping people learn to understand and take others' perspectives, to put themselves in other people's place. According to Parker, "when a diverse group of people deliberate together, they create a new 'we' in which differences are regarded as an asset, listening as well as expressing occurs, stories and opinions are exchanged, and a decision is forged together. In this way, deliberation is a *public-building activity*. Publics are groups that come together to decide what to do about common problems.... Without decision making on shared problems, an actual public consciousness is not born" (Parker, 2002, pp. 80-81).

10.   In sum, democratic education involves a diverse body of students (and teachers) in the ongoing and everyday investigation of their world with a view to improving its conditions through participating in joint deliberation and problem solving in order to address and take action on common problems.

TOOLS FOR SELF-PUBLISHING ON THE WEB

In a broad sense, everything on a Website is *published*. For our purposes, though, I am considering a set of applications and activities available, and heavily used by, youth for the purpose of publishing themselves. We will not include email and chat room postings because these are ephemeral, closer to speech conversation. Publishing on the Web includes other media than writing, but it is meant to last for some period of time, so that more than one person has the opportunity to see it. In this sense, we will consider postings on asynchronous discussion boards. Although some of these postings may be conversational, others are deeply reflective and often equivalent to small papers. In brief, these tools for self-publishing include:

• Blogs.   Millions of people around the world are now postings their thoughts, opinions, and journal entries on blogs (Weblogs), some of which allow users to post responses to each other. (See the chapter on blogs in this volume by Judith Cramer for more information and discussion of blogs.)

- Discussion boards.   There are thousands of public discussion boards for those interested in particular topics. Online course platforms routinely use them for reflective discussion. And some educational projects (like www.knowledgeforum.com) are experimenting with structuring discussions to *scaffold* learning.
- Cartoons.   Several free sites on the Web allow users to create and publish their own cartoons, and to create communities of cartoon lovers.
- Soliciting youth writing.   Many sites, like www.wiretapmag.org, actively solicit writing from youth, in order to "give young people a voice in the media" (http://www.alternet.org/about/). Youth contribute articles, personal essays, artwork, and more. The Center for Social Media at American University says that, in its survey of sites designed in any way to engage youth as citizens, nearly half "invite youth to participate online in some fashion, and almost a third provide opportunities for visitors to submit essays, articles, reviews, op-eds, or artwork to their sites" (Center for Social Media, pp. 32-33).
- Shared writing.   Sites such as www.sharedwriting.com and www.fanfiction.net allow users to submit all genres of writing for publication and peer review. Readers can often comment on submissions and start dialogues with authors about them.
- Wikis.   A "wiki" is a Website that lets anyone create and edit Web page content. This kind of open editing is exciting, according to one site, because "it encourages democratic use of the Web and promotes content composition by nontechnical users" (http://wiki.org/wiki.cgi?WhatIsWiki).
- Publishing student work.   Finally, many organizations have created structured projects to which schools or individual students submit writing to be published on a Website. The International Schools Cyberfair, for example, a project of the Global Schoolhouse Network (http://www.gsn.org/GSH/cf/), encourages students are encouraged to conduct research and publish their findings.

While the descriptions above certainly do not cover every way youth can publish themselves on the Web, they give an idea of the evolving range of tools and techniques. What is it that appeals to young people about using these kinds of publishing tools? Here are some of their attractive attributes:

- Free expression.   A simple desire to have the *whole world* see one's writing is a powerful motivating force. Even if relatively few people ever read your blog or see your cartoon, the very ability to post it in a place where anyone might see it is a radical departure from past practice. You can communicate your thoughts, opinions, and feelings, to your friends, associates, or complete strangers. These tools give at least the feeling that it is possible to reach out to the world.

- Self-discovery.   Writing, in itself, can be a wonderful path to learning about oneself. Of course, writing does not depend on computers or the Web, but if the opportunity to publish oneself on the Web motivates young people, then technology serves as a useful instigator of writing. Blogger and author Rebecca Blood writes: "Shortly after I began producing Rebecca's Pocket I noticed two side effects I had not expected. First, I discovered my own interests. I thought I knew what I was interested in, but after linking stories for a few months I could see that I was much more interested in science, archaeology, and issues of injustice than I had realized. More importantly, I began to value more highly my own point of view. In composing my link text every day I carefully considered my own opinions and ideas, and I began to feel that my perspective was unique and important" (Blood, 2000).

- Anonymity.   It has been often noted that the very anonymity made possible by the Web is a tremendous motivating force for many people. Like the old cartoon with the caption "On the Internet nobody knows you're a dog," the opportunity to write without being judged by age, gender, or appearance can, for some people, bring out more honest and forceful writing. Author and educational consultant Alan November tells the story of a girl who submitted a novelette to a shared writing site, one she had written over summer vacation. When interviewed and asked if she wrote in school, she was horrified at the idea of doing something that her peers would regard as not cool and revealing her abilities in that way (November, 2002). Over the Web, she could submit what she wrote without being found out, and others would read her work and comment on it without any preconceptions about her.

- Blending of communication and expression.   As noted several times, many if not most of the Web tools we are considering blend the expression and publication of ideas with communication of them to other people. In some cases, the two are so intertwined that it is difficult to see where one begins and the others leaves off. This is one of the areas of life that has changed most in recent years. Cell phones, instant messaging, chat rooms, blogs, discussion forums—youth have grown up being in touch in all these ways. Modern communication tools add instant or nearly instant feedback to whatever one writes, and this property enriches the writing process in several ways: the reduction in time necessary to hear other's opinions; the excitement of anticipating responses; and the ability to get feedback from many people and conduct dialogues with them about it.

- Participation. The Center for Social Media says that, "If, in relation to youth, the primary difference between the '*old*' and 'new' media could be reduced to a single word, that word would be *participation*. As opposed to the one-way print and broadcast media of the past, the new online media afford youth an opportunity to respond" (Center for Social Media, 2004, p. 32). Older media transmitted, or delivered, content to people. In this sense, newer Web-based media tools are active rather than passive, giving youth the opportunity to be respond and be involved.

DEMOCRATIC EDUCATION AND WEB PUBLISHING TOOLS

Can tools for self-publishing on the Web contribute to democratic education? The answer, I believe, is that, in terms of the attributes just described, they can be a tremendous asset, but that they supply, in and of themselves, only a part of what is needed. A serious and concerted effort by schools to educate students for democratic citizenship will entail using these tools in certain ways and for certain purposes. Through the lens of this vision, we can see that, in some ways, the tools that students use for publishing themselves on the Web contain important ingredients of democratic education, but that they lack other vital components.

- Communication. To Dewey, communication was central to life and education. People, he wrote, "live in a community in virtue of the things which they have in common; and communication is the way in which they have come to possess things in common" (Dewey, 1966, p. 4). He also believed that all communication is educative (p. 5). Still, not all communication is equal, and some kinds are better suited than others for facilitating collaborative decision-making. It is certainly true that the Web teems with communication tools, but the mere fact of communication by no means ensures democratic decision-making. The ability to communicate about blog postings and writings is indeed a marvelous addition to youths' lives, and one that may motivate them to discuss in depth and to deliberate, but this kind of activity is not inherent in the tool. Rather, it is more often a product of human will and effort.

- Information gathering.   The Web is largely a set of tools for communication and for manipulating information—finding it, storing it, and sharing it with others. Youth (and others) often search the Web for information they need in posting blog or discussion board entries, and in researching articles for posting on Websites. The very availability of information on the Web certainly can be useful in democratic education—the Web is a vast reservoir of information usable for democratic purposes. But the extent to which it is truly useful depends on what one does with the information found, and to which information presented by one person is debated and deliberated on by others, and on how people use the information in communication. Again, the tools themselves do not guarantee this kind of use.

- Deliberation and decision-making.   Young people often do deliberate with the help of Web writing and communication tools. Discussions on blogs, discussion boards, and shared writing sites may very well become deliberative, as participants read each others' points of views, present their own positions, modify their own thought and writing, and at times come to a collective decision on some action to take. When these activities occur, they demonstrate that the tools made possible by the Web can constitute a good training ground for democratic discussion and action. But, again, such occasions are not an inherent or necessary attribute or effect of the tools. Concerted effort and planning are necessary to encourage deliberation.

- Diversity.   Even though millions of sites are available to anyone who has a computer that is connected to the Web, researchers have found that availability, in itself, does not necessary increase the range of views and opinions one reads. In fact, people gravitate to sites on which others share their already existing views and not to ones with opposing views. The same tends to be true for informational sites and chat rooms and discussion forums. In this way, the Web has served more to reinforce views than to challenge them (Etzioni, 2001). Some theorists have even worried about the danger of individuals filtering out information they are not interested in, and looking only at the kinds of sites they choose, in this way fragmenting a larger public into small special-interest groups which talk and listen only to themselves (Shapiro, 1999). There are no reliable statistics on whether this is likely to be as true for younger people, but we have no reason to believe that the simple availability of blogs, discussion boards, and other Web tools serves to increase diversity. Diversity, like deliberation, needs to be cultivated.

Thus, Web tools for publishing have attributes that can strongly facilitate democratic education, but simple access to them does not ensure democratic use. Teachers must plan for their use in the context of an educational vision that values democratic learning and action. How can teachers do this? A complete answer would be lengthy, but I offer here some relatively simple ways to begin thinking about this:

- Teacher education.   First, teachers simply need to know about these tools—how to use them, how youth tend to use them, and what their possibilities for education are. Without this knowledge, they will not be used in schools.

- Structured asynchronous discussions.   Teachers can experiment with enhancing in-class discussion with asynchronous discussion boards. They can structure discussions so that students think about issues, add their own informed comments, and respond to others'.

- Expression and communication.   Students should be encouraged to express themselves through personal journals and creative writing. Blogs can be created to accompany class projects, in which students reflect on their experiences and respond to classmates' postings. Stories and poems can be shared on class Websites (or submitted to the kinds of organizational sites described above) so that others can appreciate and respond to them.

- Collaborative projects.   Classes can learn about other students around the world, and participate in collaborative projects with them, through such organizations as the International Education and Resource Network (IEARN) (www.iearn.org). This kind of activity is inexpensive and provides excellent opportunities to learn about others and make decisions with them.

- Real-world involvement.   Projects that are goal-oriented motivate students. Students can be involved in projects that are as local as studying their own neighborhood in order to make recommendations for improvements, or as large as taking steps to ease world hunger. In the process, they can work together to research these issues on the Web, deliberate and make collective analysis and decisions about what to do, get involved with organizations' Websites, and publish their own findings and recommendations on school or other Websites.

Small projects can lead to bigger projects. For teachers new to using these tools, experimenting with one of them and seeing its effects can be a good and necessary inauguration, after which others can be added as teachers see fit. Keeping in mind the goal of involving students in meaningful deliberation and decision-making about aspects of their world— teachers will find that these tools can become crucial ingredients in democratic education.

REFERENCES

Blood, R. (2000, September 7). *Weblogs: A history and perspective*. Retrieved April 15, 2005, from http://www.rebeccablood.net/essays/weblog_history.html

Center for social media, school of communication, American University. (2004, March). *Youth as e-citizens: Engaging the digital generation*. Retrieved April 15, 2005, from http://www.centerforsocialmedia.org/ecitizens/youthreport.pdf

Dewey, J. (1966). *Democracy and education*. New York: The Free Press. (original work published 1916).

Etzioni, A. (Ed). (2001). Can virtual communities be real? *The monochrome society*. Princeton: Princeton University Press.

Lankshear, C., & Knobel, M. (2003). *New literacies*. London: Open University Press.

November, A. (2002, November 13). *Preparing tomorrow's teachers to use technology*. Paper presented at the New York state consortium conference, Albany, NY.

Parker, W. C. (2002). *Teaching democracy: Unity and diversity in public life*. New York: Teachers College Press.

Rosen, J. (2004). *The weblog: An extremely democratic form of journalism*. Retrieved July 16, 2004, from http://journalism.nyu.edu/pubzone/weblogs/pressthink/2004/03/08/weblog_demos.html

Schudson, M. (2000). *The good citizen: A history of American civic life*. Cambridge, MA: Harvard University Press.

Schutz, A. (2001, April). John Dewey's conundrum: Can democratic schools empower? *Teachers College Record, 103*(2), pp. 267-302.

Shapiro, A. L. (1999). *The control revolution*. New York: PublicAffairs

Tishman, S., Perkins, D. N., & Jay, E. (1994). *The thinking classroom: Learning and teaching in a culture of thinking*. Upper Saddle River, NJ: Pearson Education.

Wilhelm, A. G. (2000). *Democracy in the digital age: Challenges to political life in cyberspace*. London: Routledge.

CHAPTER 17

BLOGS IN THE MACHINE

Judith Cramer

LOVE AT FIRST SITE

Watching as the site came into view, I was surprised. Had I expected something as strange as the sound of blog? Talking Points Memo, my first destination in the blogosphere, was already famous; here an outraged blogger had kept the Trent Lott story alive when mainstream journalists had ignored it after Strom Thurmond's 100th birthday party in December, 2002. First a khaki field filled my screen, followed by a broad white band down the middle, the blogger's writing space. It held a long, scrollable stack of messages, each labeled with a date and time. Next to the masthead there was a small portrait of the blogger, Joshua Micah Marshall. Hair uncombed, chin cupped in his hand, staring perhaps at a computer screen (the blue reflected in his eyeglasses), he looked to me like a virtual Trajan, exalted by his column.

IT'S A BLOG!

Weblogs—pet name blogs—were christened in 1997 though they were not exactly newborns at the time (Blood, 2000). Unlike other Web denizens with odd names, but recognizable pedigrees, blogs emerged spontaneously, more like geysers, say, than Google. Technical writers attribute the

Social Studies and the Press: Keeping the Beast at Bay?, 199–211
Copyright © 2005 by Information Age Publishing
All rights of reproduction in any form reserved.

stunning growth of blogs after 1999 to the availability of free software, such as Blogger and Pitas (Jensen, 2003). But others point to 9/11 as the event that turned a creative, if somewhat solipsistic Web activity into the digital *vox populi* we hear today (Welch, 2003).

Not all blogs are political, but all are journals—online diaries, frequently updated, and relying on the first person voice. They remind us anew of the common root of the words *journal* and *journalism* in the French for day (*le jour*). Blogs are being heralded now as a new form of (online) journalism, one more democratic than the conventional print or broadcast press, often derided as Old or Big Media. Blogs differ from other forms of online journalism, like those found at salon.com, for instance, or the CNN Website, not just in the way they look or sound. Though some integrate graphics, audio or even video clips, the way online newspapers' and broadcasters' sites do, and others are the work of groups of like-minded writers, the paradigmatic Weblog is the daily text- and hypertext-heavy expression of one person, with a structure all its own.

TIMELINES

A blog is simply a stack of electronic posts, or time-stamped text messages, displayed with the most recent on top. At first glance this seems to resemble the V-shaped architecture that I, like other high school journalism teachers, emphasized to my teenage reporters. Our journalism textbook told us how the V or inverted pyramid structure, with its first paragraph containing *the five Ws*, had developed along with a new technology, the telegraph. Knowing that the connection might break while a story was being sent over the wire, reporters learned to pack essentials up front, so their editors would always have something to print. Paragraphs following the meaty first ones contained information less and less important. By the time I was advising the editors of the student newspaper at the United Nations International School in the late 1990s, of course, the reason for the V structure used by reporters had disappeared—or had it? Constant exposure to the form had shaped newspaper readers' expectations, and besides, the attention span of American readers had diminished, many say as a result of television, to the point that journalists assumed that no one would read beyond the first few paragraphs anyway.

A blog magnifies one of the five Ws—*when*, or the dateline of news articles filed by reporters in the field. In their sidebars, where bloggers typically display a *blogroll*, or hotlinked list of other blogs—in this way recommending their colleagues to their readers, two groups who may, in fact, be comprised of the same individuals—they often sort such links according to criteria of timeliness: blogs that update more than once a day may be starred, or listed ahead of blogs that update only once a day. The Web medium allows bloggers to make factual corrections or modify their opinions rapidly and often, something print journalists are not able to do. While the *Errata* sections of our dailies are hardly read by anyone, except, perhaps, other papers' reporters or those readers directly affected by the errors, updates in a political Weblog are usually responses to posts from readers making use of the site's comments function—not just to call attention to errors in the original message, but also to suggest ways to make its argument stronger, or to provide links to relevant sources of information.

VIRTUAL SPACES AND PLACES

If the Weblog is characterized by a linear sequence of time-stamped posts, there is an opposite, and equally strong, if not stronger force at work in it: hypertext. It is tempting to imagine a blog's column of posts as a vertical element and its links as horizontal or spatial—and this description makes sense if you visualize the blog's structure as a two-dimensional diagram. Links take a Weblog's reader elsewhere in cyberspace: in fact, all over the virtual map. Links can add texture to a blog by bringing in other viewpoints and other kinds of documents, creating a series of diverse information arrangements, as each reader clicks on whichever links beckon.

Whiskey Bar, a lefty Weblog I discovered via a link (http://www.billmon.org), is exemplary in this regard. All I know about "Billmon," the virtual bartender on duty, is what I can glean from his posts and his blog's atmospheric look. Unlike Josh Marshall of Talking Points Memo, Billmon offers visitors neither a photograph nor a resume, but only his *nom de blog* and witty slogan: "Free Thinking in a Dirty Glass." A Bertolt Brecht quotation provides a gloss for the site's name. Besides other blogs and online versions of what bloggers contemptuously refer to as "dead tree publications"—and it is the stories in these that are the occasions for most political blogging—Billmon typically cites historical and literary works. In a few days of reading his trenchant prose, I came across quotations from or references to Tuchman's *The Guns of August,* Heller's *Catch 22,* Dickens' *David Copperfield,* Orwell's *1984,* and Melville's *Moby Dick.* I was able to make a few guesses about Billmon's age and tastes from this information and from the fact that, like other bloggers, he has a day job, which funds his night work in the Bar.

A person of formidable analytic and argumentative skills, Billmon suffers fools poorly. At Whiskey Bar, the country's paper of record is known not by the affectionate nickname *gray lady,* but by the tabloid epithet *New Pravda* (used ironically). Billmon sometimes serves up four-letter words, but the effect is colorful rather than vulgar. While saluting a select group of other liberal bloggers, like Josh Marshall and Kevin Drum, creator of the Political Animal Weblog, he delivers scathing reviews of Old Media pundits who fail to back up their opinions with facts, and of "impartial" journalists who are unaware of biases that tinge their writing. Special scorn is reserved for those who fail to take advantage of the powerful search, database, and hypertext tools that bloggers use to research and expose such faults (see, for example, "The Memory Hole," posted March 21, 2004).

The striking verbal and visual differences between Whiskey Bar and other political Weblogs of comparable quality and complexity point to a hallmark of the form. All blogs, no matter how burdened with data or studded with links, are exercises in personal expression. Bloggers do not strive for the objectivity that I worked so hard to instill in my high school journalism students, and that is still prized, though less often attained, by mainstream journalists. Rather bloggers cultivate the first-person writer's singular voice. Add to this the visual elements available in the Web medium—color, texture, typographic design, images—and you see why both bloggers and their visitors come to think of these sites as personal spaces or places.

PAGE TO SCREEN

A point made by Marshall McLuhan (1964) that has entered common discourse on media is that new communication technologies borrow content from old ones until they develop content of their own. Among the examples often cited to illustrate McLuhan's notion is the early movie, which was merely a stage play performed in front of a (stationary) camera. To help my students understand this provocative idea, I used to add the Gutenberg Bible, designed to look like a work of scribal art, even though it was produced mostly by machine; and the computer desktop, a metaphor adopted by early interface engineers to make people feel at home with digital tools. Five hundred years after Gutenberg, our books hardly resemble his at all, not even most printed Bibles, and Movable Type is the name of a software application used to create Weblogs.

My first look at talkingpointsmemo.com brought to mind McLuhan's concept. Although the terms *Weblog* and *Web page* both reference older writing technologies, it can be argued that these two digital forms represent discrete stages on a McLuhan technology continuum. With its elaborate but static visual organization, appropriate in the fixed world of ink and paper but requiring tedious coding work by designers to maintain in the dynamic digital environment, the Web page has never fit quite comfortably into the new medium. Readers who bring print-based assumptions to the Web pages they view may be disturbed by this discontinuity. It is hard to know, for instance, which parts of an individual's homepage have been updated, or which headlines in a print publication's online version are most important. Distinctions borrowed from the material realm of platens and presses make little sense when you are staring at pixels, though we continue to use them. One section of an electronic newsletter I receive is called "Above the Fold"—a tongue-in-cheek illustration, perhaps, of McLuhan's theory.

With their building blocks of posts, stamps, and links, Weblogs take advantage of the new medium's capacities in ways that Web pages have not. A post can be any length; it is easily updated; and it is built around hypertext, an essential capability of Web technology, which has itself been compared in revolutionary importance to Gutenberg's printing system (Landow, cited in Oravec, 2002). The Weblog's date and time stamp, a function of the software tool, lets the viewer zero in on the most important information. For bloggers, the post represents liberation from the spatial or word-count tyrannies of the mainstream digital page (Hourihan, 2002); and, as journalist Andrew Sullivan has argued in *A Blogger Manifesto* (2002), from interference by the many layers of authority in the Old Media establishment. In Sullivan's words, bloggers practice direct "peer-to-peer journalism" (para. 4). Sullivan describes the difference between online journalism and blogging with an analogy reminiscent of McLuhan:

> Most non-blogger web journalism is still a little like television in the 1950s. To begin with, television simply plonked radio show formats on the air, before they figured out what the new medium could do best. What many magazines and newspapers now do online is somewhat similar: They just put on a screen a pixilated version of what they already do on paper. But what bloggers do is completely new—and cannot be replicated on any other medium. It's somewhere between writing a column and talk radio.... In that sense, blogging is the first journalistic model that actually harnesses rather than merely exploits the true democratic nature of the web. (para. 16)

ROLES AND REVERSALS

Political bloggers maintain that their work's intense interactivity separates them from mainstream journalism, even in its more participatory modes. Communication among those who write and those who read and, in turn, write to the authors of Weblogs, is facilitated by comments features in blogging software, by ubiquitous e-mail options, and by a *TrackBack* function originally offered in Movable Type, and since replicated by other publishing system developers. TrackBack keeps track of bloggers' links to each others' posts. University of Tennessee law professor Glenn Reynolds has said that he started InstaPundit, his popular political Weblog, because he was frustrated by the very limited opportunities for debate offered to readers by the letters and even less accessible op-ed columns of newspapers (Seipp, 2002). Three years after he tacked up his blogger's shingle, Reynolds had more than 200,000 hits a day at instapundit.com

A space for letters to the editor was on my students' list when they began a redesign of their newspaper with PageMaker. Like Reynolds, they sought a forum for citizen engagement; and like him too, initially they found it easier to want than get. When it appeared that the school's citizens had no interest in the new reader forum, some editors wondered whether letters ghostwritten by individuals on the masthead and signed by that well-known student, "name withheld by request," might be used to fill the empty section. Our subsequent research into publishing history turned up the humbling fact that readers' letters had been printed in an English language paper for the first time in 1690. What Weblogs offer 3 centuries later is more than the opportunity to write in (or call in) provided by older technology and journalistic practice. The new medium levels the playing field and blurs the distinction between writers and their readers (listeners, viewers) in ways that are not only highly productive, but also transparent.

Readers of blogs who contribute comments become a blogger's collaborators, generally acknowledged in subsequent (updated) posts. Bloggers like Marshall or Sullivan, whose sites have no comments section, integrate emails into their posts. Others, like Markos Moulitsas, creator of Daily Kos, the most visited political Weblog, according to The Truth Laid Bear, a site that tracks blogs, may urge readers to chew the political fat in threaded discussions. Typically Kos launches several open threads every day with sly invitations like "your virtual water cooler" or "jibber jabber." Moulitsas has built into Daily Kos a number of features that serve readers interested in belonging to an online community. There is a rating system for comments, which helps keep out *flamers,* as those who launch digital diatribes are called, and a diaries function which allows readers to initiate discussions. Many in the Daily Kos community have their own blogs, a fact Kos proudly publicizes, along with a list of alumni, which includes Drum and Billmon, as well as another highly regarded liberal blogger, "Atrios," the creator of Eschaton.

Weblogs strive to replace the one-to-many model of traditional print and broadcast journalism with a participatory, many-to-many model that characterizes other kinds of communication over the Internet (see Chapter 16 in this volume by Howard Budin). A realm claimed by gifted amateurs, the blogosphere operates by a credo that is as antihierarchical (and thus, it might also be said, as anticorporate) as the hypertext that makes it run. Put another way, the map of *Blogistan*—an affectionate term I discovered reading the comments section in the PressThink site run by Jay Rosen of the New York University School of Journalism—would look more like a web than the top-down tree typically used to show the lay of the land in Big Media. In keeping with this spirit, and in contrast to most professional conferences, BloggerCon, a gathering of bloggers held for the second time in April 2004, in Cambridge, Massachusetts, was preceded only by a few sketches of agenda ideas, blogged to participants, of course, with requests for comments.

Rather than competition, a hallmark of Big Media, where the "scoop" and the "sweep" determine careers, bloggers prize cooperation. Opening a post by saying, in effect, "I'm not going to talk about *article in mainstream press (hotlink)* because my colleague *name of blogger (hotlink)* over at *name of weblog (hotlink)* has so ably covered it already," is a convention of almost all the sites on my list. This is not just charming; it is efficient. The links may introduce me to a new writer or a new topic or both. Glenn Reynolds has won praise for using his high-traffic site in this manner, often promoting emerging writers to InstaPundit's large readership. Reynolds, a conservative, believes that bloggers link as or more often to disagreeing as agreeing sites, and that the transparency that results from the constant, collaborative updating keeps bloggers honest. Old Media sites, by contrast, he says, have no interest in sending visitors off their turf, to the blogosphere or anywhere else in the surrounding Web (Wu, 2002).

THE FACTPACK

Tools like Google and Lexis-Nexis help bloggers mine the Internet to contextualize almost any topic or issue in a relatively short time. A single post, like the one made by Josh Marshall on December 6, 2002, expressing his dismay at Trent Lott's remarks at Strom Thurmond's 100th birthday party, may precipitate round after round of hyperlinked activity, each highlighting a new aspect of the story. In the few days between Marshall's post and calls from public figures for Lott's resignation as incoming Majority Leader of the Senate, a revealing history of the Mississippi politician's relationship with segregationist organizations and his anticivil rights voting record in the U.S. House and Senate was mapped with the blogosphere's powerful research technologies. Links in Talking Points Memo (December 11th and 14th), for instance, gave readers access to an interview Lott had given to the neo-confederate magazine *Southern Partisan* and to the *amicus* brief he had submitted on behalf of Bob Jones University in a landmark case.

Readers of blogs could also find Strom Thurmond's voting record, along with the platform and ballots of the segregationist Dixiecrat Party under whose banner he had run for president against Harry Truman in 1948, as Lott had enthusiastically reminded celebrants at Thurmond's party. Even before the mainstream media picked up and amplified the story, bloggers across the political spectrum called for Lott to apologize for his remarks; and then, when he failed to do so, for him to step down as incoming Republican Majority Leader. "And where's the President?" asked Andrew Sullivan in The Daily Dish, a blog bastion of conservatism. "It seems to me an explicit repudiation of Lott's bigotry is a no-brainer for a 'compassionate conservative'" ("Trent Lott Must Go," posted December 9, 2002).

By contrast to a typical news story, with its inverted pyramid structure, the saga of Trent Lott's battle with the blogs looks like a pyramid sitting upright in the sand. At the pyramid's tip, on December 6, 2002, are the brief accounts of Lott's remarks included on broadcasts by PBS (Ifill, 2002) and *ABC News*, and in ABC's online news summary, The Note, posted later that morning (Halperin, 2002). These were followed by Josh Marshall's now famous opening salvo, posted on Talking Point Memo at 3:20 pm, EST:

> But look at what Trent Lott said about [Thurmond's 1948] candidacy yesterday …

> I want to say this about my state: When Strom Thurmond ran for president we voted for him. We're proud of it. And if the rest of the country had of[*sic*] followed our lead we wouldn't of[*sic*] had all these problems over all these years, either.

> Oh, what could have been!!! Just another example of the hubris now reigning among Capitol Hill Republicans.

> —Josh Marshall

From there the story unfolds, with Marshall, Sullivan, Atrios, Reynolds, and others in the blogosphere weighing in repeatedly before the print and broadcast media echo, amplify, and add to the information. The base of the pyramid, a product of intense collaborative investigation and analysis by both liberal and conservative bloggers (and later, members of the mainstream media), is an example of what Reynolds (2003a) has elsewhere termed "horizontal knowledge."

Unlike those front page stories I taught my student editors to chisel into V-shapes meant to secure a reader's attention in the opening paragraph, the surprising narrative of Trent Lott would have to be cut from the top, instead of the bottom, where its full meaning inheres. Nothing in the story changed over the period between Lott's birthday party toast and his resignation 15 days later, except that one of the five Ws—arguably the most important one, the *why?*—was fully explored. Using the tools of their trade to contextualize Lott's remarks, and their hallmark "acid commentary" (Scott, 2004), bloggers were also voicing their opinions about what constitutes news. What is striking, case studies of the episode suggest, is that the blogs convinced Big Media to rectify its mistake in missing the significance of the Lott story by picking it up again long after the relentless 24-hour news cycle would normally have made it obsolete (Rosen, 2004; Scott, 2004).

MEDIA ECOLOGY

A criticism leveled at bloggers is that they are not journalists at all, but mere parasites in pajamas who use computers to feed on the work of those who go out and get the news first hand. None of the bloggers who took part in the transformation of Lott's remarks from nonstory to front page news had been at Thurmond's birthday party. Broadcasters made the story available to the blogosphere, and the mainstream press later put it before the general public, the argument goes. Notable exceptions to this stereotype have included some bloggers in Baghdad, such as Christopher Allbritton, whose readers at back-to-iraq.com contributed more than $14,000 to send him to Iraq as a war correspondent in March 2003, and those who received press credentials to cover the 2004 Democratic and Republican party conventions.

A good deal of bandwidth, not to mention newsprint, has been devoted to defining Weblogs' role in what is now seen as a "new media ecosystem" (Hiler, 2002; Lasica, 2003), where relationships among print, broadcast, and digital communication technologies are shifting. There is growing agreement that political blogs and Old Media outlets complement each other. While the blogosphere has human and technical resources to compensate for some of the establishment media's most obvious deficiencies—its collective amnesia and a corporate culture of laziness are two that the Trent Lott story particularly demonstrates, some critics say (Rosen, 2004)—it cannot replace the news gathering function that is the first mandate of the press. This function has been the rationale for assigning an important political role to journalists in a democratic society, a topic my students found addressed in their textbook under the heading, "The Fourth Estate."

Some observers argue that by staking a claim to news analysis and criticism, bloggers will force establishment journalism to return to its historic turf (Reynolds, 2003b). Others predict that the intimate, opinionated, decentralized model of communication epitomized by blogging may eventually displace the impersonal, objective, mass media paradigm brought in with the telegraph (Grabowicz, 2003). In a recent op-ed piece Whiskey Bar's Billmon (2004) darkly points to signs that blogging, like previous revolutionary forms of expression, will be subsumed by Big Media economics. This is unlikely, however, in the view of other analysts, such as Clay Shirky (2002), who consider blogging part of a larger phenomenon of "mass amateurization," which is destined to bring an end to the publishing industry as we know it.

The odd mix of singular, first person voices and humming, hive mind that I encountered as I traced the tale of Trent Lott is something new—and a far cry from the professional decorum I once stressed to an international group of young editors and reporters. Whereas the traditional protocol has been to edit, or filter first, then publish, the blogosphere publishes first and filters later (Lasica, 2003). This shift has also been attributed to the new medium bloggers have at their fingertips. In the words of one wag, "bloggers are like Socrates on speed" (Mooney, 2003). No doubt listening to their talk would have cheered my students, as it has me, maybe even prompted them to reconsider joining the Fourth Estate, a career choice only two of our team of 30 could defend. Assigned to analyze local newscasts and papers, my students judged American journalism to be short of the mark set by our textbook for the free press.

At the moment, blogs are in the media machine and making it work harder. Not only are newspapers and networks scrambling to add Weblogs to their online assets, but more print journalists, following early adopters like Sullivan, Marshall and Drum, are leaping into the blogosphere every day. There is some evidence that political blogs and mainstream journalism interact in ways that serve the public interest. Whether bloggers will just continue to provoke, will eventually replace, or will be co-opted by the Fourth Estate—or, keeping their edge, will become a distinct (digital) Fifth Estate—it is clear that Weblogs have earned their right to be taken seriously.

POSTSCRIPT

Making plans to go abroad last winter, I searched online for a former editor of the U.N. School newspaper, now living in London, where I was headed. Like most students, he had moved many times; I no longer had a current address or telephone number for him, and his email was not live. I had to smile when Google turned up an acerbic political Weblog with his byline. Here I could submit a (public) comment, with a tactfully hidden request to contact his old journalism teacher. In London I learned that he was applying for a fellowship to enter journalism school. I asked: is it possible that, as the proprietor of a political Weblog, you may have already joined the ranks?

REFERENCES

Political Weblogs Discussed in this Chapter

Atrios. (2004, December 22). *Eschaton: Weblog.* http://atrios.blogspot.com

Billmon. *Whiskey Bar: Weblog.* www.billmon.org
    Note: Whiskey Bar ran from April 10, 2003 until September 27, 2004,
    when Billmon put up a "closed" sign. The Weblog reopened on Octo-
    ber 29, 2004. At press time all links were live.

Drum, K. (2004, December 22). *Political Animal: Weblog.* www.washington-
    monthly.com

Marshall, J. M. (2004, December 22). *Talking Points Memo: Weblog.*
    www.talkingpointsmemo.com

Reynolds, G. H. (2004, December 22). *InstaPundit: Weblog.* www.instapundit.com

Sullivan, A. (2004, December 22). *The Daily Dish: Weblog.* www.andrewsullivan.com

Zuniga, M. M. (2004, December 22). *Daily Kos: Weblog.* www.dailykos.com

Specific Posts Referred to in this Chapter:

Atrios. (2002, December 6). Here is what Senator Lott was proud of in 1948 Mis-
    sissippi. *Eschaton: Weblog.* http://atrios.blogspot.com/2002/12/here-is-what-
    senator-lott-was-proud-of.html

Billmon. (2004, March 21). The memory hole. *Whiskey Bar: Weblog.* http://bill-
    mon.org/archives/001254.html

Marshall, J. M. (2002, December 6). I've always thought. *Talking Points Memo:
    Weblog.* http://www.talkingpointsmemo.com/archives/week_2002_12_01.
    php - 000451

Marshall, J. M. (2002, December 11). Is TPM your source. *Talking Points Memo:
    Weblog.* http://www.talkingpointsmemo.com/archives/week_2002_12_08.
    php - 000476

Marshall, J. M. (2002, December 14). As longtime readers know. *Talking Points
    Memo: Weblog.* http://www.talkingpointsmemo.com/archives/week_2002_
    12_08.php

Reynolds, G. H. (2002, December 6). Trent Lott deserves the shit. *Instapundit:
    Weblog.* http://instapundit.com/archives/005985.php

Reynolds, G. H. (2002, December 11). Lott is damaged goods. *Instapundit: Weblog.*
    http://instapundit.com/archives/006082.php

Sullivan, A. (2002, December 9). Trent Lott must go. *The Daily Dish: Weblog.* http://
    /www.andrewsullivan.com/index.php?dish_inc=archives/2002_12_08_dish_
    archive.html

REFERENCES

Bear, N. Z. (2004). *Weblogs by average daily traffic*. Retrieved September 10, 2004, from http://www.truthlaidbear.com/TrafficRanking.php

Billmon. (2004). Blogging sells, and sells out. Retrieved September 26, 2004, from http://www.latimes.com/news/opinion/sunday/commentary/la-op-billmon26sep26,1,7245002.story?coll=la-sunday-commentary

Blood, R. (2000, September 7). *Weblogs: A history and perspective*. Retrieved March 2, 2004, from www.rebeccablood.net/essays/weblog_history.html

Grabowicz, P. (2003). Weblogs bring journalists into a larger community. *Nieman Reports, 57(3)*, 74–76.

Halperin, M., Wilner, E., & Ambinder, M. (2002, December 6). Louisiana senate run-off. *ABC 2002 The Note*. Retrieved September 10, from http://www.abcnews.go.com/sections/politics/DailyNews/TheNote_Dec6.html

Hiler, J. (2002, May 28). Blogosphere: The emerging media ecosystem. *Microcontent News*. Retrieved Aug 3, 2004, from http://www.microcontentnews.com/articles/blogosphere.htm

Hourihan, M. (2002, June 13). What we're doing when we blog. *Oreillynet.com*. Retrieved March 19, 2004, from http://www.oreillynet.com/pub/a/javascript/2002/06/13/megnut.html

Ifill, G. (2002, December 6). Public broadcasting service. *Washington week*. Retrieved August 16, 2004, from http://www.pbs.org/weta/washingtonweek/transcripts/transcript021206.html

Jensen, M. (2003, September / October). A brief technological history of blogs. *Columbia Journalism Review*. Retrieved March 19, 2004, from http://www.cjr.org/issues/2003/5/blog-jensen.asp

Lasica, J. D. (2003). Blogs and journalism need each other. *Nieman Reports, 57(3)*, 70–74.

McLuhan, M. (1964). *Understanding media: The extensions of man* (2nd ed.). New York: New American Library.

Mooney, Chris. (2003, February, 2). How blogging changed journalism—almost. *Post–gazette.com*. Retrieved July 30, 2004, from http://www.post-gazette.com/forum/comm/20030202edmoon02p1.asp

Oravec, J. (2002). Bookmarking the world: Weblog applications in education. *Journal of Adolescent & Adult Literacy, 45(7)*, 616-21.

Reynolds, G. H. (2003a, June 4). Horizontal knowledge. *Tech Central Station*. Retrieved June 3, 2004, from http://www.techcentralstation.com/060403A.htm

Reynolds, G. H. (2003b). Weblogs and journalism: Back to the future? *Nieman Reports, 57(3)*, 81–82.

Rosen, J. (2004, March 14). The legend of Trent Lott and the weblogs. *PressThink*. Retrieved March 19, 2004, from http://journalism.nyu.edu/pubzone/weblogs/pressthink/2004/03/15/lott_case.html

Scott, E. (2004). *"Big media" meets the "bloggers": Coverage of Trent Lott's remarks at Strom Thurmond's birthday party*. Case Program, John F. Kennedy School of Government, Harvard University, C14-041731.0. Cambridge, MA: President and Fellows of Harvard College.

Seipp, C. (2002, June). Online uprising. *American Journalism Review.* Retrieved March 18, 2004, from http://www.ajr.org/Article.asp?id=2555

Shirky, C. (2002, October 3). *Weblogs and the mass amateurization of publishing.* Retrieved July 30, 2004, from http://shirky.com/writings/weblogs_publishing.html

Sullivan, A. (2002, February 24). A blogger manifesto: Why online weblogs are one future for journalism. *The Sunday Times of London.* Retrieved Mar 3, 2004, from http://www.andrewsullivan.com/culture.php

Welch, M. (2003, September/October). Blogworld and its gravity. *Columbia Journalism Review.* Retrieved March 19, 2004, from http://www.cjr.org/issues/2003/5/blog-welch.asp

Wu, Steven. (2002, November 22). Revenge of the blog: Keynote: Instapundits's Glenn Reynolds. *LawMeme.* Retrieved June 16, 2004, from http://research.yale.edu/lawmeme/modules.php?name=News&file=article&sid=565

PART VI

IMPROVING THE RELATIONSHIP

CHAPTER 18

PRACTICING WHAT WE TEACH

Richard Theisen

Engaging the critics of social studies education and public education in general is imperative. It may take the form of friendly dialogue over issues where both parties are willing to listen actively and reach agreement through consensus. More often though critics have an agenda they intend to implement and only see educators as road blocks in their paths. That attitude has been the norm, unfortunately, for too long.

If time is taken to examine it, the record is fairly clear that it has been appealing and often advantageous, at least in the short run, to attack education and especially social studies education, for partisan political gain. Unfortunately, media complicity in these efforts has too often been the standard, not the exception. On the other hand, the education community has often been a passive bystander, some would even say, a willing victim, more eager to complain about its victimhood than to stand, respond, and go on the offensive against those who would distort, dismiss, and oversimplify complex education issues.

Too often trust that the system will be fair, that ultimately the common good will prevail, and that each child is inherently worthwhile—all necessary qualities for educators—are undercut by powerful interest groups in the broader community. Ideologues with an agenda, religious zealots

Social Studies and the Press: Keeping the Beast at Bay?, 215–224
Copyright © 2005 by Information Age Publishing
All rights of reproduction in any form reserved.

intent on imposing their views of reality, and politicians only concerned about being reelected carry the day. Their voices are covered by the media because they provide good sound bites and fit the prevailing conflict-based definition of news stories. This is not to suggest that educators throw up their hands in dismay and become raging pessimists sacrificing the beliefs referred to earlier but, for our sake and that of the children we teach, we must learn and practice a new set of skills to accompany those beliefs.

Here are a few suggestions. First, we must overcome our fear of conflict. Conflict is not inherently good or bad. It depends on the circumstances. But to avoid it concedes the field to our harshest critics and their like-minded colleagues. Conflict, real or manufactured, attracts attention. Especially when it involves sensational charges, half truths, or comes from an author with an established reputation. A response is required. That response should include a statement of principles and values, acknowledgment of areas of agreement, and then a careful, thoughtful, and analytical response to the key distortions, exaggerations, and occasional outright mistruths.

Second, educators must actively engage in the political process outside of their classrooms and become sophisticated media consumers. We must become politically sophisticated to the point where we can and do practice the skills many of us teach our students to use in analyzing the media and taking political action. When think tanks attack public education and public school educators, when foundations have a pattern of providing financial support to education initiatives which undercut public education, when a political party (either Republican or Democrat) consistently pursues principles in its political platform that undercut public education at the state and national level, social studies teachers, and all teachers, cannot afford to be passive observers.

When you attend a government sponsored national workshop, as I did several years ago, at which virtually every speaker comes from think tanks and foundations with a common political agenda in education, it is important to be able to identify the political perspective and the common principles driving their presentations. Factual data does not speak for itself. It is presented (as it was at that conference) selectively, either reflecting the unconscious predispositions (rose colored glasses) of the presenter, or consciously promoting a personally desired political perspective. It is also true that the research we produce and use in the field of education is value laden, although peer review and professional standards should provide transparency concerning the facts upon which we base our judgments.

It is essential that we have skills which will enable us to analyze media presentations--books, films, reports, presentations, programs--fully aware of the presenter's perspective. There is no such thing as an unbiased media. That does not mean we ought to ignore the media; instead, we simply need to become more sophisticated. We must become discriminating media consumers or to put it more bluntly, we need to become skilled "crap detectors" as Postman and Weingartner (1969) suggest in their book *Teaching as a Subversive Activity.*

Third, we must acknowledge the fact that public education is one of the very last incredibly lucrative fields of potential commercial wealth that has not been privatized. If we keep this in mind it is much easier to understand the agenda and long run goal of some of our harshest critics.

Fourth, we must stop apologizing to the corporate and business community. We have much to offer each other. However, the market model and business community, in general, have their own limitations—witness Enron and the myriad of ethical and legal failures that have occurred recently. The answer for education is not the business model, certainly not as characterized by Enron, or for that matter Wal-Mart or Haliburton. On the other hand, exchanging ideas on a level playing field, based on mutual respect, is desirable.

I would add that this is a two-way street. We have as much to offer the business community as they have to offer us. An open exchange of ideas is essential and needed. However, education, should not and cannot be based on the profit motive. The market model has its place but not in the education of our children.

Fifth, we need to be prepared and organized when we engage in a debate or dialogue with our critics, and especially when there is media coverage. Having media savvy is not optional, it is a requirement. It is also true that we cannot wait for the media to come to us but instead we must follow the very successful lead of foundations and think tanks on the political right. We may call it public relations or use some other term but we must engage the wider public systematically with our ideas about the form, substance, and pedagogy of social studies education, and equally important, the value of public education.

It is also critical that we have the capacity to respond quickly and skillfully to our critics, especially when they use forums that receive significant public attention. To not respond is to suggest we agree, and that has happened too often in the past. Our muted responses to the political polemic *The Nation At Risk* (1983), and the No Child Left Behind Act of 2001 are two cases in point.

In the remainder of this chapter I will share two applications that reflect, at least in part, the previous five suggestions. The first is a presentation I made at the American Enterprise Institute on September 16, 2003. It was a forum in which each of the five participants had 15 minutes to present their formal response to a book sponsored by Chester Finn's

Thomas B. Fordham Foundation *Where Did Social Studies Go Wrong?* Mr. Finn wrote the foreword to this book, which spared little in criticizing the field. Other presenters at the forum were book contributors James Leming and Lucien Ellington, William Bennett, and Senator Lamar Alexander. After the presentations a 45 minute question-and-answer session was held. Not surprisingly, approximately two thirds of the questions were addressed to the position I had presented as a representative of the National Council for the Social Studies (NCSS).

* * *

Formal Remarks by Richard M. Theisen, past president of the NCSS at the American Enterprise Institute, September 16, 2003

Thank you for inviting NCSS to participate in this forum. It is always a pleasure to represent my profession and the many skilled and talented teachers who have just started their school year. I will first make some comments that represent the position of NCSS on many of the issues raised in these publications. I will then address our points of agreement with the texts, and finally our disagreements.

First, a statement of principles. NCSS has consistently taken the position that social studies educators should:

- Use their classrooms to teach history and social science content and the skills needed to analyze that content.
- Present multiple perspectives when teaching history or any of the social sciences such as economics and political science, where a variety of interpretations and viewpoints exist.
- Teach the principles found in the major documents of our nation such as the Constitution, Bill of Rights and Declaration of Independence.
- Teach students the relationship between those documents and their lives as citizens of the United States.
- Use the position statement of the NCSS on multicultural education as a guide in their teaching and curriculum. This is especially important because the number of immigrants and the variety of countries from which they have emigrated have increased substantially.
- Teach students that understanding causality, searching for evidence, and respecting the tentative nature of a considerable part of knowledge are valued habits of mind and heart.

- Teach students that we are not only citizens of the United States but also citizens of the broader global community. Our goal is "to prepare young people to be humane, rational, participating citizens in a world that is becoming increasingly interdependent."
- See their key role as one of teaching students the knowledge and skills which will enable them to be active, engaged citizens in their communities.
- Teach students to have effective communication skills, including the capacity to be active listeners, analytical thinkers, persuasive speakers, and effective organizers.
- Use the NCSS curricular standards to organize their curriculum and use the content standards of history and the social sciences as their guide in choosing their content standards.

Now let us take a look at the two publications of the Fordham Foundation. We strongly disagree with the overall characterization of social studies as a failed educational effort. However we do agree with some aspects of both books, or works of advocacy journalism, as I would prefer to call them.

We agree with those authors who believe that the No Child Left Behind (NCLB) law has had the effect of marginalizing social studies education at all levels, but especially at the elementary level. As one writer said, "If it's not tested, it's not taught," and since federal mandates under NCLB do not include civics or history, it is being dropped in many schools to allow more time for testing in the mandated areas. If NCLB is not modified it will have done more to eliminate history and/or social studies than any other event, person or movement. That must change. Perhaps these publications will provide some impetus for this change.

We also agree with virtually all of Diane Ravitch's summary statement, in which she says,

> Ultimately, those of us who reject indoctrination and propaganda in the classroom must recognize that these distortions may occur in any field, be it called social studies or history. Our goal must be to insist that students encounter a variety of views; that their teachers and textbooks recognize the possibility of fallibility and uncertainty; and that students gain a solid body of knowledge as well as the tools and dispositions to view that knowledge skeptically and analytically.

Few could find fault with the principles expressed in this statement, except that I would emphasize that no teacher I have ever met knowingly believes that it is OK to indoctrinate rather than educate his or her students.

We also agree that most textbooks have been almost uniformly bland and uninspiring. Textbook publishers can and must improve the quality of their work but, as Ravitch states in her most recent book, censors from a host of groups, right, left, and otherwise are continually peering over the shoulders of these writers. And frankly, it does not help matters that most publishers cater almost exclusively to large textbook adoption states. On the other hand it does create a market for good quality reference material from smaller publishers.

NCSS certainly agrees that colleges of education need to establish and follow high expectations and standards in pedagogy, and especially content. NCATE (National Council for Accreditation of Teacher Education), the nationally recognized accreditation institution, does have high standards and a very strong accountability system. In fact, the content requirements for social studies certification have increased substantially since I was certified and perhaps in the future should be strengthened even further so that teachers could only teach in areas in which they have a substantial academic background.

NCSS also subscribes to the belief that multicultural education is an important component of every social studies curriculum. Contrary to some of the representations of the authors of the books we are reviewing, the NCSS position is that,

> Multicultural education supports and enhances the notion of *e pluribus unum*—out of many, one. To build a successful and inclusive nation state, the hopes, dreams and experiences of the many groups within it must be reflected in the structure and institutions of society. This is the only way to create a nation state in which all citizens will feel included, loyal, and patriotic. (NCSS Task Force on Ethnic Studies Curriculum Guidelines, *Curriculum Guidelines for Multicultural Education*, A Position Statement of National Council for the Social Studies [Washington, DC: NCSS, 1976, revised 1991], p. 3)

We believe that the publication *Terrorists, Despots, and Democracy* has some limited merit. The statements by William Galston, Lamar Alexander, Tony Blair and Abraham Lincoln are useful contributions to a dialogue about what it means to live in a democratic society. It would have enhanced the quality of the text to have included a broader cross section of viewpoints, especially in the "what teachers should know," section but the Fordham Foundation has the right to choose its authors. Unfortunately the text does little to improve the understanding of either terrorism or despotism. I must say that Mr. Finn's introductions in both texts detract from rather than enhance the value of either publication. The same can be said about the easy use of negative labels and sarcasm by some writers in the text on social studies.

We definitely agree that the level of civic knowledge, as measured by the NAEP scores, and the political indifference and ignorance of students are concerns that must be addressed. There are a number of reasons for this behavior. A publication by The Center for Information and Research on Civic Learning and Engagement titled *The Civic Mission of Schools* addresses the causal factors and gives an extensive list of possible solutions.

NCSS certainly does support continued high quality replicated research which can be utilized to improve the quality of classroom education and particularly the quality of civic education in our schools. We believe that changes in classroom education that are based on the most current research and presented in a teacher friendly format can be extremely useful.

Where do we disagree? From my dual perspective as a social studies leader and career-long classroom teacher, the prevailing assumption in many of these articles is that:

- We do not teach the founding documents or the appropriate history, and if we do, we do not do it well.
- Colleges of education are incompetent and perhaps even conspire to produce teachers who are incompetent.
- The leaders of the social studies community include few if any classroom teachers.
- Our leaders are elitists and almost universally subscribe to left wing ideology in their teaching and theory.
- We do not teach developmentally appropriate material and we lecture too little and use constructivist strategies too often.
- Our teachers, at least in the examples provided by some, care more about the terrorists than our own citizens.
- The ideas and theory our social studies leaders promote are out of touch with the common values of the American community.
- The triumphalist narrative approach to history education is the only legitimate way to teach history.
- Progressive education, as defined by the writers, is a failure and the cause of many of today's problems.
- We do not effectively teach the unity aspect of *e pluribus unum*.
- The theory of constructivism as practiced in classrooms is ineffective.
- And, finally, that we are producing ignorant activists.

We disagree with each and every one of these assertions, as well as others I have not mentioned. There are isolated cases that would seem to support some of these criticisms, but they certainly do not apply to the typical social studies teacher or NCSS member. We do support constructive dialogue focused on improving the quality of social studies education in this country.

Why do we disagree with the above assertions? I have responded in part earlier. I will take some of my limited time to elaborate on several others here. As a classroom teacher, I taught a variety of courses, including an elective constitutional law course which required students to read, brief, and engage in a Socratic dialogue on 30-35 full length Supreme Court cases. I used a variety of teaching strategies, depending on the course and the students in that course. In my department and in most schools across this nation, original documents are used. Curriculum standards and content standards are established and followed. My colleagues at my high school used a variety of instructional strategies, including the lecture/recitation method, as do most teachers across this country. All of my colleagues thought history should be taught in a way which would increase the probability that students would not only know the facts and concepts but see the relationship of these facts and concepts to their own lives. Some used the triumphalist narrative approach, others a thematic approach oriented toward social history. Most teachers do have an interest in the ideas, theories and practical lesson suggestions of the leadership in the field, who present at local state and national social studies conferences.

I tell you all of this to make the point that my teaching experience, and that of my teaching colleagues is not atypical. We use the ideas of our leaders when appropriate in our work, we lecture when it is the best strategy for the content, we teach concepts, facts and the critical thinking that make those facts and concepts meaningful in student's lives. My work in the past 2 years on national social studies projects in which I have observed the teaching of approximately 300 teachers directly or by video tape suggests that the authors of these essays have had far too little contact with what is really happening in the classrooms of the United States. There is always room for improvement in social studies education. However, the dismal pictures drawn by the twelve critics in this text are often overstated, too often unsupported by evidence, and misleading in their depiction of classroom teachers, leadership agendas, and the leadership's ability to control and change the overall direction of social studies education in this country.

I would also like to respond to the claim that the leadership is largely made up of ideological extremists out of touch with the broader community. My experience at the collegiate level taking a large number of courses at a wide variety of colleges and universities from 1966 to 2000 belies the charge that a liberal, leftist educational agenda is the rule. That is an exaggerated statement, more hyperbole than reality. The liberal bias my colleagues speak of in this book can only be true if they take the political spectrum and move it so far to the right that former moderates are now seen as left wing radicals. My point is that it is always dangerous to use easy, ideology based labels. Most educators are not that easily categorized.

Some authors suggest that the only saving grace is that most teachers ignore the social studies leadership. The obvious first response is that, if this is true, than why attack the leadership? However it is not that simple. Ever since *A Nation At Risk* (1983) was published social studies educators have been harshly criticized for the ills of society—our inability to compete with Japan, our low voter turnout, the low performance of students on SATs (Scholastic Assessment Test), and a whole host of perceived shortcomings. Some criticisms are legitimate; others, as David Berliner points out, are distortions of reality. My point is that when you criticize social studies leaders as separate and distinct from teachers it will not resonate with most of us. We are all social studies educators and when you criticize our mentors, professors and leaders you are also criticizing us.

A dialogue which focuses on improving the quality of classroom education is something we are all interested in, especially those who are both leaders and K-16 classroom teachers. Attacks that are gratuitous satisfy the attacker but do little else. Fortunately some of the writers in this text are truly interested in such a dialogue.

And finally before I close I think it is safe to say we do not see ourselves as lunatics, Huns, Goths or other sundry labels some authors, particularly Mr. Finn heap upon us in these texts.

In closing, I do think opportunities to engage in constructive dialogue with the goal of seeking truth based on evidence and an open, respectful exchange of opinion and viewpoints are almost always of value. How could I say otherwise as a person who has taught social studies classes for 35 years?

Thank you again for offering NCSS the opportunity to participate in this forum.

* * *

The second application of the principles given at the beginning of this chapter is a short description of an education initiative that was successful in Minnesota this past year. The end result of the organized political effort led by many social studies educators, the Minnesota Council for the Social Studies (MCSS), and several citizen organizations was the adoption of social studies standards that were dramatic improvements over the department of education's original draft. The successful removal of an extremely controversial education commissioner was a secondary objective. This is a case study of the type of activity that social studies teachers should utilize at the state and national level. Other states such as Michigan have models that are based on proactive organization; this one is a reactive model.

Ultimately, the commissioner was removed from her position and social studies standards were passed and signed into law by the governor. The commissioner's standards were adopted by the House of Representatives. The MCSS alternative was adopted by the Senate. The two versions were modified in a legislative conference committee. The final result was a set of social studies standards that, while not perfect, were a substantial improvement, an understatement actually, of the original document produced by the commissioner's committee. Learning and developing a comfort level with the political process, identifying the interest groups and their agendas, organizing teachers and parents, coordinating the various interest groups, and speaking out in the media and at legislative hearings was all critical to the success of the effort. It is not enough to simply criticize a proposed course of action; an alternative must be developed. This occurred and the MCSS alternative standards were introduced in the state legislature by the senate education committee. Developing a relationship with key legislative leaders was critical. Equally important was the multifaceted communications system that united parents and teachers.

This was a successful, intense use of the political, media and communication skills referred to earlier. However, one can never rest on the laurels of past successes. Vigilance is not only the price of liberty, it is the price of good educational policy.

The expectation that decision making will be fair and open, the optimism that ultimately the common good will prevail, and the belief that every child is inherently worthwhile are foundational principles to which almost all educators subscribe. They are also principles at the core of our system of government. Ideals dependent on an informed, politically active citizenry. We need to become skillful practitioners in the political arena and equally skilled media consumers and communicators. The reality is that we must become adept at practicing what we teach.

REFERENCES

Leming, J., Ellington, L., & Porter-Magee, K. (2003). *Where did social studies go wrong?* Washington, DC: Thomas B. Fordham Foundation.

National Commission on Excellence in Education. (1983). *A nation at risk.* Washington, DC: Author.

NCSS Task Force on Ethnic Studies Curriculum Guidelines. (1976/1991). *Curriculum guidelines for multicultural education, a position statement of national council for the social studies.* Washington, DC: NCSS.

Postman, N., & Weingartner, C. (1969). *Teaching as a subversive activity.* New York: Doubleday

CHAPTER 19

COVERING THE CONFLICT
AND MISSING THE POINT

Richard Lee Colvin

The attack on the *National Standards for History* (UCLA, 1994) on the op-ed page of the *Wall Street Journal* (Cheney, October 20, 1994) by Lynne V. Cheney, the wife of vice president Dick Cheney and the former chairwoman of the National Endowment of the Humanities, initiated a controversy, framed as a patriotic defense of the integrity of American school curricula, that actually had little to do with education and much to do with politics. It was also a controversy that could not have been started or sustained without the often unquestioning help of media outlets. As many social studies educators know, Cheney's 1,500-word essay blasted the standards for making only fleeting mention of George Washington while naming discredited Sen. Joseph McCarthy 19 times and the Klux Klan 17 times. She alleged that the document gave short shrift to the U.S. Constitution and the first gathering of the U.S. Congress. Famous white, male inventors and generals were excluded. She asserted that for the sake of political correctness the standards gave "unqualified admiration" to African and other non-Western societies while rendering the American story as a regrettable narrative shaped by self-dealing scoundrels. Halting the endorsement of the standards by the federal government, she wrote, would require going "up against an academic establishment that revels in

Social Studies and the Press: Keeping the Beast at Bay?, 225–244
Copyright © 2005 by Information Age Publishing

the kind of politicized history that characterizes much of the National Standards." But, Ms. Cheney argued, "the battle is worth taking on. We are a better people than the National Standards indicate, and our children deserve to know it" (Cheney, 1994).

Ms. Cheney was a powerful figure. The agency she had headed had helped pay for the development of the *Standards*. And she had previously praised the project. So, her criticism got attention and was immediately amplified by commentators and news reports. Rush Limbaugh (October 28, 1994) dramatized his reaction a few days later by angrily ripping pages from a history textbook on television while charging that George Washington had been excised by some *secret* group at the University of California at Los Angeles (UCLA). Charles Krauthammer (1994), a leading conservative columnist, wrote a widely distributed piece three weeks later, reiterating Ms. Cheney's tallies of the named and the unnamed. *U.S. News & World Report* columnist John Leo (1994), another political conservative, wrote a widely reprinted column that also was derived from Ms. Cheney's critique. Americans, he thundered, "would be foolish to let it anywhere near their schools."

Over the next two years the mainstream press would chronicle the actual release of the American and world history *Standards* (a few weeks after Ms. Cheney's attack was published), their denunciation in the U.S. Senate by a vote of 99-1, the decision to reexamine the documents and, finally, the revision and re-release of the guides.

The purpose of this article is not to recount the history of the controversy. That ground has been well traveled. Rather, the goal is to analyze the coverage in journalistic terms and to draw some conclusions about what it tells us about how the press covers social studies as well as education issues generally. What does it say about the willingness or capacity of journalists to explain complex issues? What does it say about the status of journalism as a craft? And, finally, what can educators learn about how to deal with the media if they are ever involved in such a controversy?

BIG NEWS

Those involved in the writing of the *Standards* seemed caught off guard by the media's interest in what was essentially a guide for teachers. But to journalists the story had elements that made it irresistible: conflict, inflated rhetoric, powerful segments of society battling one another over the portrayal of national heroes and cultural icons. The culture wars had flared up after years of smoldering and this time the scene of the battle was the nation's classrooms and their role in transmitting the national culture from one generation to the next. That university intellectuals were being framed as culprits only added to the interest. Though journalists are increasingly likely to be well-educated graduates of top universities, most still cling to the notion that they are society's levelers, tasked both with elevating heroes and with laying elites low. The bottom line, at least as it was being framed by the critics of the *Standards*, was that American educators were taking it upon themselves to rewrite the American story with a different cast acting out a less triumphal narrative. So, reporters and editorial writers set to work.

The media's role in creating and sustaining this controversy has been critically reviewed elsewhere in this volume and in a number of articles and books, including at least two written by scholars from the University of California at Los Angeles who led the standards-writing project (Symcox, 2002; Nash, G.B., Crabtree, C. & Dunn, R., 1997). The attention is appropriate for there is much for the media to learn from such analyses. Indeed, looking back at a broad sample of the coverage from 10 years earlier, much of it seems superficial and lazy. Reporters focused almost exclusively on the controversy and did little independent evaluation of the critics' claims. It is obvious from the stories that many of the journalists (not to mention the high-profile critics) failed to even read the *Standards* document. As a result, readers of most newspapers would know more about what was allegedly left out, according to the critics, than they would about the vision for the kind of pedagogy and depth of student learning that the *Standards* embraced. In fact, in general, editorial writers and columnists were far more aggressive in their reporting on the content of the *Standards*, holding the critics to account for their errors and deliberate misstatements, than were the supposedly objective news reporters.

This is not to say that the *Standards* were perfect. They were not. A subsequent analysis of the *Standards* by a group convened by the Council for Basic Education (Council for Basic Education, 1996) identified politically biased language and perhaps more attention to gender, race and power issues than some might think necessary. The authors of the *Standards* also opened themselves for misinterpretation by leaving implicit much of the traditional material in the teaching examples while making explicit the personages who were added. In addition, some of the examples used "loaded, biased language" that reflected a critical, rather than open-ended, view of American history (Bain, 1996). As critics noted, one example of how students could satisfy the standard that called on them to understand the rise of big business suggested that they "Conduct a trial of John D. Rockefeller" on the charge that he "knowingly and willfully participated in unethical and amoral business practices" (UCLA, 1994, p. 139). But, though that example might have been tendentious, another asked students to "examine such companies as General Electric, the Endicott-Johnson Shoe Company, or International Business Machines to explain how new inventions, technological advances, and improvements in scientific management revolutionized productivity and the nature of work in the twenties" (UCLA, 1994, p. 181.). But few if any reporters examined the mix.

In fact, even though events gave journalists numerous chances to return to the story, few ever went beyond the charges and counter charges of the critics and the defenders of the *Standards* to look at them independently.

At their best, journalists seek to discover truth by systematically gathering data and evidence and authoritatively weighing its meaning. But what are we to make of the fact that these failures on the part of reporters were so widespread? Is it possible that so many journalists were simply lazy? Were they afraid to challenge the assertions of a powerful conservative figure, for fear of being labeled liberal? Or is it true, as many educators contend, that even though individual reporters describe themselves as liberals that the institutions they work for are inherently conservative?

CONSERVATIVE BIAS?

Many educators who criticize the way journalists covered the *Standards* battle believe that to be the case. They decry a trend toward corporate, rather than independent, ownership of media outlets. Books have been written arguing both positions—that the media is too conservative and thus unwilling to question the nation's apparent political shift to the right or too liberal and therefore reluctant to embrace big business and the war in Iraq (See Coulter, 2002; Alterman, 2003).

Such efforts to label journalists liberal or conservative go back decades, to the Civil Rights movement if not before. But for all the evidence of systematic bias assembled by each side in this debate, what the arguments usually come down to is different views of the role of the media in a free society. To conservatives, the media's role is to push forward their agenda of small government, unregulated markets and individual, not group, rights. To liberals, and to many journalists, the role of the media is to stick up for the underdog and to work to improve society. Often, this involves an important role for the government in protecting the weak from the strong and in leveling the playing field to provide equal opportunities.

But, more concretely, what both conservatives and liberals really seem to want is for the media to give greater weight and prominence to their views. They want to read and hear and see criticism of views they disagree with and unchallenged representations of the views they embrace. This is true of much of the criticism of the media's performance in general; it is also true of analyses of the debate over the coverage of the national history *Standards*. A 1999 content analysis in the journal *Social Education*, for example, tallied the *voices* quoted in a small sampling of articles on the national standards debate and concluded that conservative voices were overrepresented (Avery & Johnson, 1999, pp. 220-224). Nash, as the principal author of the *Standards*, was quoted 31 times in this sample and Ms. Cheney was quoted 23 times; the analysis found 13 indirect quotes from authors of the standards and 13 indirect quotes from critics of the standards. But the authors of the review added up the quotes from other sources they considered conservative and said they were not balanced by quotes from liberal groups. Therefore, the authors concluded that the coverage was biased.

Ironically, that is the approach Ms. Cheney and other critics applied to the examples included in the *Standards*. But objectivity is more than keeping score or giving equal weight to all sides by counting quotes. Objectivity requires that journalists keep an open mind, weigh the evidence and then reach a conclusion based on a thorough evaluation of that evidence. Judged that way, much of the coverage of the *Standards* controversy fell short. It conveyed a superficial balance that did little to inform readers of the important educational, social and historical issues involved. The critics said their piece. Then the authors of the *Standards* were given a chance to respond. The readers were on their own in trying to sort things out, something the coverage left them ill-equipped to do.

THE ATTACK

Most nonsubscribers to the *Wall Street Journal* or those who had not seen Mr. Limbaugh on television first learned of the controversy from an Associated Press story published in newspapers throughout the nation on October 26 or 27 (Cass, 1994). That story coincided with the release of the American history standards but it contained no details about the standards themselves. "A proposed set of national teaching goals is supposed to take history beyond the biographies of great men," the wire service story began. "But critics fear America's great men will be abandoned in a rush to political correctness." The second paragraph quoted Ms. Cheney saying that "people like Daniel Webster and Thomas Edison don't appear at all" because "they are politically incorrect white males" (Cass, 1994).

Unnamed, the creators of the standards responded in the fourth paragraph of the story, claiming their work was being misrepresented. Their intent was not to list names and events but rather to outline "broad historical themes."

The story was balanced according to what has become the unfortunate norm of much contemporary journalism—Ms. Cheney's claims were paired with the responses of the historians and teachers who worked on the *Standards*. But the fulcrum for the story's balance was selected by Ms. Cheney and she had specific, concrete examples that served to tip the story in her favor. She did not just say that McCarthy got more attention than Washington (Cheney, 1994). She said McCarthy was mentioned precisely 19 times, a claim repeated in dozens of articles, including some published a decade later, in the fall of 2004 (Schlafly, 2004). Such details are like jewels to journalists. They offer convenient shorthand for conveying abstractions. Ms. Cheney's numbers and her invocation of famous names, wrapped together by her outrage and her claim of political correctness, created a seemingly unassailable reality, one which the creators were forced by the conventions of journalism to respond to.

The headlines on the initial wire service story about the national history *Standards* favored the point of view of the critics because they had initiated the controversy. "Don't Know Much About History" was the headline on the story in *The Salt Lake Tribune* (1994, p. A14).

"'Politically Incorrect' White Males Ousted from History Guidelines," was the headline in the *Chicago Tribune* (1994, p. 2), the quote marks the only indication that politically incorrect was a characterization, not a fact. The *Seattle Times* headline said the *Standards* were "too trendy," which it attributed to a "critic" (1994, p. A8). The headline in the *Buffalo News* conveyed the idea that both knowing facts as well as their context is impossible. "Critics Fear New Goals Ignore Great Men But Curriculum Creators Say Students Should Study Themes, Not Trivia," the headline said (1994, p. A4).

The *New York Times* published the wire service story but the *Washington Post* and the *Los Angeles Times* both produced staff-written accounts on October 27, the day the American history standards were to be released. Those versions of the story were longer and better written. But the hook was the criticism of the standards. The *Los Angeles Times* story said the release of the standards came "amid complaints from conservatives that political correctness prompted the slighting of such familiar historical figures as Ulysses S. Grant and the Wright brothers" (Merl, 1994, p. A1). The *Post* story led with UCLA's Nash saying that the standards were meant to "create a second 'American revolution.'" Cleverly, the second sentence said that "Some prominent conservatives are already in open rebellion" (Gugliotta, 1994, p. A03). The next day neither newspaper carried a story about what the standards document actually said.

CONTROVERSY VS. CONTENT

This early coverage shows how thoroughly the critics commandeered the story such that the political story was given greater weight than the educational one. Little mention was made of why the *Standards* were deemed necessary, who wrote them, what teachers thought about them or how classroom lessons would have to change if the *Standards* came to be widely used. The 31 standards for American history were, on the whole, substantive, challenging and open-ended and certainly surpassed the intellectual rigor of the curriculum of most of the history classes in schools at the time or even a decade later. What the critics objected to were the supporting examples, which were meant to give teachers some practical ideas for how to teach the broad concepts of the *Standards*. Nash has explained many times that the audience for the *Standards* was, principally, teachers (Nash, et al., 1997, p. 177). Sample lessons were included at their suggestion. But in the published version of the *Standards*, the standards and the examples are intertwined so it is completely understandable why critics treated them as all part of a singular whole. If the authors of the document truly wanted them to be viewed separately—and not as part of the main document—they should have published them in an appendix.

But the biggest failure of journalists was their apparent unwillingness to read the *Standards*. Journalists usually have little time to read books about the subjects they are covering. That is why journalists contact academics and ask them for information. But, in this case, the book-length *Standards* and what they said or did not say was the focus of the story. In the earliest days of the controversy it is likely the journalists did not have copies of the books. After all, a number of stories were written before they were released and in 1994 the Internet and email were not as widely used, such that embargoed copies could have been made available electronically. Given that the controversy continued for nearly 2 years, however, it would seem that journalists could find a few hours to read the volumes and consider which side in the debate had a more solid argument. But a search of major national and regional newspapers turned up almost no stories which included evidence that the reporter had done so. Ms. Cheney's basic assertions went unquestioned. This work would not have involved great intrigue or even much enterprise. It would only have required reporters to read the *Standards* and think about the claim that students taught in accordance with them would not only know less history, they would be more inclined to be critical of the United States.

Had they done so, journalists would have learned that, despite what Ms. Cheney and Mr. Limbaugh said about Washington's disappearance from history, the first president was prominent throughout. Nash acknowledged that Ms. Cheney's numbers were accurate. But that is not really the issue. It would be impossible to talk about the nation's origin without mentioning the Founding Fathers, including Washington. But the standards went much further, asking fifth and sixth graders to "identify and compare the leadership roles of at least two major political and diplomatic figures such as George Washington, Benjamin Franklin, Thomas

Jefferson, John Adams, Samuel Adams, John Hancock, and Richard Henry Lee" (UCLA, 1994, p. 76).

Nash (1997) noted that the *Standards* "tout the age of Washington 'as the culmination of the most creative era of constitutionalism in American history,' 'the embryo of the American two-party system,' 'the beginnings of a national economy,' and an 'exuberant push westward.' Washington, Nash notes, "was intimately involved in every one of the above-mentioned developments."

Moreover, much more material on the "father of our country" was included in the standards for kindergarten through grade four: "The two books taken together encouraged students to study his life, military leadership, and presidency through stories, biographies, documents, national symbols and library research." But, Nash noted, "it was difficult to explain all this in a few seconds of broadcast time."

As to the frequency with which McCarthy or McCarthyism appeared, that was a canard. The assertion that this unfortunate period of the nation's history was emphasized beyond its importance was one of the critics' most common complaints. But looking at the document itself one gets a different picture. All of the 19 appearances of the two nouns came on only two pages of the 271 page *Standards'* document. And 17 of the citations are in the sample lessons, which are divided by grade level. This fact, however, was not reported until a year after Ms. Cheney launched her crusade and only then in *Education Week* (1995), a publication primarily for educators.

SOME POSITIVE EXAMPLES

There were a few notable exceptions to this doleful recounting of journalistic performance. The first substantive story appeared in mid-November in the *New York Times* (Thomas, 1994) in connection with the release of the world history standards. The lead of the front page story by Jo Thomas announced the release of the standards and said they "keep William the Conqueror and the Battle of Hastings" but "also give emphasis to non-European hallmarks like China's Sung dynasty, which developed paper currency, gunpowder and woodblock book printing from the tenth to the thirteenth century."

"Two years in the making," Thomas wrote, the standards "ask teachers to broaden their scope beyond Europe and ask students to go beyond rote memorizing and explain, analyze and explore historical movements around the world." The article gives a nod to the brewing controversy in the fifth paragraph but only as part of the context for how the *Standards*, and their focus, might be received. The author of the article notes that those most vocal in criticizing the standards to that point had not even read them.

The article reports that the standards give teachers suggestions for how to achieve the ambitious educational aim of the documents. And it concludes by providing a gentle warning that the standards may be too ambitious for the average classroom. "It's an impossibly ambitious and rich curriculum they're putting before high school teachers and students," the article said, quoting an emeritus professor from the University of Chicago (Thomas, 1994).

Another story that tried to explore the educational issues at hand appeared in the *Christian Science Monitor* on November 18th of that year (Henderson, 1994). Although the story began with the controversy, it then addressed how the standards were developed. No secret group, came up with the standards, as Mr. Limbaugh had ominously charged. In fact, the article reported Nash saying that hundreds of teachers and professors discussed and debated the content of the documents for more than two years. The story also was unusual in that it quoted a teacher involved in the process. "Kids can think, they really can," the teacher was quoted saying. "History is very messy, and kids have to get in there and wrestle with the material." As to the controversy, the teacher said that "it's wonderful to see people arguing about what we're teaching kids."

WHAT REPORTERS WANT

Early on in the controversy, Princeton history professor Theodore K. Rabb wrote a lengthy essay for the Sunday edition of the *Washington Post* that drew on interactions he had with reporters who asked him to comment on the world history standards (Rabb, 1994). Rabb served on the National Council for History Standards and was an adviser to the standards-writing process. He said he was confident that the document achieved his goal, which was to "create curricula with a solid Western foundation."

Reporters, however, were not interested in hearing that debate over the past is "the historian's bread and butter." What made the story a story, in their minds, was that a new front had been established in the culture wars. If historians routinely argued and debated the substance and meaning of history it would not have been newsworthy. Reporters were more interested in the right vs. left faceoff than they were in issues of education, Rabb said.

"If, as news organizations seem to believe, the main story worth reporting about the standards is the argument over their content, then the nation will miss the main point: Do we really care whether schools teach much history, and whether they do it well?"

He noted that three states had at the time no history requirement for high school graduation and that 25 others required students to take only one course but no reporters asked him about that. Rabb wrote that the standards alone would not improve history teaching. Also needed would be more training for teachers and better, more interesting, materials. "This, of course, is not the kind of issue that attracts the nation's battle-happy reporters," he wrote. "If it did, though, we might actually get some-where."

Robert Bain, a high school teacher at the time who was asked to be part of the Council for Basic Education panel that critiqued the standards, made a similar point. "The sound and fury obscured the pedagogical dis-course," he wrote. "When the political debate fades and pundits lose interest, the real educational questions will remain. What is good history teaching? How should students study history? How do they learn history? What activities best capture the discipline of history?"

But the focus on the controversy and the content made it "improbable, if not impossible" for such questions to be discussed (Bain, 1996).

EDITORIAL WRITERS CHALLENGE CHENEY

In early 1995, the historian Jon Wiener wrote an essay about the contro-versy that appeared in the New Republic and in several newspapers, including the *Rocky Mountain News* in Denver and the *San Francisco Exam-iner* (Wiener, 1995). Wiener wrote that "even a cursory look at the stan-dards suggests that the assault by Cheney and her allies was flawed."

It was appropriate that Wiener's piece appeared on the op-ed page, where this controversy began. In fact, editorial pages in general did a bet-ter job of clarifying the issues raised by the attack on the standards and, perhaps more surprising, editorial writers did a better job of reporting on the content of the standards.

In their retrospective, Nash and his co-authors quote editorials in a number of papers that disputed the critiques of conservatives. "We are happy to report that this new inclusiveness... entails no new, politically correct exclusions," the *Los Angeles Times* opined (cited in Nash, et al., 1997, p. 194).

The *Minneapolis Star Tribune* wrote that Ms. Cheney, Limbaugh and others "should be embarrassed" (cited in Nash et al., 1997, p. 195). "With a nit-picking focus on whiffs of political correctness, critics like Cheney have missed the new standards' huge contribution—a whole new peda-gogy, far more rigorous, challenging and involving than the dates and names approach of past classroom practice," the editorial said. The *Seattle Post-Intelligencer* called the claims of those who attacked the world history standards "xenophobic trash" (cited in Nash, et al., 1997, p. 195). The authors also quote a *New York Times* editorial that boldly stated that "Ms. Cheney skips over" the rich materials of the sample assignments and "ridicules through misrepresentation" (Nash, et al., 1997, p. 196).

Such endorsements were not just heard on the coasts. In Nebraska, the *Lincoln Star* said the standards were intellectually demanding and "expect senior high students to begin exploring the shades of truth, to look at how the values of a bygone era affect behavior of that time, to learn the difference between facts and interpretations of those facts" (Nash et al., 1997, p. 195).

Even Debra J. Saunders, a politically conservative columnist at the *San Francisco Chronicle* syndicated nationally who often defends traditional approaches to education, praised the standards for their rigor and their demand that students think about history. (Saunders, D., 1994) Her column demonstrated she had read and analyzed the standards and even that she knew something about history. "What I have seen from reading the standards for three periods in world history—1000 B.C. to 300 A.D., 1750 to 1914 and the 20th century—is a body of work that explores history from various perspectives without robbing events of personality," she wrote in a November 16, 1994 column. Though she was writing specifically about the world history *Standards*, she was endorsing the approach of the entire effort. "The standards do a laudable job of blending two philosophies of history—one that applauds great men and women for changing the tide, and the other that sees events as the result, not of personality, but inexorable social forces. By addressing the lives of the great and the small, the standards paint a complete picture—of cause and result—and make for good story telling."

Later, when revised standards were released, Saunders also stepped up to praise them, judging them on their educational, rather than political, merit and bolstering her argument with specific details from the *Standards* (Saunders, 1995).

To be sure, there were many exceptions to this relative clarity on the editorial pages. Instead of emulating the effort of the newspaper in Lincoln, the paper in Omaha, Nebraska essentially parroted the complaints of Ms. Cheney, using the same examples. Unfortunately, reporters were more likely to produce stories that did the same thing.

In March of 1995, for example, six months after the controversy surfaced, the *Rocky Mountain News* of Denver carried a 400-word article reporting on a speech by Ms. Cheney given the previous month. "When Lynne Cheney visited Denver last month, she questioned the image of the United States presented in proposed national history standards," the story began. It went on to say that Ms. Cheney charged that those who learned history according to the *Standards* "would not know George Washington was the first president," a charge that was not only false, it could have easily been proven false (Morson, 1995). The standards, according to the story, had set off a national debate over "whether the role of white men is minimized in American history and whether the United States is compared unfavorably with other nations, as charged by Cheney." Even a casual reading of the volume would have shown that white males are represented on virtually every page.

An article published in March of 1995 on the front page of the *Times-Picayune* in New Orleans demonstrated in a particularly stark way this unwillingness to write anything that might appear to be taking a stance on such easily proved issues (Coyle, 1995, March 13). The 1,500-word article was a roundup of the events of the previous months. The article seems balanced and, if anything, more sympathetic to the standards than to the claims of the critics. But it led off with the critique by Ms. Cheney and her camp and followed that with a statement in defense of the *Standards*. The rest of the story was in the form of a debate in which both sides stated their opinions about the *Standards* without quoting the standards at all. In other words, a story published 5 months after Ms. Cheney's column followed the format of the Associated Press story that appeared on October 26th, before the *Standards* were released. It would be easy to dismiss this as simply a particularly egregious example of laziness. But the newspaper also published a sidebar that listed actual standards from the document, which belied some of the claims made by the critics in the story itself

FALSE OBJECTIVITY

In an essay on his journalism weblog, former *New York Times* reporter Doug McGill (2004) addressed this apparent paradox—of editorial writers doing more in-depth reporting than the news reporters themselves. He asserts that journalistic objectivity, a noble tradition and worthy goal, has broken down into a he-said, she-said "pseudo-objectivity" that lets reporters avoid figuring out where the weight to the evidence lies. But editorial writers do not have the luxury of remaining an agnostic or simply taking someone else at their word. They have to figure things out for themselves.

"Are we served as citizens of a democracy when reporters feel their job is done, merely to report 'both sides' of a given public issue?" McGill asks. "What if the reporter, himself or herself, was deeply convinced—or would be deeply convinced if he or she took the time to look into the issue more closely—that one side in the argument was right? That is, that one or the other side had the actual facts of the matter on their side? Would it be the reporter's obligation then, to point this out?"

This false objectivity is most stark in coverage of presidential campaigns, in which the comments of one candidate are offset by the reaction of the other. But many journalists, regardless of the topic they cover, have fallen victim to the he said-she said formula. This characterizes much of education coverage. The "whole language" crowd makes a claim about its philosophy with the phonics supporters asked to respond. Few reporters ever make an effort to learn enough about beginning literacy to identify what research has discovered about how children learn to read. The "math wars" are covered in similar fashion. The math reform camp calls for more hands-on explorations, more emphasis on understanding, and less memorization of math facts and standard algorithms. Backers of more traditional lessons, meanwhile, paint the proposed reforms as lacking rigor or substance. Few reporters learn enough about what is known—and not known—about effective math instruction, about the importance of teachers knowing math and being able to communicate it well, about the value of knowing math facts as well as how to apply them. And so rather than reporting authoritatively about the issues involved in improving students' academic achievement, journalists assemble the back and forth with little explanation. As a result, their stories leave readers unable to understand the curricular and pedagogical issues affecting their children and schools. The same was true of the coverage of the history *Standards*.

SHORTCOMINGS AND EXCEPTIONS

The coverage of the standards was deficient in other ways.

For example, few reporters ventured into classrooms, which might have made it possible for them to explain how the updated pedagogy envisioned by the standards looked in practice. By watching teachers in action, reporters could have contrasted a typical lesson of the day with the more ambitious lessons laid out in the standards.

One story that was based in a classroom and showed how much could be learned there appeared in late November of 1994 in the *Orange County Register*, the newspaper serving the affluent, fast-growing county south of Los Angeles. Betsy Bates, the reporter, spent time in an award-winning high school history class and reported that, indeed, hagiographies of traditional heroes were less central than they'd been in the past. Instead, students were being encouraged to think more deeply about the meaning of past events (Bates, 1994).

To prepare to write essays about the causes of the civil war, students in the classroom had "read documents such as the Fugitive Slave Law of 1850 and the Ostend Manifesto, studied the pre-Civil War economics of the North and the South and pondered Abraham Lincoln's ambiguous words about slavery in his debates with Stephen Douglas." Had the students been asked about the causes of the Civil War, they would "all give you different answers based on states' rights, 250 years of Southern culture, tariffs and economic systems and … slavery," the teacher said. "I don't want them to stop at the facts. I want them to ask good questions and to really think about both sides of the issues." Such a story gave readers a glimpse of the new approach to history teaching, helping them better understand what was being proposed.

In April of 1995, as the *Standards* were being revised, Jo Thomas, the *New York Times* reporter who wrote the initial in-depth story the previous November, visited history classrooms in six high schools in New York and environs. The resulting story showed that some of the methods and content debated in the abstract on the editorial pages were already a reality. The story noted that this less didactic, more discussion-oriented mode of teaching was not always successful. Teachers' ambitious plans for debates sometimes ran up against the fact that students knew little about historical reality, had weak vocabularies and poor reading skills. But the story also noted that these methods have "long been used by some of the best teachers to challenge students." The story implied, though it did not say so explicitly, that less than stellar teachers, or those whose own knowledge of history was limited, would find the new approaches to teaching to be more challenging for them as well as for their students (Thomas, 1994).

But such stories from classrooms were almost entirely missing. This is a shortcoming of much of the coverage of education. Reporters tend to be wary of classroom visits. Going into classrooms takes a lot of time, both to set up and then to carry out. Increasingly, principals and superintendents try to shut out reporters. It is difficult to know if one classroom or even a dozen are representative. Reporters always worry that they are being sent to the classrooms of only the very best teachers, not those who are just average or worse. In the absence of such visits, reporters quote academics and policymakers, who often disagree with one another. The silly facts vs. understanding debates that have wracked not only history teaching but math and science look different amid the hustle-bustle of classrooms, where theory must bow to brutal pragmatism. Journalists who write about education can help remind the educational theoreticians as well as the political demagogues of that simple truth, by visiting classrooms and simply recording the interactions they see.

Journalists also did a poor job of comparing the proposed national standards to what already existed in their states. The newspaper in Riverside, California did just that, which produced a helpful guide to both documents. (Chiang, 1996)

In addition to allowing the coverage to be framed by the critics, failing to report on the content of the standards themselves, slighting the educational issues involved and not spending enough time in classrooms, reporters also did a poor job of putting the standards into a historical context. Debates over what should be included in history classes had wracked American education throughout the twentieth century. Jonathan Zimmerman (2002) documents in his book, *Whose America? Culture Wars in the Public Schools*, that battles over the content of textbooks had been fought over how the British were portrayed in recounting the Revolutionary War, the New Deal, the Cold War and the treatment of the role of African Americans in U.S. history (Zimmerman, pp. 55-134). In 1952, the conservative William F. Buckley wanted to eliminate what he called "collectivism" in textbooks. Others wanted textbooks to eschew support for the United Nations and for integration. Throughout the 1950s, newspapers including the *Chicago Tribune* and the *Indianapolis Star*, both owned by political conservatives, ran series attacking so-called "subversive" textbooks and sparked campaigns to withdraw them from classroom shelves (Zimmerman, pp 81-106).

But Zimmerman concludes that, for the most part, the "history wars are vastly exaggerated."

"In the rarefied atmosphere of universities and think tanks, admittedly, theorists joust angrily over the proper balance of unity and diversity in the public school curriculum. Out in the schools themselves, however, this battle was settled long ago. Throughout the twentieth century, campaigns to diversify history instruction almost always served to enhance, not to erode, its "patriotic" quality" (Zimmerman, p. 7).

Reporters also seemed to ignore another long-running educational debate—that between social studies and history. Indeed, some in the social studies camp criticized the history standards not for being too politically correct but rather for being too traditional and excessively oriented toward the past (Evans, R. W., & Pang, V. O., 1995). No reporters took note of the fact that social studies teachers often think studying history is a waste of time for most students. Nor did they report that the writing of history standards was aimed, in large measure, at restoring history classes to greater prominence.

The national history standards were revised and reissued in the spring of 1996. The teaching examples, which had caused the most controversy, were eliminated. Although not all critics were satisfied, most were. Both Arthur Schlesinger Jr. and Diane Ravitch, who had been among the critics of the original standards, wrote a piece for the *Wall Street Journal* in which they agreed that the revised version was essential to "the education of our children and to the uniting of America" (Schlesinger & Ravitch, 1996).

Tens of thousands of copies of the revised version were distributed, in addition to the 40,000 copies of the original that had gone out. Professional organizations of educators embraced the revised standards and, according to various accounts, the standards influenced the writing of state level standards.

With the controversy over the national history *Standards* settled, more or less, reporters moved on. But journalists had learned a lesson. Covering the writing of academic standards could lead to controversy and to front page stories. After all, a lot was at stake. And the process of deciding what students should know and be able to do was destined to be messy.

OTHER CONTROVERSIES

Journalists have wrestled with similar debates over social studies or history standards in Georgia, Massachusetts, Mississippi, Virginia and other states in recent years, with greater or lesser sophistication. In 2003, for example, a reprise of the debate over the national history standards arose in the state of Minnesota. A group of University of Minnesota professors had put together a standards document that expressed broad themes but gave classroom teachers leeway to determine what specifics students should know. Some legislators criticized the document, alleging that it had "not been looked at by the public" (Draper, 2004). They offered up an alternative, and the *Star Tribune* reported that the major difference between the two proposals was "in the number of people, places and events kids are required to know." The alternative version "stirred up controversy over what critics contend is its Republican-white-male bias and Trivial Pursuit-like emphasis on meaningless facts." No examples of either of the sets of standards were included in the article so that readers might better understand the dispute.

In 1998, California adopted a set of history standards that built on the 1980s curriculum guide that, in turn, had influenced the creation of the national history standards. The article on the new set of standards that appeared in the *Los Angeles Times* stands out because although it gives a passing nod to the national contretemps, its main theme was educational. In a rare bit of context, the article notes that "breadth vs. depth" is a perennial academic debate. The article also observes that "whether teachers will fit the new material into their lessons remains to be seen. Though they provide a road map for state policy, the standards are voluntary" (Anderson, 1998).

With no sign that the standards and accountability movement is going away, journalists will probably continue to pay attention to standards and to the tests and test scores connected to them. Meanwhile, the nation's student population will continue to grow more diverse through immigration and differential birth rates. And the center of the nation's political discourse is to the right of where it was in 1994—all of which means that the discussion over what this nation wants its children to know about its history is not yet ended. So, journalists will continue to face the challenge of communicating the substance and direction of that conversation.

EDUCATORS' RESPONSIBILITY

Social studies educators, therefore, should take seriously their interactions with journalists and, as with journalists, seek to learn lessons from their past mistakes.

One lesson, certainly, is that educators who are in a position to influence the public debate about issues of concern to them should get out in front and not wait for controversy to show up on their doorstep—or in their electronic mailboxes. Those involved in the writing of the national history standards, or any other standards documents, for that matter, should keep key reporters briefed on their progress and on issues, as they arise. This process of deciding what students should know should be illuminated by the light of public discourse along the way, not just after the standards are released.

It is clear from the coverage of the controversy involving the national standards that it is crucial that educators provide the frame for the story they want to tell. They cannot expect journalists to see the story they want them to see. They cannot assume that journalists understand the education issues involved. Ms. Cheney provided a story and then stuck by it and that was the story the journalists told. Educators should tell the education story—not the political or ideological story—that they want told if, indeed, their goal in these controversies is educational.

Another lesson is that educators should remember something that their day to day experience has already taught them well: they are not the sole arbiters of what students should know. They bring their expertise and experience to the table but the will of the community is more than an irritant and must be engaged as decisions about what is to be taught are made.

A few weeks before the reelection of George W. Bush in the fall of 2004, the *Los Angeles Times* reported that the U.S. Department of Education had destroyed 300,000 copies of a parent's guide to history teaching that suggested consulting the reissued national history standards (Merl, J., &

Alonso-Zaldivar, R, 2004). The newspaper's sources said the publication was shredded after receiving an inquiry from Ms. Cheney's office. A new version of the publication was issued with all references to the standards removed. A few weeks later, the ultraconservative commentator Phyllis Schlafly posted on her website an attack on the history standards that praised the shredding of the parent guides and echoed Ms. Cheney's essay from a decade earlier (Schlafly, 2004). Ms. Schlafly once again trotted out the charge that Senator Joseph McCarthy had been mentioned 19 times. But Ms. Schlafly a decade later labeled McCarthy an "anti-Communist" and seemed angry that the mentions of the senator were "unfavorable" rather than favorable. She repeated the charge that the national history standards made the 1848 feminist declaration at Seneca Falls, New York as prominent as the U.S. Constitution, a false statement.

All of the statements Ms. Schlafly made had appeared in newspaper stories a decade earlier and were never prominently rebutted by journalists.

The day Bush was reelected, the conservative former congressman Newt Gingrich wrote a column in *USA Today* that called on the schools to teach history and eschew politically correct multiculturalism (Gingrich, 2004). It was the huge congressional victories won by Gingrich's forces in the fall of 1994 that helped fuel the attack on the national history standards. After the election, Dick Cheney asserted that the Bush Administration had won a broad mandate for its agenda, so history lessons will continue to make it onto the front page. Journalists need to learn from their own history in order to do a better job of covering the issue each time it arises.

Educators can help them do that—by inviting them in to classrooms to see lessons in action, by always arguing that facts and dates are as important as understanding of the meaning of those facts, by upholding heroes but also making those heroes human and by making the case as aggressively as possible that a strong democracy is able to withstand scrutiny. Journalists are motivated, more than anything else, by good compelling stories. And educators should not take a back seat to ideologues in helping them find and tell such stories.

REFERENCES

Alonso-Zaldivar, R., & Merl, J. (2004, October 8). Booklet that upset Mrs. Cheney is history. *Los Angeles Times.* Retrieved October 11. 2004, from newspaper's Website.

Alterman, E. (2003). *What liberal media: The truth about bias and the news.* New York: Basic Books.

Anderson, N. (1998, November 25). History's lessons: For standards panel, name of the game was deciding who and what students need to know. *Los Angeles Times*, p. B2

Avery, P., & Johnson, T. (1999, May/June). How newspapers framed the U.S. history standards debate. *Social Education. 63*(4), 220-224).

Bain, R. (1996). *Beyond the standards wars: Politics and pedagogy in the national history standards' controversy.* Retrieved December 7, 2004, from http://w3.iac.net/~pfilio/bain.htm

Bates, B. (1994, November 27). Disputed approach to history finds home in O.C. class. *The Orange County Register.*

Cass, C. (1994, October 26) New York: The Associated Press. Electronic version retrieved from Lexis/Nexis academic database September 25, 2004.

Cass, C. (1994, October 26). "Politically incorrect" white males ousted from history guidelines. *Chicago Tribune*, p. 2.

Cass, C. (1994, October 27). Don't know much about history. *Salt Lake Tribune*, p. A14.

Cass, C. (1994, October 27). History-teaching standards are too trendy, critic says. *Seattle Times*, p. A8.

Cass, C. (1994, October 27). Critics fear new goals ignore great men but curriculum creators say students should study themes, not trivia. *Buffalo News*, p. A4.

Cheney, L. V. (1994, October 20). The end of history. *Wall Street Journal*, p. A26.

Chiang, S. (1996, April 14). History lesson: U.S. follows state's lead in classroom. *The Press-Enterprise*, p. A03

Coulter, A. (2002). *Slander: Liberal lies about the American right.* New York: Crown.

Council for Basic Education. (1996). *History in the making: An independent review of the voluntary national history standards.* Washington, DC: Council for Basic Education.

Coyle, P. (1995, March 13). History project debated: Proposed national history standards come under fire. *Times-Picayune*, p. A1.

Diegmueller, K., & Viadero, D. (1995, November 15). Myths and realities. *Education Week.* Retrieved December 7, 2004, from www.edweek.org

Draper, N. (2004). Senate approves history standards. *Minneapolis Star-Tribune*, p. 1B.

Evans, R. W., & Pang, V. O. (1995). National standards for United States history: The story of controversy continues. *The Social Studies, 86*, (6), 270.

Gingrich, N. (2004, November 3) Real change is best medicine. *USA Today*, p. A25.

Gugliotta, G. (1994, October 28). Up in arms about the "American experience": History curriculum guidelines play down traditional heroes and focus on negatives, critics say. *Washington Post*, p. A03.

Henderson, K. (1994, November 18). The making of history standards. *The Christian Science Monitor,* p. 15.

Krauthammer, C. (1994, November 4). History hijacked. *Washington Post*, p. A25.

Leo, J. (1994, November 8). The pc crowd is trying to hijack American history. *The Times-Picayune*, p. B7.

Limbaugh, R. (1997). Transcript of television program broadcast October 28, 1994. In G. B. Nash, C. Crabtree, & R. E. Dunn (Eds.), *History on trial: Culture wars and the teaching of the past* (p. 5). New York: Alfred A. Knopf.

McGill, D. (2004, October 24). The fading mystique of an objective press. *The McGill Report*. Retrieved from http://www.mcgillreport.org/objectivity.htm

Merl, J. (1994, October 27). Debate greets standards for history classes. *Los Angeles Times*, p. A1.

Nash, G. B. (1997, July/August). The national history standards and George Washington. *The Social Studies, 88*(4), 159-162.

Nash, G. B. (1997, July/August). The national history standards and George Washington. *The Social Studies, 88*(4), 159-162.

Nash, G. B., Crabtree, C., & Dunn, R. E. (1997). *History on trial: Culture wars and the teaching of the past.* New York: Alfred A. Knopf.

National standards for United States history: *Exploring the American experience.* (1994). Los Angeles: Regents, University of California, Los Angeles.

Morson, B. (1995, March 5). History standards: The debate goes on. Critics contend effort to adopt U.S. guidelines snubs role of white men. *Rocky Mountain News*, p. 26a

Rabb, T. K. (1994, December 11). Whose history? Where critics of the new standards flunk out. *Washington Post*, p. C5.

Saunders, D. J. (1994, November 16). History rewrites itself. *San Francisco Chronicle*, p. A10.

Saunders, D. J. (1996, April 8). New curriculum actually challenges students. *Atlanta Journal Constitution*, p. A08.

Schlafly, P. (2004). *Trying to teach kids history.* Retrieved December 7, 2004, from http://www.eagleforum.org/column/2004/nov04/04-11-03.html

Schlesinger, A., Jr., & Ravitch, D. (1996, April 3). The new, improved history standards. *The Wall Street Journal*, p. A14.

Symcox, L. (2002). *Whose history? The struggle for national standards in American classrooms.* New York: Teachers College Press.

Thomas, J. (1994, April 5). History on the march: New standards, attacked on the right, stress the neglected. *New York Times*, p. B1.

Thomas, J. (1994, November 11). A new guideline on history looks beyond old Europe. *New York Times*, p. A1.

Wiener, J. (1995, January 11). Who decides what will be history? *Rocky Mountain News*, p. 38A.

Zimmerman, J. (2002). *Whose America?: Culture wars in the public schools, 7*, 55-134. Cambridge: Harvard University Press.

CHAPTER 20

DOWN FROM THE TOWER AND INTO THE FRAY

Adventures in Writing for the Popular Press

E. Wayne Ross

"I read the news today oh boy ..."
—Lennon & McCartney

Over lunch my colleague Larry told me, "If the *Times* is going to run your letter, they'll call you first."

"Well, I doubt they will, but at least I feel better for having written it."

When I returned to my office the little red message light on my phone was blinking. Indeed, *The New York Times* had called to confirm that I wrote the letter and on the following Sunday it ran:

Old Medicine in N.Y.

To the Editor:
The plan of New York State's Education Commissioner, Richard P. Mills, to increase high school graduation requirements seems hard to argue with (news article, Sept. 16). After all, increasing the number of credits for grad-

Social Studies and the Press: Keeping the Beast at Bay?, 245–261
Copyright © 2005 by Information Age Publishing
All rights of reproduction in any form reserved.

uation and requiring more study of math, science and foreign language sends a strong message.

The problem with his approach is that it relies on the logic that merely by ratcheting up graduation requirements, learning will be improved. Requiring more seat time does not necessarily make an educational experience more effective. Mr. Mills ignores symptoms showing the old medicine doesn't always work.

His proposals divert attention from issues like the equitable distribution of state money for public schools.

E. WAYNE ROSS
Binghamton, N.Y., Sept. 17, 1997

I had written scads of letters to politicians (to no avail), but despite a long personal history of whining about newspaper stories and opinion pieces I had never written a letter to the editor. Since then I have logged a long list of letters, opinion pieces, and reviews in newspapers and popular journals—local and national in circulation—from publications like *The New York Times*, *The Chronicle of Higher Education*, *Education Week*, and *Z Magazine*, as well as various Knight-Ridder, Gannett, CanWest, and Hearst newspapers, to the monthly fanzine of underground punk rock and critical politics *MAXIMUMROCKNROLL*.

In this chapter I want to share some of what I have learned about why it is critical that academics, particularly social educators, become more engaged in the popular discourse on education, culture, and politics; provide some examples of how I have stepped into the fray; and offer a bit of advice about what you might expect if you have not yet—but as a result of reading this book—decide to challenge "the beast" on its home turf.

THE CORPORATE PRESS, PUBLIC SCHOOLS, AND DEMOCRACY

The central concern of democratic theories of all types is how people can have the information, knowledge, and forums for communication and debate necessary to govern their own lives effectively. The media and schools (particularly social studies education) are key mediums in the pursuit of a democratic society, and if these systems undermine democracy then it becomes "difficult to conceive of a viable democratic society" (McChesney, 2000, p. 2). So there is reason for the public to be concerned about the state of democracy as they read story-after-story in the press about broken public schools, while prominent papers such as *The New York Times* and *The Washington Post* are writing *mea culpas* for allowing themselves to be too easily misled in their coverage of the case for war in Iraq. Both of these institutions appear to be failing the public. But there are two key issues we must always remember when considering the ideals (and failures) of these pillars of democracy.

The questions to ask about the media and public schools are: (1) In whose interests do they operate? and (2) do these institutions provide and promote *informed* social criticism? Public schools are certainly not above criticism and a democratic free press must be critical in its examination of key social institutions, a practice that should be the responsibility of every member of a democratic society. My concern in this chapter is with the media.

CORPORATIZATION OF THE NEWS

The most fundamental issue, which determines the answer to the first question (and which in my view undermines much of the mainstream media coverage of education), is the corporatization of the news. For-profit corporations own almost all of the media that reach large U.S. audiences. Herein lies a critical distinction between the media and public schools. While both the media and public schools function as critical institutions in the dissemination of knowledge, information, and ideas, the mainstream media will continue to be privately owned and operated, at least in the foreseeable future. As a result, the public will always find it extremely difficult, if not impossible, to influence their editorial policies.

Public schools, on the other hand are public. That is, insofar as they continue to be operated under public control, the public can wield considerably more influence over the policies that impact educational practices within public education than it can ever hope to wield over the corporate media. It is this circumstance, for example, that largely fuels the growing movement to privatize schools. Privatization would effectively transfer the control of schools from public hands to corporate hands.

Legal scholar Joel Balkan (2004) points out—and Noble Prize winning economist Milton Friedman agrees—that corporations are legally mandated to pursue, without exception, their own economic self-interests, regardless of the harmful consequences it might cause to others. The "best interests of the corporation" principle is a fixture in the corporate law of most countries, forbidding any other motivation in corporate decision-making:

> whether to assist workers, improve the environment, or help consumers save money. [Corporate managers] can do these things with their own money, as private citizens. As corporate officials, however, stewards of other people's money, they have no legal authority to pursue such goals as ends in themselves—only as means to serve the corporation's own interests, which generally means to maximize the wealth of its shareholders. *Corporate social*

responsibility is thus illegal—at least when it is genuine. (Balkan, 2004, p. 37, emphasis added)

As a result, one can quite easily argue that corporations are incompatible with democracy, at least participatory democracy, which involves paying attention to the multiple implications of our actions on others—what John Dewey called "an associated way of living." The primary responsibility of democratic citizens is, as Dewey argued, concern with the development of shared interests that lead to sensitivity about repercussions of their actions on others around them (Dewey, 1916).

As Balkan (2004) points out, "only pragmatic concern for its own interests and the laws of the land constrain the corporation's predatory instincts" (p. 60). Routine and regular harms caused to others—unlike Enron-like corporate scandals that are clearly not in shareholders' best interests—are considered an inevitable part of corporate activity and known to economists as "externalities." Milton Friedman describes an externality as "the effect of a transaction...on a third party who has not consented to or played any role in the carrying out of that transaction" (Friedman quoted by Balkan, p. 61). The bad things that result from corporate pursuit of profit—illness, death, poverty, pollution, and textbooks written with profits rather than accuracy in mind—are categorized as externalities, "literally other people's problems" (Balkan, p. 61). Balkan (2004; Achbar, Abbott, & Balkan, 2003) describes corporations as "psychopathic creatures" that "can neither recognize or act upon moral reasons to refrain from harming others" (2004, p. 60). It is clearly impossible for corporate *persons*—as currently defined under law—to be democratic citizens, particularly in the Deweyan vein of an "associated way of living."

A further complication is "the media monopoly"—the concentration of media control in an increasingly smaller number of corporations. In 1983, Bagdikian reported that media ownership was in the hands of 50 transnational corporations. Today, that number is down to nine. Five huge corporations dominate most of the U.S. media (Bagdikian, 2004). And, Canadians have been told that one perspective is enough. CanWest owns 14 large dailies, 120 weeklies, Global TV network (Canada's second largest private broadcaster), plus international holdings in Australia, New Zealand, and Ireland. After acquiring the Southam and Hollinger newspaper chains, CanWest chair Israel Asper told shareholders that "on national and international key issues we should have one, not 14, editorial positions" (Winter, 2002). The chair of CanWest's publication committee, David Asper, invoked rock group R.E.M. in responding to criticism of the dramatic concentration of Canadian media by saying "It's the end of the world as we know it, and I feel fine" (Winter, 2002).

The continued concentration of media ownership reduces the diversity of media voices and increases the power of a few large conglomerates, with holdings in many industries. The existence of monopolistic media conglomerates also increases the conflicts of interest in news coverage, for example, media corporations have significant levels of interlocking directorates, sharing members of their boards of directors with defense, banking, investment, pharmaceutical, and technology companies (FAIR, 2001).

There is a huge economic, social, cultural, political, and educational price to be paid for the devotion to profit, which results from the legal imperative that every corporation serve the bottom line. The relationship between mainstream corporate media and education must be informed by this fact. In addition, we must pay close attention to how corporate interests have infiltrated public schools via the state regulation of knowledge and the accountability driven educational reform movement that is trying to mold learners into "Stepford" employees for global corporations (e.g., Ross, Gabbard, Kesson, Mathison, & Vinson, 2004, in press; see also Saltman & Gabbard, 2003). To do otherwise will distort our efforts to understand how these two institutions affect our potential to achieve a democratic society.

SEPARATING THE INSTITUTION AND THE INDIVIDUALS

When you look at a corporation it's just like when you look at a slave owner, you want to distinguish between the institution and the individual. So, slavery for example, or other forms of tyranny, are inherently monstrous, but the individuals participating in them may be the nicest guys you can imagine—benevolent, friendly, nice to their children, even nice to their slaves, caring about other people. As individuals they may be anything.... In their institutional roles they are monsters because the institution is monstrous. (Noam Chomsky, quoted in Achbar, Abbott, Balkan, 2003)

Can this searing indictment of corporate managers and directors be fairly applied to the corporate press or to those who work on education issues in the interests of the corporate state rather than the public? Certainly it applies in some important circumstances (e.g., Chomsky, 2003; Gabbard, 2003; Herman & Chomsky, 1988). The more important issue is to recognize that there are differences between institutions (media/schools) and individuals (editors, reporters/superintendents, principals, and teachers).

Despite the best efforts of many individual journalists, there is much evidence that education reporting is not as well informed as it should be. Just as the limited curriculum and poor pedagogy that one can easily find in public schools is often not solely the result of individual teachers' lack of knowledge and skill, substandard journalism cannot be blamed on individual editors or reporters alone (at least in most cases). Editors and reporters, like teachers, often become victims of institutional contexts that fail to provide adequate resources or deskill them in various ways. That said, it is still important to examine the roles of individuals within these institutions.

In the film *Anchorman*, Will Ferrell portrays local TV news anchor Ron Burgundy, who Frank Rich (2004) describes as "every newsman who's ever told us 'This is what's happening in your world tonight!' while remaining clueless about anything happening beyond his own teleprompter" (p. 1). While *Anchorman* is a farce, Rich points out that the "Burgundy principle of pandering" is no laughing matter. It was evident in the infamous White House news conference of March 2003, when not a single reporter asked George W. Bush a tough question, even though he conflated 9/11 with the impending war on Iraq eight times. The basic Burgundy principle is "don't do anything that might make you less popular with your customers."

As Rich points out, the principle has two variants, the first is that ideology drives the media. The prototype for ideological pandering is, of course, Rupert Murdoch's media empire, particularly, Fox News Network.[1] However, there are also many examples of ideological pandering to be found in print journalism across North America. The second, perhaps more insidious, version of the Burgundy principle is when the media give the people what they want in an effort to keep circulation, ratings, and, most importantly, profits up by pleasing their customers. Covering what is actually happening in the world, as opposed to giving the people what they want, might entail financial risk.[2]

Berliner and Biddle (1998) describe the deficiencies in press coverage of education issues arguing that there is a journalistic mindset of "if it bleeds, it leads." This results in a persistent negative treatment of public schools by the media. In particular Berliner and Biddle point to three key deficiencies in reporting:

1. simplistic and incomplete view of the education issues;
2. an "appalling" lack of knowledge of statistics and social science research; and
3. ignorance of the role of poverty as the root cause of many of the difficulties in our schools.

Gene Maeroff (1998), former National Education Correspondent for *The New York Times*, agrees that there is "the tendency of education writers to simplify." Simplification can reduce issues to "caricatures." He notes that this is the case in all journalism. Aleta Watson (1998), former president of the National Education Writers Association, confirms that there is truth to the contention that journalists have not done a good job on stories about student achievement. Watson notes, "few reporters are comfortable with statistics." Maeroff adds, "It must be noted that some of those who report on education may not ask the right questions because they do not always know the questions to ask" (p. 6). This is, in part, the result of a revolving door of reporters at the education beat, but one has to wonder whether newspapers would tolerate the same level of ignorance among financial or even sports reporters.

Education reporters themselves agree that their own coverage of the issues leaves a lot to be desired. When asked to rate the quality of their reporting on teaching in their local communities 74% of education journalists said the coverage was only fair to poor. On curriculum issues 54% rated the quality of their coverage similarly. Only one in five education reporters is "very satisfied" with media coverage of public schools (Farkas, 1997).

There is no doubt that journalists, like teachers and other workers, have experienced intensification of their work. Watson describes how the emphasis on speed in daily reporting results in "analysis on the fly." Press journalists frequently complain about the inadequate time and resources for in-depth analysis. Bill Kovach, the curator of the Neiman Foundation for Journalism at Harvard, told the *Washington Post*, "There is a rising level of concern about the degree to which work in the newsroom is pressured and shaped and interfered with by the pressures of the marketplace" (quoted in Wadsworth, 1998). The compounding problem, Watson observes, is the lack of space in newspapers devoted to providing nuanced analysis of education issues, which leads back to oversimplification on complex stories. While editors and reporters may strive to act responsibly, the time pressures of reporting, competition for column-inches of space, and lack of knowledge on complex education issues create circumstances in which the press is susceptible to "journalism by press release."

THE PRESS AND MOVEMENT CONSERVATISM

Waiting in the wings to capitalize on these conditions is an impressive network of over 100 conservative foundations and think tanks with tremendous influence on public policy discourse. David Berliner and Bruce Biddle point out a key problem in media coverage of education when they ask, "Who speaks for education?" Recent research has illustrated how right-wing foundations and think tanks exercise a tremendous influence on the media's coverage of education, thus shaping discourse on educational policy and practice (e.g., Berliner & Biddle, 1995; Bracey, 2001; Vinson & Ross, 2003).

In *Political Agendas for Education*, Joel Spring (2001) describes how conservative think tanks, like the Manhattan Institute and the Heritage Foundation, work to discredit public schools and promote privatization via their policy and research papers. Spring points out how the web of money, op-ed writers, federal political appointments, and the press come together to establish an agenda for education that undermines public interests. Research by Eric Haas (2004) in the *Journal of Critical Educational Policy Studies* supports this conclusion and points out how corporate media:

> consciously manipulate the news by selecting bits of pre-packaged news disseminated by advocacy groups like conservative think tanks that they can use to create news-like populist entertainment. The new media outlets utilize conservative think tanks for their populist entertainment because they provide free, ready-to-use, and engaging material on social and political issues. Whether it is accurate, is less important than whether it is entertaining. (Haas, 2004, online)

Social studies education in particular has been a target of movement conservatism, with the most recent example being the Fordham Foundation's report *Where Did Social Studies Go Wrong?* (Ross, 2000; Ross & Marker, 2005). But the spectacular success of the "high standards, high-stakes testing" approach to educational reform, culminating in the No Child Left Behind Act of 2001 (NCLB) is the premiere example of an aggressive and persistent campaign by corporate interests via The Business Roundtable, think tanks, and supposedly "non-partisan" outfits like Public Agenda, Public Education Network, and others (Emery & Ohanian, 2004).

The strongly bi-partisan NCLB has received little critical scrutiny in the mainstream media that would alert the public to its insidious policy implications. NCLB, the progeny of *A Nation at Risk*, is creating important changes in schools, in part because its advocates have been successful in reconfiguring the discourse of educational reform via the press. NCLB has effectively established the boundaries of what should be the appropriate or legitimate function of schools in our society, at least in terms of how the politicians and the media present education issues. For example, the primary goal of schooling, student learning, has been redefined as "test scores" rather than authentic knowledge, skills, or abilities. As a result, the school curriculum has also been narrowed to focus merely on what is tested. A further implication is that teachers' have been deskilled (e.g., their professional autonomy is eroded) by requirements to teach from scripted lesson plans keyed to test content. The discourse of standards has reshaped the way many people think about students as learners, teachers as professionals, the nature of the curriculum as well as the appropriate indicators of "educational progress."

Turning back to the questions posed at the outset, this brief and necessarily incomplete overview of the corporate media supports the conclusion that at the very least corporate journalism suffers from serious conflicts of interest—the private interests of shareholders versus the interests of the public. While this contradiction does not completely disallow corporate journalism in the public interest, it seriously constrains how public interests are defined, and thus undermines the rhetorical ideal of the fourth estate. More specifically, on issues of education there is evidence that reporting lacks what might be described as informed social criticism and is often reflective of the interests of the few rather than the many.

STEPPING INTO THE FRAY: WHY DO I BOTHER?

Many journalists respond to press coverage of educational (and other issues) by repeating a dictum that goes something like this: "The press might reinforce existing opinions, but that is not the same as molding views in the first place." For example, Maeroff (1998) says that "it is unclear exactly how much the media could sway public opinion in a direction toward which it is not already inclined. People who are leery of the public schools may find credence for their perceptions in the media. The original source of their wariness may have little to do with the media" (p. 5). Deborah Wadsworth (1998) of Public Agenda, puts it this way, education is an issue that most people believe they are qualified to discuss and Public Agenda's research says that parents, in particular, have a "pretty good fix on the strengths and weaknesses of schooling in America" (p. 67).[3]

The existing level of media subordination to corporate interests and state authority (most recently exemplified in the *mea culpas* over pretenses given for the current war in Iraq), combined with a spate of high-profile fabrications by reporters at *The New York Times*, *Boston Globe* and *The New Republic* undermine the trust journalism is built upon.[4] The objections of many journalists notwithstanding, Herman and Chomsky (1988) have meticulously illustrated the ways in which corporate media manufacture public consent. Herman and Chomsky do not offer a conspiracy theory, rather they make a compelling argument that the U.S. media do not function in the manner of the propaganda system of a totalitarian state. Rather, they permit—indeed encourage—spirited debate, criticism, and dissent as long as these remain faithfully within the system of presuppositions and principles that constitute an elite consensus, a system so powerful as to be internalized largely without awareness.

NCLB is a triumphant example of manufacturing consent. NCLB has established the boundaries of educational reform discourse based on a system of presuppositions and principles that in many cases run counter to accepted standards of educational practice, based upon an extensive research literature (e.g., Berliner & Biddle, 1995; Ross, Gabbard, Kesson, Mathison, & Vinson, 2004).

As a social educator, I have always been concerned with social institutions and how they control human conduct, channeling it in one direction as opposed to many other possible directions. The controlling characteristics inherent in governmental and economic structures, social relations, systems of education and mass media, for example, must be targets of sustained, critical analysis as part of our efforts to realize democracy. As a result, I have come to understand writing for the popular press, not as a sideline, but a central part of what it means to be an engaged social educator.

THE MEANING OF TEST SCORES: AN EXAMPLE

The topics, formats, and authorial voice I have adopted in my popular writing have varied greatly. Nearly all of the topics I address are social issues that comfortably fit within the realm of social education, for example, state regulation of knowledge via high-stakes testing, racism/segregation, labor rights, and academic freedom, but I have rarely written about social studies education directly. I have contributed letters to the editor, op-ed articles, and longer articles that have incorporated both policy analysis and reports on events and activism. I nearly always write in my role as an education professor, sometimes offering basic education on particular issues, while at other times I aim to make recent research findings relevant for general readers. I am often engaged in (what I hope is) informed criticism of what passes as conventional wisdom.

For example, in August 2003 newspapers across Kentucky reported that students' scores on the Comprehensive Test of Basic Skills (CTBS) were up slightly, an important story in the context of NCLB. This result was widely touted as a signal that schools across the state were improving. Kentucky's third-, sixth-, and eighth-graders scored at the 63rd, 54th, and 52nd percentiles on the CTBS and every press report included the important, yet subtle, inaccuracy that "the national average on the CTBS is 50." This prompted me to write an op-ed article for one of Kentucky's major newspapers, explaining the differences between norm- and criterion-referenced tests and, most importantly, why norm-referenced tests like the

CTBS were not appropriate measures of schools' improvement (see Ross, 2003, September 2). In addition, I described the deleterious effects of inflated emphasis on any one measure of achievement (particularly standardized tests).

A month later, following the release of Kentucky's Commonwealth Accountability Testing System (CATS) scores, Louisville's *The Courier-Journal* published a report by one of its education writers, which implored parents to focus on their children's CATS scores because "educators say it's the best way to find out how well your child is doing" in school. In response, I wrote a letter to the editor that disputed this claim, invoked the *Standards on Educational and Psychological Testing* regarding fallibility of single test scores, briefly outlined the harmful effects of standardized tests as a simple effort that fails to account adequately for the complexities of learning and teaching, which are laced with issues such as inequitable distribution of opportunities to learn, and described alternative models of accountability that are more authentic (Ross, 2003, October 11).

The same week, *The Courier-Journal* published an editorial claiming the CATS results showed no relationship between test scores and poverty:

> a scatter chart showing the distribution of Kentucky elementary schools by poverty and achievement shows no big correlation. We have poor and wealthy schools performing at high levels. We have poor and wealthy schools performing at low levels. There is no concentration of wealth schools among the high performing (KERA—Restoring Hope, 2003, p. A10).

This is an example of truth being trumped by a well-intentioned campaign on the part of a statewide newspaper. The paper's claim, without reference to specific evidence, contradicted the findings of research on the relationship of poverty and student achievement as measured on standardized tests, including recent research on Kentucky schools (Munoz & Dossett, 2001).

The Courier-Journal has devoted a tremendous amount of resources to promoting educational reform in Kentucky, a state that has long been plagued by high illiteracy and dropout rates. The Kentucky Educational Reform Act along with the CATS tests have been consistently promoted by the newspaper as key instruments in the campaign to reform schools. As a result, the editors latched on to increased scores on CATS as "positive proof that great and important things are happening in Kentucky's public schools" (p. A10).

Three days after the editorial, Sandra Mathison and I submitted an op-ed length response to *The Courier-Journal*. Our concern was that the paper's longstanding support for improved schools had crossed the line into uncritical boosterism for policies that, despite broad acceptance, are based on unsound principles and constitute educational malpractice. We presented an analysis of test scores (as published in the paper) and poverty rates of Kentucky schools (from the Kentucky Department of Education) that illustrated extremely high correlations of these two factors[5] and demanded more responsible journalism:

> Your editorial also claims that the gains on CATS, CTBS, etc are "real gains." We don't dispute the numbers per se, only what the numbers truly mean. The questions to be asked are: What accounts for the distinctive performance of the three high-poverty schools in the top ten? Are these scores accurate reflections of authentic increased achievement? Or, are these scores an artifice of instruction narrowly aimed at improving CATS scores?... we believe the public deserves ... responsible journalism that investigates the meaning of test score increases (or decreases). (Ross & Mathison, 2003).

The Courier-Journal did not publish our analysis nor did they respond or modify their claims about the relationship between poverty and test scores in Kentucky schools.

SO YOU WANT TO BE A PUNDIT?

These examples, drawn from the course of a couple of months, illustrate various forms, voices, successes, and failures one can experience when engaging the press. Stepping into the arena of public debate has sharpened my thinking and writing. Communicating clearly and efficiently, while not highly prized in academic journals, is a necessity in writing for the popular press. The challenge I have found is how to deal fairly with hugely complex issues, while avoiding clichés and academic jargon, and consistently raising questions about the controlling characteristics of our social institutions—a guiding idea in my work as a social educator. And, like my experiences in the academic world, I have learned more lessons of patience and persistence.

As with all kinds of publishing, there are some particularities that will enhance your chances of getting your point of view into the opinion pages:

- Track the news and look for opportunities. Newspaper op-eds and other kinds of commentary articles for the popular press must be timely; editors are looking for perspectives on the news of the day. Some circumstances though are predictable: For example, you can be prepared in advance for issues that arise at the start of the school year or during testing season.

- Focus on a single point and do it well. This is perhaps the most important guideline in writing for the opinion pages. Many of my colleagues have commented on my op-eds by pointing out issues that I did not mention. Covering multiple topics is a luxury not allowed in the op-ed format.

- Stake out a clear position. Some editors are quite interested in views that challenge the newspaper's editorial stance or that of its columnists—they are often looking for different voices. Do not equivocate.

- Look for the local angle on a wider topic. Local newspaper editors prefer to hear from people in their own community and are interested in how issues of national or international import play out for their readers.

- Shorter is always better. Editors are usually looking for op-ed articles that are 700-750 words (and letters that are under 200 words); remember it takes longer to write a shorter article.

- Write a lead that hooks the readers and close by summarizing your point. It is important to tell readers why they should care about the topic you are writing about. State your point up front then provide the supporting evidence.

- Leave academic discourse behind. Aim for clear, powerful, direct language. Your writing must be accessible to have an impact. Avoid jargon. Use shorter sentences and paragraphs and the active voice.

- Offer specific recommendations. Use concrete examples and do not offer non-substantive conclusions such as "more research is needed."

- Accuracy is key. Tell readers where the information in your article comes from. On occasion I have offered to supply the editor with background information on the topic, such as a list of references keyed to claims made in the article, but this is usually not necessary. Personal experience is a compelling source (try writing in the first person) and often is less tedious than attempting to translate research findings.

- Be cautious when using humor, but do not write with solemnity. Your article does not need to be lighthearted, but avoid sounding grave. I have found sarcasm and irony to be useful tools.

- Exclusivity. Some newspapers and almost all magazines want you to submit your article for exclusive consideration. Newspapers with national circulation (*The New York Times*, *The Washington Post*) often will take only a few days to a week to decide on your article (if you do not hear from them in a specified time, that means "no thanks").

- Build relationships with editors and reporters. It helps to build relationships with editors and reporters by writing to them on particular news articles or editorials, not with the intent of having comments published, but to elaborate or inform them on issues. Once you become a "known quantity" (at least in a positive way) you will likely have greater success getting published.

- Inquire before you write. As a general rule this guideline is more important for magazine writing, but newspaper editors are many times interested in hearing your idea before they receive your manuscript.

My experience in writing for newspapers and popular magazines is about much more than just sharing opinion and moving on to the next issue. My writing has resulted in deeper engagements in a variety of communities. I have had the chance to develop relationships with editors, reporters, folks who think like me and not a few who do not.

The number and kind of responses I get from readers of my newspaper op-eds and articles published in *Z Magazine* has surprised me. Yes, there are often anonymous (and sometimes ominous) letters sent to me or complaints made to the Provost or Dean, but these are the exceptions. I have been pleased by my ability to raise the ire of folks at the Business Council of New York or Rod Paige (2003), who have responded to my work in quite critical ways. A friend has told me to be as proud of who my enemies are as I am of my friends.

On the other hand, I have had numerous phone conversations and extended email exchanges with a wide variety of people who are deeply concerned by issues I have written about. Some of these people just want to share their thoughts; others have questions they want to ask. It has been rewarding to work with these folks, who come from all walks of life. Another kind of response has been from reporters, particularly in broadcast media. It is not unusual for me to get calls from radio or television producers who are interested in a topic I have just written about, followed by appearances on various kinds of public issues programs. These experiences have opened up opportunities for me to learn and become more actively involved in various local and national networks of activists for social justice, democracy, and progressive education.

This aspect of my work as a social educator is exhilarating because it often produces immediate and potent responses to—and from—me and most importantly it provides me with a way to embody the principles I have long taught and written about. The traditional classroom-based practices of social educators remain crucial to the struggle for democracy, but some *new medicine* administered via the press can only help the cause.

NOTES

1. See Robert Greenwald's documentary *Outfoxed: Rupert Murdoch's War on Journalism*.

2. In the same article Frank Rich reports that the news-consulting outfit Frank N. Magid Associates released a survey of 6,000 TV viewers to its clients, which reported news coverage of protests against the war in Iraq was the least popular news topic.

3. Wadsworth's (1998) claim regarding parents' funds of knowledge about public schools is disingenuous, especially in light of the prominent role her organization took in advising the corporate leaders of the National Educational Summits on how to make accountability-driven education reform more palatable to the public. In a paper prepared for the 1999 National Education Summit, Public Agenda declared that parents are insignificant players in the educational reform movement and said "most are not especially well-informed or vigilant consumers, even concerning their own child's progress" (Johnson, 1999, p. 5). For more on this issue see Ross (2000, March).

4. Here I am referring to Jayson Blair (*The New York Times*, 2001), Stephen Glass (*The New Republic*, 1998), Patricia Smith (*The Boston Globe*, 1998), and Jay Forman (Slate, 2001) all of whom followed in the footsteps of Janet Cook (*The Washington Post*, 1980) as journalists who fabricated all are parts of their published reports (see Shafer, 2003).

5. Our analysis included every school in Jefferson County Public Schools (Louisville) and all schools *The Courier-Journal* reported as "top 10" and "bottom 10" achievers from across the state. We found very strong correlations between wealth and CATS scores across JCPS schools at all levels: JCPS elementary schools ($r = .72$); JCPS middle schools ($r = .89$); JCPS high schools ($r = .91$). The correlations between wealth and CATS scores for the reported top and bottom ten achieving schools in Kentucky were: Elementary schools ($r = .81$); Middle schools ($r = .71$); High schools ($r = .93$).

REFERENCES

Achbar, M. (Producer & Director), Abbott, J. (Director), Balkan, J. (Writer). (2003). *The corporation* [Motion picture]. New York: Zeitgeist Films

Apatow, J. (Producer), & McKay, A. (Director/Writer). (2004). *Anchorman: The legend of Ron Burgundy*. Glendale, CA: Dreamworks Pictures.

Bagdikian, B. H. (1983). *The media monopoly*. Boston: Beacon.

Bagdikian, B. H. (2004). *The new media monopoly*. Boston: Beacon.

Balkan, J. (2004). *The corporation: The pathological pursuit of profit and power*. Toronto, CA: Viking Canada.

Berliner, D. C., & Biddle, B. J. (1995). *The manufactured crisis*. Reading, MA: Addison-Wesley.

Berliner, D. C., & Biddle, B. J. (1998). The lamentable alliance between the media and school critics. In G. I. Maeroff (Ed.), *Imaging education: The media and schooling in America* (pp. 26-45). New York: Teachers College Press.

Bracey, G. W. (2001). *The war against America's public schools: Privatizing schools, commercializing education*. Boston: Allyn & Bacon.

Chomsky, N. (2003). The function of schools: Subtler and cruder methods of control. In K. J. Saltman & D. A. Gabbard (Eds.), *Education as enforcement* (pp. 25-35). New York: RoutledgeFalmer.

Dewey, J. (1916). *Democracy and education*. New York: Free Press.

Emery, K., & Ohanian, S. (2004). *Why is corporate America bashing our public schools?* Portsmouth, NH: Heinemann.

Fairness and Accuracy in Reporting. (2001). *Interlocking directorates*. Retrieved from http://www.fair.org/media-woes/interlocking-directorates.html

Farkas, S. (1997). *Good news, bad news*. New York: Public Agenda.

Gabbard, D. A. (2003). Education is enforcement. In K. J. Saltman & D. A. Gabbard (Eds.), *Education as enforcement* (pp. 61-78). New York: RoutledgeFalmer.

Greenwald, R. (Producer & Director). *Outfoxed: Rupert Mudoch's war on journalism*. [Motion picture]. New York: Disinformation.

Haas, E. (2004, September). The news media and the Heritage Foundation: Promoting education advocacy at the expense of authority. *Journal of Critical Educational Policy Studies*, 2(2). Retrieved from http://www.jceps.com

Herman, E. S., & Chomsky, N. (1988). *Manufacturing consent: The political economy of the mass media*. New York: Pantheon.

Johnson, J. (1999). *Standards and accountability: Where the public stands*. New York: Public Agenda.

KERA—Restoring hope. (2003, October 10). *The Courier-Journal*, p. A10.

Maeroff, G. I. (Ed.). (1998). It's all in the eye of the beholder. In *Imaging education: The media and schooling in America* (pp. 1-9). New York: Teachers College Press.

McChesney, R. (2000, November). Journalism, democracy, ...and class struggle. *Monthly Review*, 52(6). Retrieved from http://www.monthlyreview.org/1100rwm.htm

Munoz M. A., & Dossett, D. (2001). Equity and excellence: The effect of school and sociodemographic variables on student achievement. *Journal of School Leadership*, 11(2), 120-134.

Paige, R. (2003, March 17). Bush education law will help black students. *Lexington Herald-Leader*, p. A8.

Rich, F. (2004, July 15). Happy talk news covers a war. *New York Times*, section 2, pp. 1, 7.

Ross, E. W. (2000). Diverting democracy: The curriculum standards movement and social studies education. In D. W. Hursh & E. W. Ross (Eds.), *Democratic social education: Social studies for social change* (pp.203-228). New York: RoutlegeFalmer.

Ross, E. W. (2000, March). The spectacle of standards and summits. *Z Magazine*, 12(3), 45-48.

Ross, E. W. (2003, September 2). Don't inflate CTBS's meaning: Scores don't necessarily signal school improvement. *Lexington Herald-Leader*, p. A11.

Ross, E. W. (2003, October 11). Standardized tests "are harmful." *The Courier-Journal*, p. A7.

Ross, E. W., Gabbard, D. A., Kesson, K., Mathison, S., & Vinson, K. D. (Eds.). (2004). *Defending public schools* (Vols. 1-4). Westport, CT: Greenwood.

Ross, E. W., Gabbard, D. A., Kesson, K., Mathison, S., & Vinson, K. D. (in press). *Saving public education—saving democracy. Public Resistance!*

Ross, E. W., & Marker, P. (2005). (If social studies is wrong) I don't want to be right. *Theory and Research in Social Education, 33*(1), 142-151.

Ross, E. W., & Mathison, S. (2004, October 13). Response to *The Courier-Journal*'s "KERA—restoring hope." [Unpublished manuscript]. Louisville, KY: University of Louisville.

Saltman, K. J., & Gabbard, D. A. (2003). *Education as enforcement: The militarization and corporatization of schools*. New York: RoutledgeFalmer.

Shafer, J. (2003, May 8). The Jayson Blair project: How did he bamboozle *The New York Times*? *Slate*. Retrieved from http://slate.msn.com/id/2082741/

Spring, J. S. (2001). *Political agendas for education*. Mahwah, NJ: Erlbaum.

Vinson, K. D., & Ross, E. W. (2003). *Image and education: Teaching in the face of the new disciplinarity*. New York: Peter Lang.

Wadsworth, D. (1998). Do media shape public perceptions of America's schools? In G. I. Maeroff (Ed.), *Imaging education: The media and schooling in America* (pp. 59-68). New York: Teachers College Press.

Watson, A. (1998). The newspaper's responsibility. In G. I. Maeroff (Ed.), *Imaging education: The media and schooling in America* (pp. 13-25). New York: Teachers College Press.

Winter, J. (2002, May/June). Canada's media monopoly: One perspective is enough, says CanWest. *Extra!* Retrieved from http://www.fair.org/extra/0205/canwest.html

ABOUT THE AUTHORS

Michael J. Berson is an associate professor in the Department of Secondary Education at the University of South Florida. He serves as a vice president of the Society for Information Technology & Teacher Education and is a former chair of the College and University Faculty Assembly of the National Council for the Social Studies (NCSS). His research focuses on technology in the social studies and global child advocacy. He can be contacted at berson@tempest.coedu.usf.edu

Ilene R. Berson is an associate professor in the Department of Child and Family Studies at the Louis de la Parte Florida Mental Health Institute of the University of South Florida. She serves as the director of the Consortium on Child Welfare Studies and is the chair of the Florida Professional Society on the Abuse of Children. Her research focuses on the prevention and intervention of child abuse and victimization as well as behavioral health services and supports available to young children. She can be contacted at berson@fmhi.usf.edu

Howard Budin directs the Center for Technology & School Change at Teachers College, Columbia University, which works with schools to help them integrate technology into their curriculum. He taught in New York City schools for 10 years, and helped started alternative public schools in the city. For many years he has taught courses and workshops about technology and education at Teachers College, including online courses. His areas of interest include the history of technology in our educational system, using technology for problem solving and collaboration, and technology and democracy.

Richard Lee Colvin is the director of the Hechinger Institute on Education and the Media at Teachers College, Columbia University. As a journalist he covered education for three newspapers over a period of 20 years including an 8-year stint covering state and national education issues for the *Los Angeles Times*. He also has written about education for a number of popular and trade magazines, *Education Week* and others. He is a graduate of Oberlin College, where he earned a bachelor's degree in English and American studies, and the University of Michigan, where he earned a MA degree in journalism and, in 2000, was awarded a mid-career fellowship.

Catherine Cornbleth was a former high school history-social studies teacher in Texas and Connecticut, and faculty member at the University of Pittsburgh's School of Education. She is now professor at the Graduate School of Education, University at Buffalo, State University of New York. Her research and publications have addressed questions of curriculum politics, policy, practice, and change from a critical perspective. Cornbleth's most recent book is *Hearing America's Youth: Social Identities in Uncertain Times* (Peter Lang, 2003), based on interviews with more than 60 high school juniors and seniors in New York and California.

Judith Cramer, the educational technology specialist at Teachers College, Columbia University, taught journalism and advised the award-winning student newspaper at the United Nations International School in New York City. A contributor to publications on the arts and education, Cramer currently serves as editor of *The Interpreter*, the online journal of the New York City Museum Educators Roundtable (NYCMER).

Margaret Smith Crocco is associate professor of social studies and education at Teachers College, Columbia University. Most recently, she has authored (with Arthur Costigan and Karen Zumwalt) *Learning to Teach in an Age of Accountability* (Lawrence Erlbaum Associates, 2004). She has written extensively about issues of gender, diversity, and teacher education in the social studies.

Ronald W. Evans is professor in the School of Teacher Education at San Diego State University. He is author of *The Social Studies Wars* (2004), served as first editor of *The Handbook on Teaching Social Issues* (1996), and has published numerous articles and book chapters. He is currently working on a biography of Harold O. Rugg.

Tedd Levy is a former public school teacher and (NCSS) president. He was a feature writer and columnist for 4 years with a Connecticut weekly newspaper and is currently an educational consultant and freelance writer.

Gene I. Maeroff is senior fellow at the Hechinger Institute on Education and the Media at Teachers College, Columbia University. He was the founding director of the Institute in 1996. His most recent book is *A Classroom of One: How Online Learning Is Changing Our Schools and Colleges*, published by Palgrave Macmillan.

Merry M. Merryfield is professor of social studies and global education at The Ohio State University. Her research interests include teacher decision-making in global education and face to face and online cross-cultural experiential learning. See her Website at http://www.coe.ohio-state.edu/mmerryfield and www.teachglobaled.net for resources on global education.

James McGrath Morris has been a journalist, editor, and teacher. He was most recently a member of the Social Studies Department of West Springfield High School in Fairfax County. He is now working full-time on a biography of Joseph Pulitzer.

Richard J. Paxton is an associate professor in the Educational Foundations Department at the University of Wisconsin Oshkosh. A former high school history teacher and journalist, Paxton's research targets the teaching and learning of history. He teaches classes in educational psychology and research methods.

Michael Pezone is a social studies teacher at the Law, Government and Community Service Campus Magnet High School in Queens, New York, and an adjunct instructor and cooperating teacher at Hofstra University. He is a graduate of Brown University and has a MS in Education from Hofstra University. He has written and presented widely on teachers as activists.

E. Wayne Ross is professor in the Department of Curriculum Studies at the University of British Columbia. He has also worked on the faculties of the State University of New York and the University of Louisville, where he served as a distinguished university scholar. He has written numerous articles, book, and CD reviews for newspapers and magazines and is a frequent contributor to *Z Magazine*. He is general editor of the four-volume book set *Defending Public Schools* (Praeger, 2004) and co-author of *Image and Education: Teaching in the Face of the New Disciplinarity* (Peter Lang, 2003). Ross coedits two online journals: *Workplace: A Journal of Academic*

Labor (www.workplace-gsc.com) and *Cultural Logic* (www.eserver.org/clogic).

David Sadker is a professor at The American University (Washington, DC) and with his late wife Myra Sadker gained a national reputation for research and publications concerning the impact of gender in schools. Dr. Sadker has degrees from CCNY, Harvard University, and the University of Massachusetts. The Sadkers' book, *Failing at Fairness: How Our Schools Cheat Girls,* was published by Touchstone Press in 1995, and their introductory teacher education textbook, *Teachers, Schools and Society* (McGraw Hill) is now in its seventh edition. The Sadkers received the American Educational Research Association's award for the best review of research published in the United States in 1991, their professional service award in 1995, and their Willystine Goodsell award in 2004. The Sadkers were recognized with the Eleanor Roosevelt Award from The American Association of University Women in 1995, the Gender Architect Award from the American Association of Colleges of Teacher Education in 2001, and several honorary doctorates (www.american.edu/sadker).

Mark Sass has been a public high school teacher for 8 years, all of them teaching in the North Denver metro area. Prior to teaching he was an advertising photographer for 12 years, and prior to that a truck mechanic for 4 years. He lives with his wife Gina, and two children, ages 5 and 3, in Denver, Colorado.

Doug Selwyn is a professor of education at Antioch University. He was a teacher with Seattle Public Schools for 15 years and was Washington State Council for the Social Studies teacher of the year in 1990-91. His latest book is *History in the Present Tense* (written with Jan Maher, published by Heinemann 2004). He has also written *Social Studies at the Center* (with Tarry Lindquist, Heinemann 2000), and *Living History in the Classroom* (Zephyr 1993). He can be reached by email at dselwyn@antiochsea.edu.

Alan Singer is a professor of education in the Department of Curriculum and Teaching at Hofstra University in Long Island, New York, and a former New York City high school social studies teacher. He is a graduate of the City College of New York and has a PhD in American history from Rutgers University. He is the editor of *Social Science Docket* (a joint publication of the New York and New Jersey Councils for Social Studies), author of *Social Studies for Secondary Schools: Teaching to Learn, Learning to Teach* (2nd ed.), and editor of the "New York and Slavery: Complicity and Resistance" curriculum guide.

Linda Symcox is an associate professor in the Department of Teacher Education at California State University, Long Beach, and director of the Graduate Program in Curriculum & Instruction. She serves as the history education scholar for two Teaching American History grants and was formerly the associate director of the National Center for History in the Schools at UCLA (1989-1996), where she served as assistant director of the National History Standards and oversaw the NCHS curriculum project. Her research examines the interplay between curriculum theory, policy, and reform. Professor Symcox is author of *Whose History? The Struggle for National Standards in American Classrooms* (Teachers College Press, 2002), and has published numerous articles and curricula in the field of history and social studies education.

Rick Theisen was a high school social studies teacher in Minnesota from 1966-2000. He was the president of NCSS in 1999-2000, and a member of the board for 9 years. Most recently he has been a consultant on a variety of national social studies projects, including several funded by Annenberg, C.P., which focused on NCSS's national curriculum standards and high school civics.

Printed in the United States
37341LVS00004B/1

9 781593 113360